FAITH IN THE AGE OF ARTIFICIAL INTELLIGENCE

Christianity Through the Looking Glass

DAN SCOTT

ELEISON
PRESS

FREE BOOK OFFER

Are we living in the end times?
Is there anything good about AI?
What are the implications of church scandal?

Pastor Dan Scott answers some of the world's most burning
questions in his free book, The Great Falling Away.

www.pastordanscott.com

To my father, Daniel Scott, Sr., and my friend, Joe Cook, who have remained unafraid of the changing world.

What is real?
AN INTRODUCTION

Our world has stepped through a looking glass.

Like Alice in the famous story, many Christians experience things on this new side of the glass as utterly reversed. When they try to communicate, things don't come out right. What others say doesn't make sense either. They feel dizzy and disoriented.

Some desperately want to go home.

Artificial intelligence symbolizes all that is weird and befuddling about an age determined to rewrite reality. Much more than AI is involved—neural-links, bioengineering, the metaverse, and radical social change, just to name a few—but a robot is a convenient face for all the rest.

These emerging technologies (and the culture they empower) threaten to further disillusion and divide Christians already stressed by decades of endless social change. They represent major leaps forward. They also contain unimaginable dangers. Christians will be forced to continually rethink how they experience and explain their faith. Moments of existential vertigo will certainly increase.

Many Christians are unhappy about this.

Indeed, it's easy to assume that their ancient faith has little to say in such a world. I believe the opposite.

Christianity hasn't had as much to say since the days of the apostles. To deliver its message, however, we must learn much more about our own faith and its implications. We also must resist becoming defensive about the knowledge and assumptions of our changing times.

It's no small task, especially as old definitions of words like justice, fairness, democracy, love, and many, many others, are perpetually shifting. Like a new Tower of Babel, our language now often seems to hinder, rather than facilitate, conversation.

Believers disagree about which side of any given social conflict is most compatible with their faith. Many seem unaware that their faith might offer an entirely different perspective than the secular alternatives.

In this book, we will not only look at emerging technologies. We will also connect them to the major *social* changes of our "looking glass world," which we categorize under the label of *postmodernism.* It's a slippery concept. It literally means nothing more than, "after modern."

If, like me, you grew up thinking of the word modern as a synonym for "contemporary," you may be wondering what could possibly be more up-to-date than modern. However, for our use here, the word modern will not carry the street meaning of "up-to-date." It will describe the culture of the era we are leaving behind.

Since we'll be looking at other moments in history when Christian faith was forced to reexplain itself, we need a brief introduction to three terms that describe why a fresh explanation of faith became necessary. The terms *premodern, modern,* and *postmodern* are references to how the peoples of the Western World have experienced and explained reality within given periods of time.

Premodern refers to the perspective of our ancestors during the centuries before the modern era. They derived meaning and purpose from their culture's tradition, religion, and mythology. Technology gradually advanced during this period but was powered by animal power, running water, and wind. It was a world in which community was more important than individuals.

Modern. The modern era began around 1600 with an intense focus on science, technology, and industry. Among the important values promoted by people during the modern period were reason, logic, and continual technological progress. This was a world in which the individual became more important than community but remained responsible to community.

Postmodern. Postmodernism describes the emerging era we have just entered. It challenges many of the ideas of the modern era, including any belief in absolute truth or fixed ways of looking at things. Postmodern culture insists on making room for diverse perspectives, and is fairly certain that one's view of reality is shaped by society. Ours is thus an era in which community must continually adapt to the needs of continually changing individuals.

People living within one of these three eras of history were rarely inclined to question what reality was like. They had a *common sense* about what was real and what was not. Life during the decades between the eras, however, was more challenging because people were divided about how to experience and explain reality. They no longer held *sense in common*. Some were inclined to defend older ways of seeing things. Others were ready to move toward newer ways of seeing things. Until the shift was complete into a new *sense in common*, there was considerable disagreement about nearly everything.

We are living through such a season now.

Although a massive cultural shift has been gradually occurring over the last few decades, it recently reached a tipping point. The new postmodern perspective is no longer marginal. In fact, in the age of AI, it is the older, *modern* way of looking at things that is marginal.

Let's unpack that a bit more.

Until the late 1550s, the peoples of the Western World thought of reality as a synergistic web of visible and invisible parts. God was in control of the web, and so everything worked as it should. Every part of the universe reflected the whole. "As it was in the beginning, is now, and shall ever be, world without end," as the old prayer puts it.

That was, as we have seen, the *pre*modern era.

Then, from about 1600 AD, Europeans began to think of reality in a different way. In the new perspective, individual things became the focus of attention. A system was now merely the sum of its parts, or a machine, we could say. Although all facets of the universe were worthy of scientific interest, the meaning of the universe had become a topic for philosophy or religion.

That is a fifty-thousand feet view of the modern era.

Since that was the era that formed the way most older people in our society think, we need to say more about it.

In the early decades of the modern age, everything seemed possible. For example, one could suddenly imagine not only a new nation but a new kind of nation. If individuals were more important than systems, then the purpose of a state should be the flourishing of its citizens. That is why the Declaration of Independence said the United States was being created for "the pursuit of happiness."

The founders assumed that a group has no entitled existence in the world. Individuals voluntarily create the kinds of groups they believe benefit them. As the modern period progressed, this idea became irrefutable. All groups—the state, the church, and ultimately the family—would be expected to affirm it.

In the modern era, no group, not even a nation, was thought to have an absolute right to exist. Human beings, rather than gods or God, called nations into existence. The Constitution of the United States says that very thing in its opening line, "We the People . . ."

If this seems like common sense, it is because we feel that they are, as the founders of the United States put it, "self-evident." When the Constitution was written, however, such ideas had only recently become "self-evident." They had not been self-evident to the grandparents of the nation's founders. Something had changed between the premodern and the modern era and it was not the level of people's intelligence. It was a shift from experiencing reality as a synergistic whole to experiencing it as individual components.

The people of the modern period continually challenged their culture's traditional beliefs and practices, especially ones rooted in religion. Rather than invite the wrath of God, as their ancestors would have feared, the challenges led to scientific progress. Individual freedoms increased. Curiosity grew. Wealth spread. Technology flourished.

Unfortunately, modernism's focus on individual things also drained the Western World of meaning and community. By the end of the nineteenth century, the autonomous, sovereign individuals found it difficult to imagine that much of anything mattered. Individualism had led to fragmentation. Mental health declined.

The postmodern age began to emerge as the modern era was fading. By the early decades of the twentieth century, several discoveries had forced scientists to redefine reality. This knowledge, that reality was different than how previous generations had imagined it, was contained at first within intellectual circles. As the decades passed, however, that information slowly seeped into public awareness. As the twentieth century unfolded, philosophers, artists, religious leaders, and politicians began reassessing and revising the culture's assumptions and behaviors.

By the early decades of the twenty-first century, the peoples of the Western World had grown uncertain about what is real. On both the right and left, political leaders harvested the power of the resulting disruption and polarization. Religious institutions, including Christian ones, proved incapable of mitigating the strife. In fact, they often contributed to it.

Meanwhile, scientific discovery and technological innovation continued. The atomic bomb, the transistor, space travel, lasers, personal computers, the internet, the mapping of the human genome, and artificial intelligence propelled each successive generation into new ways of understanding the world and themselves. Because the modern era had succeeded so well in demonizing the past, the Western World purchased this growing knowledge at the cost of its inherited wisdom. The more we learned, the less it mattered.

As William Butler Yeats prophesied, the center could not hold. Indeed, for postmodern people, there was not, and had never been, any real center anyway.

If synergy is the descriptive word for *pre*modernism, and *machine* describes the perspective of modernism, then *ephemeral* may be the best word to describe *post*modernism. Although not an often-used word, it points to a common contemporary experience. Let's call it the Cheshire Cat effect. While Alice was talking to the animal, it began to disappear. Finally, nothing was left but a smile. Nonetheless, the conversation continued.

Like Alice's Cheshire cat, much of contemporary technology continually increases its efficiency as it decreases in size.

Ephemeralization, in other words, separates an object's ephemeral function from the material object. For example, not so long ago, sound engineers worked in studios filled with complicated gadgets and wires, large spools of tape, and recording devices covered with endless knobs and meters. Today, these are all software functions. The tangible knobs and meters of the old equipment became images on a screen. The engineer of a sophisticated sound project may be a kid with an iPad.

Ephemeralization affects much more than technology though. It affects institutions as well. Take your bank, for instance. In the decade you have been its customer, it has been bought, sold, renamed, consolidated, and reorganized. You don't know anyone who works there, and no one there knows you. It was once a large, beautiful building downtown, filled with workers. Later, it became a branch near your house with a half a dozen employees. It then became a network of ATM machines. Today, it is a computer link. If you phone your bank, it's unlikely you will connect with anyone living in your area, perhaps not in your country. Increasingly often, the voice that answers a call to your bank isn't even human.

In the postmodern world, meaning itself is ephemeral. The names of the political parties remain, but their narratives continually change. Many politically-active people don't really notice because they are more emotionally tied to their brand than to a specific narrative. The label, rather than the narrative, is the anchor of the group's identity.

In the postmodern world, narratives emerge to meet specific situations. One must not therefore impose any narrative on others, or even on one's future self. This includes text, which is a flexible, individually interpreted narrative rather than a fixed message for everyone of all times. The same holds true for morals, ethics, and art. For a growing number of people, even one's experience of reality is simply a useful narrative. If George therefore wants to think of the world as flat, then challenging that narrative is an act of aggression.

So where does this leave Christianity, the heir, translator, and carrier of *pre*modern thought? In this postmodern age of AI, tradition in any form is viewed as at best irrelevant and at worse, toxic. Our society is increasingly repulsed by any treatment of beliefs, practices, places, or roles as sacred.

Understandably then, many Christians see postmodernism as incompatible with their faith. Watching the news or conversing with neighbors feels to them like trying to imagine six impossible things before breakfast.

I felt this way not long ago. However, I have come to believe that the postmodern age offers fresh opportunities for our faith. Although there is considerable incompatibility between Christianity and the secular, contemporary world, nostalgia is not an appropriate response. The only healthy way forward is engagement.

In other words, Christians must accept that this is the era in which we live. Indeed, it is the era God has called us to serve. Jeremiah told the Jews in Babylon to "pray for the inhabitants in whose land you dwell, that it may go well with them." Unlike Alice, we will not be returning to the world we knew on the other side of the glass. So, it is probably better to take our lesson from Jeremiah.

In any case, it is dishonest to critique the faults of the contemporary world without acknowledging its blessings. We know things our ancestors did not. It was twenty-five years after George Washington's death before anyone knew that dinosaurs had existed. Two hundred more years passed before we learned that life is a language, written upon and executed through the millions of cells that constitute every living thing.

Also, I am not writing these words with a quill. I am writing them on a keyboard. As I write, I am erasing my mistakes. I don't know where those mistakes go. Then again, they never really existed. They were just ephemeral symbols on a screen hanging suspended between real and unreal. Soon, I will be co-writing with some form of artificial intelligence.

We cannot pretend that such changes will not affect how we view, practice, and explain our faith. That's why nostalgia is not a healthy form of piety. Since even the most fervent fundamentalist asks for Novocain before dental surgery, honest faith must acknowledge the benefits of contemporary life.

Information technology is one of those benefits. It is not an unmixed blessing, to be sure. Nonetheless, Christian's use of computers and the internet implies their unspoken endorsement not only of the technology but of the science that made it first imaginable and then possible.

We know in our heart of hearts that successful technology does not emerge from falsehood. Technology advances because science makes a new connection to reality. An honest person therefore will not use information technology for denouncing the science from which it emerged. New discoveries, and the inventions that we derive from them, have implications about reality.

This is problematic, however, because the science behind this technology has raised questions that are about to provoke considerable discomfort within the Christian community. Some of that discomfort will be warranted. AI programs, for example, force us to wrestle with what it means to be human. The core reason for most of our discomfort though is a fear that faith is not up to the task. Indeed, faith as sentiment and rule-keeping is utterly incapable of even sustaining itself, much less of answering serious contemporary questions.

What can comfort contemporary Christians, though, is the experience of believers who along ago wrestled with similar questions. Their responses will help us serve our own times.

From the moment Christian faith moved beyond Jerusalem, it has been forced continually to wrestle with other cultures and systems of thought. The interaction always provoked new developments within the Christian community. Christianity is not therefore an unaltered deposit sent by the first century to the contemporary world. This is why African Christians worship differently than

Swedes and French Canadians. It's why Russians cover churches with onion domes and Southern Baptists prefer steeples.

The postmodern world—the Age of AI—is simply the newest environment in which the Christian faith has been called to give "an answer for the faith that lies within us." Its questions—both new and old—deserve a respectful response.

In the first volume of his *Orthodox Dogmatic Theology*, Dumitru Staniloae says that a contemporary theologian should not ask "What did the Fathers say long ago?" but rather "What would the Church Fathers say now?"[1]

Of course, imagining what our spiritual ancestors might have said about contemporary issues requires us to know what they said about the issues of their own time.

C. S. Lewis used the term *Mere Christianity* to describe the core Christian assumptions that most believers throughout history would affirm. It was an echo of St. Vincent's definition of healthy faith: *that which has at all times and in all places been believed by the whole people of God.*

By picking up my book, it's likely you're interested in finding a spiritually healthy way to understand and respond as things in our culture get "curiouser and curiouser."

To learn how to survive and thrive, we will need advice from our spiritual ancestors. We will learn from our postmodern neighbors. Most of all, we will need a fresh encounter with the Holy Spirit, the Lord, The Giver of Life, who broods over things yet unformed to prepare them for the coming of Light.

One thing for sure, if God has called us to this moment, then we, like Alice, have been pulled into an adventure. It will sometimes get scary, but it will also transform us. Then again, as Alice and all explorers of all times and places always discovered, that is what adventures are designed to do!

Looking Through the Lens
HOW MIND MIRRORS THE WORLD

The light of the body is the eye: if therefore thine eye be single, thy whole body shall be full of light.
Matthew 16:22 (KJV)

WHEN I WAS A BOY, THE CONVERSATION I HEARD AROUND ME WAS full of quotes from "the Holy Bible." That means the Authorized Version, better known as the King James Bible.

Later on, I lived abroad. So, I read scripture in other languages. After returning to the United States years later, I read contemporary English translations. Still, when I remember the Bible's best-known passages, I nearly always hear them in that regal cadence of this most singularly influential book our language has yet produced, The King James, Authorized translation of the Holy Scriptures.

Perhaps that's why, as I began writing this chapter, that I heard the voice of Jesus speaking in that familiar dialect: "if thine eye be single, thy whole body will be full of light."

No contemporary translation clarifies the passage's cryptic message. The New Living Translation, for example, says it this way:

*"Your eye is like a lamp that provides light for your body.
When your eye is healthy, your whole body is filled with
light."*

That doesn't help much. So, what can help us understand the passage?

The Superman comics I used to keep under my bed!

Superman has X-ray vision. I could tell when he was using this power when dotted lines came from his eyes. Ancient Mediterraneans would have understood! They believed that our eyes are like flashlights. Tiny beams travel from our eyes to whatever we want to see.

Early Christian teachers assumed that Christ was describing spiritual wisdom with this understanding in mind. They thought by "eye," Jesus meant "conscience," "soul," "mind," or "heart." That would make the literal meaning of this passage read something like this: "If your soul develops integrity, it will light up your entire life."

That does not fully capture the meaning of Jesus's words. Rendering scriptural metaphors as literal statements nearly always impoverishes their meaning. What we do see in these words though is this: comprehension always involves more than what one looks *at*. It also involves what one *looks through*.

As William Blake put it:

"If the doors of perception were cleansed, then everything would appear to man as it is, infinite. For man has closed himself up, till he sees all things through narrow chinks of his cavern."

C. S. Lewis, in his *Meditation in a Toolshed*, tells us what he learned by watching a beam of light shine through a crack in his toolshed. He realized that he could look either *at* the beam or, *because* of the beam, look at everything in the shed. This taught him that *looking at* something is different from *looking through* it. Lewis learned that we cannot see anything without a means by which we see it. Therefore, there are times when we need to take a break from looking at things in order to pay attention to what we are looking through.

Whatever else Jesus may have meant by the phrase "If thine eye be single," we can be certain that he wanted us to be aware of what we look through and to remember that what we look through profoundly affects what we see.

As children we learned that wearing yellow sunglasses changed how one saw the world. What many of us do not know is that everyone is always wearing some sort of sunglasses.

Our "sunglasses" is the web of assumptions through which we experience reality. It is called a worldview. Although we rarely think about the filters through which we experience reality, they shape our every thought, emotion, and experience. The reason our neighbors experience the world differently than we do is because their sunglasses are colored differently than ours.

To understand what reality looks like through our neighbor's worldview, we must try on their sunglasses. Doing that may radically change our perspective about things. In fact, that is what the New Testament calls *metanoia*, or repentance. It's a deliberate change of worldview.

One thing for sure, once we know that people experience the world through a lens, we cannot return to the innocent assumption that how we see things is simply the way things are. Jesus shatters that assumption. He tells us that we have been looking at reality through a distorted lens and so must learn how to see things differently.

Jesus also tells us to accept his yoke. That means to make him the leader of our life. If we do that, he promises to teach us how to see and respond to reality in a life-giving way.

Christianity is thus more than a community of people sharing spiritual experiences or affirming certain ethical and moral principles. Christianity is (or is intended to be) a philosophical school that trains us how to relate to and respond to reality. Spiritual life involves much more than intellect, of course. It is first and foremost a response to grace. However, responding to grace leads to the engagement of our will, our intellect, our intuition, and our behavior.

Many contemporary Christians seem unaware that Christianity, like Judaism before it, involves the intellect. Because this part of the Christian life was seriously neglected throughout the modern period, few contemporary Christians view the world differently than their non-Christian neighbors. A conservative Christian and a progressive one may embrace different aspects of the secular world-view, but often they are equally secularized in terms of how they experience life.

If we want to respond to postmodernism in ways that are faithful to Christian teaching therefore, we must recover much more of that teaching than most of us were taught. That will require us to think about what we have been looking through before we jump to conclusions about what we are looking at.

What Exactly is a Christian Worldview?

Nineteenth century philosophers coined the term worldview (or *weltanschauung*, if we want to show off). In their age of a growing interconnection among the world's peoples, it became apparent to them that a Navajo shaman in 1830 viewed reality through a different lens than a French neurologist living in 2021. Likewise, a Japanese Zen practitioner and a Swedish physicist necessarily differed in how each viewed reality. These differences in perspective, moreover, was not merely about who was smarter. It was about the assumptions through which each experienced the world.

In the decades since, the social sciences have explored how human beings become embedded within their culture, gender, and socioeconomic placement in the world. All these things affect how individuals interpret the world and respond to it. Although an individual may change over time, how that individual begins will influence him or her throughout life.

Like all cultures, Christianity makes certain assumptions about reality. A Christian experiences the world through those assumptions. Some of these will strike a non-Christian as incredible, perhaps even outlandish.

Throughout history, human beings have not generally expected a dead person to walk out of a tomb and ask for breakfast. If that really happened, even only once, then the universe works differently than the way non-Christians assume.

The Apostle Paul said as much. He insisted that Christianity doesn't have much to say if Christ did not resurrect from the dead. That makes the resurrection the foundational Christian worldview. Christianity makes other shocking claims that we will consider in the following pages. However, the resurrection is already a huge belief to swallow.

Christians must therefore accept the fact that faith is more than a comforting community. It is a collection of claims about reality. Intellectual integrity thus requires believers, as well as unbelievers, to examine their worldview. This can be terribly uncomfortable. It requires us to shift from looking through a Christian lens at things and to take a look at the lens itself. It forces us to face the possibility that our lens may distort reality rather than clarify it.

Keep in mind that we are trying to look at what reality looks like when *one assumes Christianity to be an accurate way of viewing the world*. One can appreciate the value of a Christian subculture whether or not Christianity offers an accurate picture of reality. All communities are *socially* important, whether or not its stated beliefs make sense. That is why an atheist visiting at a church potluck with his family may have a good time. Indeed, if everyone starts singing songs he knew as a child, tears may come to his eyes. A social connection like that is meaningful, whether or not one shares a Christian worldview. Thousands of Japanese belong to gospel choirs because they enjoy the music. Over time, some of them become Christians. Most of them do not.

In other words, people attend church for reasons other than a personal belief in or knowledge of Christianity.

Why does this matter? Well, when the surrounding culture more or less affirmed Christianity's moral teachings, it actually didn't seem to matter to most people. Most people celebrated Christmas and Easter then. They knew the major stories of the Bible. So, Sunday worship was just icing on the cake.

Today, a professing Christian feels increasing pressure to explain his faith to himself. Enjoying potluck suppers and gospel music is no longer enough. This is particularly true in areas where few attend church.

The Importance of Theory

All systems of thought (theories) are interpretations of data. There are therefore few things in life as useful as a good theory. A theory organizes our thoughts. Theory also leads to action. Fantasy, which most of us enjoy in some form or another, does not do those things. I have already confessed that I once enjoyed reading comic books. Fortunately, that didn't influence me to jump from a tall building. (I did wear a cape at school once, however.)

Fantasy, in contrast to theory, isn't based on data. Even if complex and compelling, fantasy has no clear connection with reality. In fact, we enjoy fantasy because we understand that difference. We reassess our view of reality only when we can no longer fit reliable data into our present theories.

If I wake up in the morning to find myself floating above my bed, I will know that something radically new has occurred. It will be inconsistent with reality as I have experienced it so far. It will challenge everything I know about gravity, for example. So, I will need an explanation.

"Perhaps I am having a psychotic episode," I will say to myself. "I'll call for help."

"Well, maybe not. It could be that while I was sleeping, I was transported to outer space somehow. Or I may have died in the night. In that case, I will soon see a tunnel of light stretching into the distance."

"Or . . . My naughty friend slipped some LSD into my tea."

The only thing I will know for sure is that floating above my bed does not fit anything I've been taught or have personally experienced. Floating above my bed, therefore, will seriously challenge my worldview.

If I have acquired an ability to float above my bed, it will force me to develop a new understanding of physics. If I can reliably demonstrate this new talent to others, *everyone* will be forced to change their understanding of physics!

Gravity is part of our core beliefs about reality. It is so deeply embedded in our view of reality that we rarely even think about it. Only very smart (or mentally unstable) people question why gravity exists.

Einstein was one of those. He decided gravity was a depression in space-time, something akin to placing a metal ball on a stretched piece of thin rubber. As it turned out, Einstein was *not* crazy. So, I'm not saying that one cannot question our culture's view of reality. I'm only saying that one must have a credible reason for doing so.

Gravity, which is one of the so called "laws of nature," is not something we usually question. It just is. It's part of our *common* sense.

We call such core beliefs "givens."

An ideological system's givens are what determine what a particular culture deems relevant. They also predetermine the data we notice, which categories we use to sort data, and what all this implies about reality. A given is the starting point of a system of thought. If a system's givens are found to be false, the entire system must be reconstructed and perhaps even abandoned. This will be the case even if the system is otherwise internally consistent and eloquently stated.

Unaided levitation repudiates a fundamental given of how we experience the world. If it is false, then everything resting on it must be reexamined.

Like all thought systems, Christianity emerges from a few "givens." If we want to understand the Christian worldview, we must therefore begin by examining those givens. For an unbeliever, this is a shift from looking *at* the faith to looking *through* it. For the believer, it is the opposite.

The Givens of the Christian Worldview

The first line of the Bible states the first "given" of the Christian worldview. "In the beginning God created the heavens and the earth." Both the Apostles Creed and the Nicene Creed begin by affirming this statement because it is the core of the core of Christian faith: the universe was purposefully created by God.

Christianity's second "given" comes from the first line of *The Gospel According to St. John*: "In the beginning was the Word and the Word was with God and the Word was God." This statement is another affirmation of the core belief that God created everything. The Apostle John, however, modified the statement by telling us that the Word (*Logos* in Greek) was with God when things were created and indeed, was God. He goes on to say that this had something to do with how and for what purpose God created the universe.

The relationship between the opening lines of Genesis and St. John's Gospel establishes the Christian worldview. That relationship claims that the universe (and all it contains) exists because God created it through Logos. The Apostle John then adds that in Jesus Christ, God has entered into and become a material part, of God's creation.

These statements led believers to embrace a particular way of viewing reality. If one believes the statements to be true, they shape how one experiences reality.

Of course, not everyone who reads the Bible is a believer. It is possible for a reader to accept the Bible's assumptions about reality provisionally, for the purpose of engaging the text on its own terms. The Bible may be important to such a reader because he views it as a mythopoetic piece of literature.

So, let's take a few lines to think about what it's like to view scripture as a mythopoetic statement about ethics, morals, and the meaning of life. This is the way readers approach fantasy literature or science fiction because entering an artist's imaginary world requires a momentary suspension of critical thought. That is also how a Christian reads religious literature from other traditions, such as the Bhagavad Gita or Tao Te Ching. Non-Christians may read Genesis or St. John's Gospel in the same spirit. They enjoy the mythical imagination of ancient writers or want to understand how Jews and Christians think. This sort of reader will not expect to learn from the Bible much that is objectively true about the universe.

Christians, on the other hand, do expect to learn things from the Bible that are objectively true. Although they disagree among themselves what parts are meant to be objective and what parts are offered as allegory, they all believe that God speaks through scripture. This belief shapes one's life differently than reading the Bible as merely a human product.

Of course, at one level, even the most devout believer reads scripture as a mythopoetic narrative. If a reader does not acknowledge the Bible's intentional use of metaphor and poetry, he misses both its moral instruction and its objective claims. That is why reading the Bible requires preparation. Reading scripture naïvely, as though it were a contemporary newspaper or a textbook, distorts its message. Even the most fundamentalist believer sometimes asks the text the question the disciples asked of Jesus, "Lord, why do you speak to us in parables?"

Later on, we'll look at how to read scripture. For now, let's simply say that we should not expect Genesis to address questions about reality in the same way as one does in physics or paleontology. Nonetheless, Christians agree with Jews that the universe is a purposeful creation. Christians furthermore believe that the Creator has become a part of creation.

All this to say that Christians read and pray the Bible as something more than a mythopoetic statement about morals, ethics, and spirituality. It's part of the lens through which we understand reality itself.

Three Ways of Viewing Reality

After reading an early draft of this book, a professor urged me to emphasize the importance of the following section. He thought it was the foundation of the rest of the book. He was probably right. So, as you read through the following pages, think about what reality looks like when we view it through each of three lenses below.

Let's begin with this: one's view of reality emerges from how we respond to the question, "What is real?"

Surprisingly, there are only three basic answers.

One is *materialism*, which views reality as material.

Einstein's famous formula ($E = mc^2$) told us that energy and matter are different modes of the same thing. Therefore, a more precise label for this worldview would be *physicalism*. However, since the term materialism has been more commonly used, let's stick with it.

In a materialist view, non-material entities are seen as concepts we invent to make sense of our life. An idea is thus not "real," at least in the sense that tables, trees, and kangaroos are real. This means that "good" is always an adjective, describing things that please us. Good is a useful term to be sure but refers to nothing outside the human mind. The same is true of qualities like love, truth, beauty, and so forth.

For a materialist, disembodied intelligences such as angels, demons, and God are personifications of human thought and emotion. They are at best useful metaphors that help us imagine a culture's values. They are not, objectively speaking, real.

Materialism, in other words, reduces reality to matter.

Another response to the question "what is real?" is *idealism*. An idealist believes that things like ideas, spirit, and information are real. Material is a manifestation of non-material reality.

From this idealist perspective then, material things are experienced as temporary expressions of information (or spirit, if the idealist is religious). To use Owen Barfield's example (which we will explore later), a rock and a frog are not essentially different from a rainbow in that all three are examples of phenomena. Our sense that a rock is more real than a rainbow is due simply to its longer duration. Human beings don't live long enough to observe the formation and disillusion of a rock. The rock therefore seems more solid, more "real" than a rainbow. In truth, however, rainbows, rocks, and rhinos are all phenomena, as indeed, are we.

For the idealist, in other words, phenomena emerges from (and resolves back into) some immaterial source. Depending on how religious we are, we call that source spirit, information, or idea.

The final response to the question "what is real," is the Abrahamic one. By that I mean the worldview roughly common to Jews, Christians, and Muslims. Let's call it the *incarnational* worldview. It is the perspective that reality is an interpenetration of both matter and spirit. In this view, all visible things, including human beings and human societies, emerge from material and nonmaterial sources. Other levels of reality may be nonmaterial, but they are related to and influenced by matter, though in ways we do not always comprehend.

Among the Abrahamic religions, Christianity is particularly impacted by its insistence that God has become a human being. That is the basic worldview this book assumes, though we will look seriously at several important contributions (and valid questions) that the other views offer Christians for understanding ourselves and the universe in which we live.

In summary then, these are the world's three major responses to the question "what is real?"

1. Materialism
2. Idealism
3. Incarnationalism

During the European Enlightenment (roughly 1690 to 1815) educated Western peoples increasingly leaned into materialism. As a result, the present language of our scientific disciplines, including the social sciences, reflect this materialist perspective. That can make it challenging to express other perspectives in ways that seem competent or compelling. That is why any Christian who intends to converse with those of other persuasions should think deeply about how reality appears through each of these three perspectives.

The contemporary question most affected by these competing worldviews is this: "What does it mean to be conscious?"

2

A Mirror That Shapes What It Sees

HOW HUMAN CONSCIOUSNESS INTERPRETS REALITY

Human beings are conscious: that is to say they are aware of self, of other conscious beings, of the natural world, and of where they are, have been, and may yet be located in time and space.

ANDY WEIR'S NOVEL, *PROJECT HAIL MARY*, BEGINS WITH A BARELY conscious man becoming aware of a voice that repeatedly asks, "What is 2+2?"

"I don't . . . ahh," responds the man.

"Incorrect!" the voice says. "What is 2+2?"

The man is still unable to answer, and the voice again coldly says, "Incorrect."

After many hours, the frustrated man shouts an answer. "FOUR!"

"Correct," the voice says. "What is your name?"

Once more, the interrogated man struggles to respond. Yet again, his efforts are met with that same cold rebuke: "Incorrect."

As the inquisition continues, the man gradually becomes aware of his hands, feet, and legs, which allows him to explore his surroundings. He learns he is the sole survivor of a spaceship crew.

He also learns that he has been asleep for a long time but can remember nothing about anything that happened before then.

It is weeks before he recalls his name, Dr. Ryland Grace. With this insight, he begins to recover a sense of his self. His unseen torturer then introduces itself as the spaceship's central computer. Its sensors show that Dr. Grace is now fully conscious and capable of assuming full control of the vessel.

The bewildered astronaut is left trying to figure out how this vessel arrived in an alien galaxy, and why.

Ryland Grace's experience is not so different from our own. There was a time for us too when things and people seemed strange and mysterious. We also discovered our body before making much sense of the world. We learned to control our movements and began repeating the sounds of others. Slowly, we began using words and gestures to express ourselves. As we did all of this, we began to form a sense of self, emerging from a fog.

We have been experiencing the world as an "I," as a self, since those early, shadowy days. We know that our mind was interacting with its environment for some time before that. However, we do not recall ourselves as a self before this point of self-identification. In fact, when we try to recall what it was like to form a self, we enter a mystery.

In counseling, I often ask my clients to talk about their first memories of life. Most of the time, the client is a bit perplexed by my question. It is rather like that biblical phrase "in the beginning;" we can barely imagine the moment when we first recognized our own selfhood. Thinking about ourselves before that is nearly impossible. We may see pictures of ourselves before we knew we were a self, but it is challenging to make a real connection with the image as truly related to us.

So, when precisely did I become a self? What does that even mean?

Philosophers and religious teachers have been pondering such questions for millennia. Now, scientists are joining the conversation.

Is the Mind Simply the Brain at Work?

You probably have the sensation that you peer out at your environment from behind your eyes. Although you cannot describe where exactly you are located, it seems to be somewhat different than the environment you experience and evaluate. That is a nearly universal experience, for all human beings in all cultures and all ages. Even when we say, "my body," we express that there is something in us that is other than body. We may not be correct about that, but that is how we experience ourselves.

For decades, scientists have told us that our sense of self is formed in our brain. Most of us accept this, though something about it seems incomplete. Even the neurologists making this claim rarely report experiencing themselves as programed meat. They may insist that science forces them to this conclusion, but love and music seems to undermine it, at least when they are not in work mode. Somehow, the concept of mind feels to most of us like something larger, and something different, than brain.

Some philosophers of science explain our reluctance to equate brain with mind as an evolutionary adaptation. In this view, human evolution requires us to deceive ourselves about the true nature of our mind. The conviction that we are immaterial selves peering through a body motivates us to stay alive long enough to procreate. Experiencing ourselves as we truly are—biological machines reacting to stimuli—would not have motivated us enough to keep ourselves alive. Some have proposed that our body and mind are simply the means by which human gametes extend themselves into the future. That would imply that sperm and egg are the core forms of human life, making the body and mind into something like the fruit and fragrance of plants.

A popular expression one hears in graduate school is: "the mind is simply the brain at work." This implies that mind is an *emergent* property of brain.

Here is an analogy: fragrance is an emergent property of a flower. If we smell a flower at a distance, we may not know where the fragrance is coming from. Nonetheless, we know by experience what produces that sort of fragrance is a flower. In the same way, according to this materialist view, we can be aware of the workings of the mind without knowing much about the brain. Nonetheless, mind, which is more like a verb than like a noun and more like a process than an object, emerges from a material brain.

One cannot simply dismiss this materialist explanation of mind. It is a possible conclusion to draw from the neurological knowledge we have. However, all we've learned so far about neurological structures and processes does not inevitably lead to this materialist conclusion. Science cannot yet corollate the workings of the mind with brain processes. We only know that mind and brain are interlaced. We also know that scientists, like everyone else, evaluate data through a worldview.

Neurology is at a similar juncture faced by physicists toward the end of the nineteenth century. At that time, most physicists believed light moved through a medium called "ether." Some of the world's greatest scientists spent an entire career devising tests for defining and measuring the ether. Those attempts ended abruptly after Einstein proved that light didn't require a medium through which to move.

One cannot fit new data into old categories. It's like finding a place for new books in an old bookcase. At some point, one needs a new bookcase! Once we build that new bookcase, we discover that even these old books must be rearranged. That is what Einstein did with the old knowledge about the universe. He built a new bookcase. We have been trying to arrange old and new information into that bookcase for over a hundred years.

That is what has been happening in neurology, psychology, and cognitive science. We have gathered a lot of data, but we have no place to put it. Our theories, in other words, are not keeping pace with our discoveries. In this new age of artificial intelligence, that is particularly true concerning human consciousness.

We suddenly cannot agree about a common definition for consciousness. For several decades, neurologists doubted that we even have a mind, something nearly all human beings had always taken for granted. Their materialist point of view required a material explanation for mind. So far though, neither the psychologists, nor the philosophers have agreed on one. The opinions of plumbers, priests, artists, and businesspersons, though they claimed to be conscious, didn't really count.

Today, a growing number of scientists, philosophers, and cognitive researchers, most of them committed to a materialistic perspective, acknowledge the challenges of knowing how, or at what stage, consciousness emerges from matter. They have proposed various theories. One of them is called panpsychism. It says that our sense of self emerges from neurological processes that are themselves conscious. Just as our two cerebral hemispheres (under normal conditions) unite to present a single sense of self, so does the brain stem, central nervous system, and other parts of our neurological system.

This view leads to places no scientist wants to go. We could ask whether neurotransmitters and hormones are conscious, or the molecules that form them, or even the atoms that form the molecules. In the end, the panpsychist perspective flips the old problem of brain/mind on its head. It forces us to ask, is mind merely using biological material as an interface to the material world?

Buddhists may smile at this, but most neurologists will not!

An explanation like panpsychism ultimately leads to a mystical worldview, which makes many neurologists nervous. However, ideas like this have been emerging from within, rather than from outside of, the scientific world. There just seems to be no way of acknowledging the existence of consciousness without addressing what we call "the hard problem," how human beings have a sense of being something more than a body.

There is, to be sure, a good deal of agreement among scientists concerning what we have learned about the human brain in the last few decades. In spite of this progress, however, perhaps even *because* of it, the human brain remains the universe's most mysterious entity.

Except for a handful of people (Buddhists prominently among them) most people have been content to look *at* the world *out from* their consciousness. Few have thought about looking *at* consciousness. Today, however, the peoples of the Western World have joined their Eastern counterparts in the quest for knowing where the mind comes from and why it exists.

One of the contemporary discussions about consciousness involves what we call "the zombie problem." In this case, zombies are not the characters of a horror film. They are imaginary participants in a thought experiment.

The experiment begins with a question: "From the evolutionary point of view, why should human beings need to be self-conscious?" Our biological drives—fear, hunger, reproduction, and so forth—would operate just as effectively (arguably more effectively) without a sense of self. Consciousness, or at least self-consciousness, seems unnecessary for the existence (or even the maintenance) of biological life.

If I were to meet someone lacking a sense of self—a zombie—I might not sense that anything was missing. When imagining the inner life of another, I rely on their self-disclosure. I assume they are telling the truth about how they experience themselves. Why? Because I am aware of my own inner life. It is possible I am the only conscious human being on the planet, surrounded by people who are either lying or are programed to respond in ways that make them appear conscious. However, healthy people do not come to this conclusion.

Although most of us don't believe in zombies, this thought experiment makes us aware that one can only experience his own consciousness. This leads to an important study we call phenomenology, which we cannot unfortunately explore here. It is enough to say that if I doubt I am a computer made of meat, I must assume that other human beings have the same sort of inner life as the one I experience.

As we will see, this zombie question becomes truly important when we think about the possible consciousness of computer programs.

And yes, scientists and philosophers actually talk about zombies and "machines made of meat."

How Mind Affects Brain

Whatever our beliefs about consciousness, most of us are certain that changes in the brain affect the mind. A blow to the head, a stroke, or even a nasty virus alters how we think, behave, or present ourselves to the world. What we have not known until recently is how the changes in the mind affect the brain. Modern Western thought has had no place for that sort of reverse causation.

I am referring to what we call *brain plasticity*, the potential of a brain to alter itself in response to an environment. It is a relatively new concept. William James, the father of American psychology, did indeed insist, over a hundred years ago, that the brain continually changes itself throughout life. Most neurologists and psychiatrists at the time didn't buy it though. Now, we know James was correct. Even more surprising has been the discovery of neurogenesis, that the brain has a life-long ability to grow new cells and form new connections.

Until recently, most neurologists believed the brain reached its greatest level of functionality in young adulthood. After that, they assumed, the brain began a gradual and irreversible decline. After a serious injury (or the onset of most cognitive declines due to aging), the brain is usually incapable of significant recovery.

None of this was true, as it turns out.

What changed?

An important component of these neurological breakthroughs was the growing experience of physical, occupational, and speech therapists. These hands-on practitioners discovered that stroke victims could recover in ways neurologists insisted was impossible.

My wife was a test case. After suffering a subarachnoid hemorrhage in 2004, Trish had the great fortune of receiving care from creative and persistent therapists. They insisted she would get her life back. Then, they worked hard to achieve that.

A gifted surgeon stopped the bleeding by inserting a platinum coil into her brain. He also rerouted her cerebral fluids by implanting a shunt. After recovering from the ten-day coma that followed, Trish began a long and arduous journey to recover her cognitive and motor functions.

Barrows Neurological Center Phoenix, where Trish was hospitalized, had been among the first to incorporate the findings of cutting-edge neurological research. Some of the most productive research had been conducted in Silver Springs, Maryland under Dr. Edward Taub. Due to an animal right's controversy, his work remains divisive. What is not debatable is Taub's discovery that the brain is dynamic rather than a static organ that continually shapes itself in response to novel situations.

The research of people like Taub supported and deepened the convictions of therapists that the brain has an enormous capacity to renew itself. The treatment of brain injury has made great strides in the last twenty years because of this finding. Many patients, who before might have permanently lost any freedom of movement or clarity of thought, instead returned to near-normal life.

Unfortunately, these breakthroughs have not settled our disagreements about the relationship between the mind and the brain. For some, they prove that mind is merely the brain doing what it does. Repair a damaged brain and behold—mind reemerges! For others, the notion that healing from brain trauma requires not only good surgeons and experienced therapists but the patient's engaged and cooperative mind, indicates that something more than the material brain is involved.

I believe neurogenesis and brain plasticity are the result of both physical and mental processes. Neurological healing, in other words, involves the combination of physical movement guided by competent coaches and a patient's cooperative attention. Most physical, speech, and occupational therapists will agree with me about this.

Therapists know that if a brain-injured patient insists on defending and maintaining the distortions of thought that follow a brain injury, the effectiveness of his therapeutic care will decline. On the other hand, a patient who accepts that they are temporarily experiencing the world through a damaged brain, and is motivated to cooperate with therapists, teachers, and loved ones to recover their full self, will usually experience recovery.

The mind can, in other words, train the brain. Most people need a coach for doing that, but a patient's will to heal is the most critical component of recovering brain health. This implies that the mind can evaluate the health of its own brain. It can learn to "fact check" judgements the brain makes about one's inner and outer environment. This is hard and discouraging work, but it can be done. This principle is the basis not only for neurological healing but for all types of athletic, musical, linguistic, and academic training. Growth and healing require an engaged and an informed mind. Indeed, the brain physically adapts itself to the movements of one's mind.

So how does this work?

One morning after waking from her coma, my wife told me that her roommate's family had taken all the furniture out of the room during the night. When I insisted this didn't happen, Trish laughed. She didn't berate herself. Neither did she argue about what had occurred. Instead, she became more motivated to recover her sound judgment.

Trish decided that during recovery, she would continually compare her perception of the world with the perceptions of those she trusted. She knew that her perceptions were the temporary results of a damaged brain. They were, therefore, unreliable. She didn't assume that this would be her permanent condition. She would do what she could to heal and recover herself.

It's not only brain-damaged people that distort reality. Success in life requires everyone to balance a reasonable level of confidence in their own convictions with a reasonable level of doubt. That is what we call wisdom, an essential quality in all intentional transformations of the human self. Recovery from brain trauma is in this way a powerful model for all types of human transformation.

In *A Beautiful Mind*, John Nash, the Nobel prize winning mathematician, learns to fact-check his schizophrenia-generated perception. At one point, Nash asks a student whether the student can see the man in a green hat standing beside them.

"No!" the startled student replies.

"Right," says Nash, who then turns toward what the student

sees as empty space. The startled student hears Nash say firmly, "You are not here! Go away!"

I have referred to this scene countless times while helping clients develop reality-checking techniques. Schizophrenia is a brain disease and requires medication. Mental force alone is inadequate for dealing with the physical realities of this particular brain dysfunction. Nonetheless, when a patient dealing with any sort of brain disorder accepts the fact that he has a diseased brain, he makes a giant step toward managing his disease.

Patients who refuse to accept their diagnosis, or who give up all sense of personal agency because of their diagnosis, usually will stop taking medication. Nearly always, this results in a steady decline in the patient's ability to discern reality.

My wife was a trained psychotherapist who had been working in drug rehab the morning she collapsed. She was confused when she awoke. During the time she had been unconscious, she had undergone two serious operations and had weathered a dangerous event called vasospasms—from which she nearly died. This had been followed by pneumonia. Understandably then, she had a difficult time distinguishing daydreams from reality. Fortunately, somewhere inside (or perhaps from beyond) her damaged brain, was a psychologically educated self who knew that stroke victims do not always perceive things accurately. That awareness directed her to compare her perceptions with those of her loved ones, nurses, and therapists.

Trish was fortunate because by the time she experienced her aneurism, stroke rehab had been transformed into a type of high-intensity coaching. Her therapists formed intimate relationships with their patients. This created what we might call a wireless neurological interface through which therapists worked to restore the patterns of thought and movement eroded by the brain injury.

Surgery is often required after a brain injury. So are drugs. These are physical responses to a physical organ. They cannot be minimized. Without them, the brain rarely heals. However, something else is also required: the active engagement of the patient's mind. For this we usually need trained and intuitive coaches. From this combination, the mind regains its sense of self and becomes capable of reshaping the brain.

This explanation of the relationship between the mind and the brain, will resonate more with therapists than with neurologists. It is not so much a scientific explanation as it is a functional one. I believe neurology will eventually support it, though at present we can only insist that science does not rule it out.

What we know is that mind and brain are not different ways of talking about the same thing. What that implies depends on one's worldview.

Jeffery Swartz

Most therapists, together with a growing number of neurologists, ignore the question about how the mind and brain are related. They simply treat the mind as something different than the brain because that seems to motivate patients to care for themselves. Therapists know that patients who believe the brain and the mind are different things find it easier to manage their illnesses and dysfunctions. So, they leave questions like "the hard problem of consciousness" to philosophers.

Dr. Jeffery Swartz is one of the most successful advocates of this approach.

Swartz formed his view of mind after working for years with patients suffering from obsessive compulsive disorder. Many of his patients seemed to experience a breakthrough after hearing his assurance that they were not crazy. Swartz insisted that though a part of their brain sometimes malfunctioned, their mind was good. He would remind them that it is difficult to pick up an object with a broken hand. It is just as challenging to discard obsessive thoughts and behaviors when a small part of one's brain is broken. Frustration and shame only add to the burden, he said.

Swartz's patients found this reassuring. They could accept that a part of their brain was not functioning as it should. That it was uncomfortable, but manageable. The insight transformed their suffering into an adventure. As a result, most of his patients learn to minimize the impact of OCD on their daily lives.

When I first heard about his approach, I assumed Swartz was Buddhist. In those days, most mental health workers were behaviorists. Behaviorists thought the idea that we have a mind was an antiquated, unscientific construct. Real scientists, they said, study behaviors that can be measured, such as stimulus and response, or attraction and aversion. In contrast, the Buddhists (mostly on the West Coast in those days) drew their insights from a centuries-old heritage of observing and labeling mental states.

To my surprise, Swartz was a Christian. I don't know whether his faith directly influenced his therapeutic model, but it is consistent with what Christianity teaches about one's interior life.

The early teachers of our faith insisted that mental healing is about much more than repairing a biological machine. It is mostly about embracing a life of cooperation with grace within a spiritual community. This is why Jesus once asked a lame man, "Do you want to get well?" (John 5) He was inviting the man's participation.

Like physicians through the ages (and unlike a growing number of physicians in America's health-business system) Swartz develops the sort of intimate relationship with his patients that Irvin Yalom calls "the therapeutic bond." For Swartz, acknowledging a patient's dignity is an essential part of forming the therapeutic bond through which healing occurs.

OCD patients are intelligent people. They are painfully aware that touching their doorknob a hundred times before leaving their house doesn't make sense. That is why they seek help. They feel crazy because their thoughts and behaviors are sometimes difficult to control. However, Swartz knows they are not crazy. If they were, they would not recognize the irrational nature of their thoughts and behaviors. That is why Swartz congratulates a new patient for having good judgment about their need for help. He tells them that noticing that one's brain doesn't always work as it should, is an indication of a healthy mind.

Swartz seeks to shift the patient's sense of identity from "I am so crazy that I have to touch a doorknob a hundred times before leaving my house," to "a diseased part of my brain sometimes insists that I touch a doorknob a hundred times before leaving my house." The patient moves from feeling defeated and crazy to empowered and curious. It then becomes possible to find a strategy for managing the disease.

The kind of therapeutic care practiced by Swartz and the stroke-rehab therapists we have mentioned, would not be effective if they didn't align with something real about human nature. Although more neurological research is needed for learning why these relational, hands-on coaching approaches promote brain healing, the common assumption behind them is simple: the human mind, though obviously interrelated with the brain, is nonetheless something different from it. Furthermore, changes in one leads to changes in the other, implying that our brain not only gives rise to our mind, but that our mind forms our brain.

What the Heck IS Consciousness?

When mental health workers, doctors, and philosophers talk to one another about consciousness, they quickly discover they are using the same word to refer to different things. This makes it challenging to agree upon a clear, common definition.

For example, is a tree conscious?

How one answers this depends on one's definition of consciousness. If by consciousness we mean an organism's potential for taking action to preserve or enhance its existence, then a tree is certainly conscious. Something nonetheless seems missing. Does a tree *decide* to connect with the water or the sun, or are these "zombie" operations of a biological machine? Many of us can be persuaded to agree that a frog is conscious. But a tree?

If we define consciousness as an organism's awareness of its relation to its own mental processes, then the term "self-conscious" will be more descriptive. Although we have learned that trees respond to light and soil in ways that seem purposeful, trees are apparently unaware they are doing these things. Frogs seem to fall somewhere in-between humans and trees in terms of their self-awareness and intentionality. Research in animal intelligence has seriously eroded our past assumption that consciousness is a quality unique to human beings. The more we learn, the smarter the animals seem to be.

We will assign the term *self-consciousness* then for "an awareness of one's own awareness." We are quite certain that trees do not have this level of awareness. We do not know about the frog. Other animals fall at various places on the spectrum from zombie to self-conscious. There is much we still do not know.

What we do know is that self-conscious beings respond purposefully to changes in their environment as well as to changes within their own mind. They are also aware that they are doing such things. Put in a simpler way, a self-conscious being anticipates change and forms strategies for responding to it. The change may be a shift in the weather or the adjustment of one's own opinion about something.

Self-consciousness then involves an awareness of one's own internal mental processes. However, this begs the question about *awareness*. What does awareness really mean, scientifically speaking?

As far as we know, human beings are the only life form that is fully aware about being aware. That means that humans can speculate on what awareness means, as we are doing here.

We continue to learn that many animals exhibit signs of an inner awareness of themselves. For example, they can identify themselves in a mirror. Likely, we will learn much more about the cognitive abilities and emotional lives of other animals. Even so, the self-reflecting nature of human awareness—the awareness of one's own awareness—seems unique in many ways.

We do not expect an octopus or an African gray parrot to write a novel, for example. If that occurs, I for one will read it. I can't imagine it would make less sense than some of the literature I have encountered.

Whatever we learn about animal intelligence though, questions about human self-consciousness will remain. We all want to know why each of us experience a profound sense of self. We also would like to know why most of us find material explanations for the phenomena disturbing. Even when we are committed to an honest assessment of the data, it requires an indoctrination in materialist philosophy to convince ourselves we are nothing more than a biological machine.

It would be reasonable to expect that a book about Christian worldview would begin with a chapter about God. We learned in *The Sound of Music* that one should always start at the beginning because that is a very good place to start. However, since this book is about how Christianity responds to the postmodern age, I decided to begin with a reflection on consciousness.

I am convinced that all other discussions in the postmodern world, including those about God, eventually return to the question of what consciousness means. If human consciousness is a mirage, mere hiccups of electrical and chemical data processing, then it is difficult to imagine what Christianity means or what it would matter. Indeed, it is challenging to know why anything matters.

Most of us can agree that consciousness seems to function like an intelligent mirror. It reflects, records, recalls, and reconstructs the contents of one's experienced world. It also forms potential responses to anticipated developments.

However, if early Christians (such as Augustine) were right, then consciousness is also a person's awareness of himself. It is an awareness that one has gradually individuated himself from tribe and from a specific time and place. It is the conviction that one is in the process of becoming a unique self and should choose how that process should proceed.

From the Christian perspective, consciousness does more than reflect. Consciousness seeks to shape itself, its environment, and other selves. Furthermore, it evaluates the appropriateness of its own thoughts and deeds by a system of values it embraces and seeks to embody. Finally, a Christian view of consciousness revolves around a core awareness that one's Creator holds one accountable for how one makes his way through life.

How Consciousness Affects Material Reality

A few words here about quantum mechanics may be helpful. That is the field of physics that deals with subatomic reality. Few outside the field grasp even its most basic concepts, and the implications continually expand. With that cautionary confession in mind, we will proceed.

One cannot discuss contemporary culture without wrestling with this monumental achievement of the early twentieth century. Along with the theory of relativity, genetics, and information theory, quantum mechanics has utterly altered how we view reality.

That consciousness became such a major topic for physicists came as a surprise. The reason this occurred, however, is that the universe, at least at the subatomic level, seems to react to consciousness. Many physicists wish this were not true. Some continue to insist it is not. The evidence so far though seems to indicate that consciousness indeed plays a role in how subatomic particles behave.

We call this the Copenhagen interpretation of superposition.

I know it's a mouthful! But it is a vital component of contemporary knowledge.

Superposition means that until observed, the state of a subatomic particle is undetermined. In simple, perhaps imprecise words, the state of a subatomic particle didn't only unknown but unknowable until one observes it. Until then, a subatomic particle exists potentially in any one of several states. In other words, it is conclusively present nowhere. Observation causes the suspension to collapse, forcing the particle to move from a potential to a definitive state.

The Copenhagen interpretation isn't the only way to describe this phenomenon. However, it remains the most widely accepted explanation. To help non-physicists understand the Copenhagen interpretation of superposition, Erwin Schrödinger told a famous parable about a cat.

Schrödinger's cat is in a box. From outside the box, one cannot say whether the cat is dead or alive. That is not merely because we don't *know* whether it's dead or alive but because the cat's state is non-determinable.

We can say either that the cat is suspended somewhere between being dead and alive or that it is both dead and alive. The cat is not yet assigned to either state. It's when we open the lid that the super-position collapses. In other words, something has forced reality to make a choice. That is when we discover that the cat is either alive or dead.

Please don't get angry with me! It was Schrödinger's cat!

All sorts of nonsense has been written on this topic. I don't want to add to it. So, I will add only that quantum mechanics isn't some sort of bunny trail. Countless experiments over many decades have demonstrated that quantum mechanics accurately describes the subatomic world. If the Copenhagen theory continues to hold—as it has now for several decades—consciousness will remain an impor-tant topic in contemporary physics. As, indeed it will be in many contemporary fields of study.

Computers and Consciousness

In 1947, Claude Shannon published an article in *The Bell System Technical Journal*. He called it *A Mathematical Theory of Communication*. It was about how information becomes distorted as it travels. Noise, in other words. Shannon's immediate goal was simple: he wanted to describe a way to keep the nation's growing telephone communica-tion clear and intact over long distances. He drew upon mathemat-ical and mechanical knowledge that most people would have thought unrelated to the problem Shannon wished to address.

Shannon thought of himself as a tinkerer rather than a theorist. He had no idea that his paper would prove to be as groundbreaking as it was. The surface matter of the article was simply about how to share information—any kind of information—without loss of content. He didn't realize that he had laid the groundwork for redefining information altogether, or that people would soon come to identify information as an irreducible aspect of reality.

In retrospect, we can see that Shannon's gift for synthesizing theories and technology had been evident for some time. Early in his career, he had worked with a huge mechanical calculator at Bell Laboratories. Once powered by steam, the gadget was by that time run by electricity.

Shannon soon realized that none of the calculator's wheels, levers, and gears were now necessary. All that was needed for calculation was the electricity itself and a switch capable of turning the electricity on and off. By assigning the on position a value of one and the off position a value of zero, calculations could be processed in binary, or base two instead of the customary base ten.

In base two, the number sequence for 1, 2, 3, 4 becomes 1, 10, 11, 100. The number 562 thus becomes 100010010. For a while, this was a theoretical insight without a practical application. What sort of switch could turn electricity on and off quickly enough to do even simple calculations?

Not long after Shannon thought about this, it became possible to mass produce the transistor, a small (and rapid) switching device. A few decades later, microchips—even smaller and even faster switching devices—allow us to build calculators that switched electricity on and off millions of times per second.

The use of base two, or *digital* computation, could be used for processing algebraic formulas. That made it possible to create, store, and send not only numbers, but words, sound, and pictures. Shannon's famous article explained how all such information might be sent, even over long distances, without loss of content. There would be no more separation between local, national, and global communication. There was just endless information traveling from everywhere to everywhere.

Shannon may have been, just as he claimed, more of a synthesizer than a discoverer. Even so, the synthesis was an act of genius. Although analogue computers had existed for at least a couple of centuries, they were far removed from the digital computers we have now. More than anyone else, Shannon made this imaginable.

It was not long before people in other fields would draw on Shannon's work to understand human cognition. New fields such as cognitive psychology and artificial intelligence began to emerge as a result. Some became so impressed with information theory that they began to wonder whether the human brain was simply a biological switching device. From there, it became possible to think of artificial intelligence as an emerging form of consciousness. Put another way, perhaps consciousness was simply the "software" of a biological computer housed between human ears.

Major Theories About Consciousness

In this chapter, we have looked at how several contemporary disciplines are now focused on consciousness. Once confined to religious and philosophical discussions, there is now scarcely a field that does not wrestle in some way with what consciousness is and does. This attention has not yet resulted in a common understanding of consciousness. In fact, it has left us with more questions.

As we conclude this chapter, let's summarize the major hypotheses currently in vogue.

1. Substance Dualism

Substance dualism is what most Western peoples would have, until very recently, thought of as "common sense." It was best articulated by Renee Descartes in the famous sentence: "I think; therefore I am." In this view, human consciousness is the quality of a real person peering out through a body and into the world. Whether the person is delusional, mistaken, or a genius, Descartes says, he cannot help but be aware of his own existence. This includes his awareness that his own body is something somehow separate from his core self. Mind and matter are thus different kinds of things.

Descartes does not explain how mind and matter connect, at least not in ways that seem satisfying to most of us.

Substance dualism and Christianity are reasonably compatible, though many would argue that it goes too far in separating the human person into separate material and spiritual components. Both the ancient Hebrew definition of soul and the New Testament definition of sanctification and resurrection assumes a much more unified being than what Descartes presents. Nonetheless, this viewpoint is widespread in most Christian groups.

2. Material Monism

Material Monism is a view held by many cognitive psychologists, usually in a form called *functionalism*. In this view, mind is simply an emergent property of brain and is often expressed in the phrase that "mind is simply the brain doing its job."

Most of its proponents would agree that material monism is incompatible with Christianity. If there is no spiritual realm, and if the human mind does not survive the loss of the body, Christianity seems unsustainable as much more than an aspirational (and largely unobtainable) system of ethics.

3. Idealist Monism

Idealist Monism is a view encountered in many traditional Eastern religions and philosophies. Hinduism and Buddhism are well known examples, though some Western philosophers (Arthur Schopenhauer, for example) have held it. In this view, idea precedes and structures matter. Some proponents of idealism go so far as to say that matter is an illusion. Deepak Chopra, for example, once said, "Body is the printout of mind."

In this view, the brain becomes something like an interface that connects the spiritual being temporarily inhabiting the body with the natural and social world.

This view, at least in its most radical forms, is incompatible with orthodox Christianity. Nonetheless, it has always enjoyed considerable influence. One detects it sometimes in Christian funerals: "This is not Bob, lying here in this box. It's only the body Bob used for a while!"

As theologians are often quick to point out, this view is a form of Gnosticism, a spiritual philosophy that early Christians rejected.

4. Neutral Monism

Several important scientists and philosophers have developed a view called neutral monism. (Bertrand Russell and William James are notable examples.) Neutral monism views mind and brain as separate entities, though neither can be denied in favor of the other. Unlike substance dualism, however, neutral monism proposes that mind and brain, and therefore thought and matter, emerge from a common, unknown source.

This view is compatible with Christianity, though it begs the question of the missing link from which it proposes that both matter and mind emerge. It would present no real problem for Christianity were physics to discover such an underlying substance. Of course, we would have to rewrite tons of textbooks. That has happened before and is likely to occur again.

Neutral monism is the view of a wide spectrum of thinkers, including both religious and anti-religious ones. We can expect then that it will be with us for a while. Some are proposing that information is the common source of both matter and mind. This view presents no problem for Christian theology, though neither does it necessarily lead to theism.

5. Panpsychism

Panpsychism is a relatively new perspective. At least it is a new take on an ancient idea. Despite its name, it is not a form of pantheism. It is, in fact, a respected theory held by a few (mostly younger) scientists and philosophers.

In this view, consciousness (but not necessarily self-consciousness) exists wherever information becomes dense enough to self-organize. Also, consciousness is viewed as a spectrum rather than as a category. An atom is "conscious" in that it carries information and can interact with other atoms in ways that complexify information.

This view comes close to the way St. Maximus and John Scotus Eriugina viewed reality. They based their view on the implications of Logos being present in all things because of the universe having been spoken into existence. As Eriugina put it, "The world is an epiphany of God," or as Maximus more thoroughly expressed it,

> *"The world is a sacrament of God's presence, a means of communion with him, a theophany; all created things are God's garments[1]."*

Note that Eriugina did not claim the universe was an incarnation, but rather an epiphany. An epiphany is a revelation of some aspect of God. Incarnation is God in a material form. The distinction, though important, didn't protect Eriugina from charges of pantheism.

If panpsychism were to gain more traction in the Western World, it would provoke a major restructuring of the current secular worldview. Many believe that such a restructuring is at any rate inevitable, but that is mere speculation at this point. A so-called "theory of everything" is still a distant goal. Nonetheless, panpsychism is an early contender for future explanation of how information becomes conscious. So, we're likely to hear more from proponents of this view in coming years.

Chapter Summary

Contemporary studies on consciousness have until recently leaned heavily toward either material monism or neutral monism. The "bad boy" of contemporary consciousness studies, often beaten up in the town square and left for dead, is substance dualism. Nonetheless, it lurks around every corner. When in an unguarded moment a neurologist falls in love or is moved by Mozart, the old familiar way of viewing one's own self as something real can magically remerge in all its glory. It's challenging even for brilliant scientists to reduce love and music to something akin to neurological flatulence.

Idealist monism also has its proponents. Even the most dedicated materialist will often question his accustomed view of reality after ingesting the right kind of mushroom. A near-death experience or a left hemisphere stroke can have the same affect. Such experiences often lead one to entertain an idealist point of view.

In short: consciousness studies are indeed presently in a muddle. So far, no one has thoroughly proven any of the viewpoints described here. Meanwhile, we keep learning, so we will all have to stay tuned.

In the meantime, there is another Christian "given" we should explore: the fact that human beings experience themselves as inhabitants of a cosmos. Something inside most of us is in awe of something outside us. Although the various human cultures have explained human experience differently, they all agree that the universe seems put together rather well.

Christians believe they know the reason.

3

Participation in Reality
THE MIND'S GRASP OF A COMPLEX
UNIVERSE

We began the previous chapter with a scene from Andy Wier's *Project Hail Mary*.

I have found that sci-fi literature provokes scientific and philosophical imagination. It seems to bypass our tendency to dismiss what we find threatening or uninteresting. Its weird settings and creatures hold our attention as the authors slip novel ideas into our head. The reason this works is simple: whether or not aliens exist, or teleportation ever occurs, future human beings will have philosophical, emotional, and relational questions. That is why we are still reading Homer and Plato.

The best sci-fi authors usually have been well-informed about the scientific innovations of their time. They have also had a good idea about where things were headed.

Chester Gould's *Dick Tracy* series (1931-1977) contained technology that looks suspiciously like a smart watch. Julies Verne's submarine, the robots of the 1927 movie *Metropolis*, and depictions of thinking machines decades before the advent of the modern computer, are pretty impressive. It may be that sci-fi writers have not been prophets as much as hypnotists. It could be that Gould correctly predicted the smart watch, or perhaps he ignited the imagination of little boys like Steve Jobs.

We do know that imagining the evolution of technology cultivates an appreciation for science and technology. Most computer science innovators read sci-fi as children. What many of these innovators missed in sci-fi literature was the warning that in the hands of unethical and amoral people, advanced technology leads to disaster. Advanced technology is cool. It demonstrates a civilization's knowledge and creativity. It says nothing about a people's wisdom or ethical life.

What we notice in science fiction then is that people in the future are much like those of the present and the past. Two hundred years from now, in a galaxy far, far away, people still use math and logic to figure things out. Some of them are wise and some of them are fools. Some seek goodness; others, merely power. All of them must learn how to count. All of them must develop reason and strategies for solving problems.

In *Project Hail Mary*, Dr. Ryland Grace is confused when he awakes from a long sleep. When he figures out that he is on a spaceship, he begins to explore it. It doesn't take him long to realize that the light pouring through the ship's windows is not from the sun he has known all his life, but from the sun of a strange galaxy. He is very far from home!

Although he is in a novel situation, Grace discovers where he is. He then begins to work through a few possible reasons for being there. Not once does he ask himself whether mathematics will work in this strange galaxy. Grace is a scientist and knows that the principles of physics describe reality *everywhere*.

How does he know this?

Grace understands that this strange galaxy is part of the universe. Because of this, research, analysis, experimentation, and logic work—

On earth.

In space.

Underwater.

Everywhere.

Reason leads to solid connections to reality—whatever one's inner conflicts or external challenges. Neither the limitations of one's prior experience nor existing knowledge can prohibit the human mind from engaging with any part of the universe. The human mind transcends its natural environment—if the mind does not subvert the process.

That is why we need thinking tools.

Thinking tools help the mind avoid self-deception. We need that help because the mind naturally resists information that appears to conflict with what it already knows. Thinking tools keep emotional reactions at bay while gathering and evaluating information. This forces the mind to work deliberately, step by sequential step, avoiding preferences or prejudices that might otherwise highjack one's quest for truth.

A pilot flying a plane that's experiencing mechanical difficulties, a surgeon removing a complicated tumor from a child's brain, and a space traveler waking up in a strange galaxy must all rely on thinking tools for evacuating the situation and arriving at a solution. Admirable human sentiment, loyalty to one's traditions, and personal taste become potential hazards in such cases.

So, what are these thinking tools, and how do they work?

The Human Mind Reflects a Seen and Unseen Universe

Christians believe that the human mind's ability to comprehend and respond to both visible and abstract realities indicates that we live within an ordered creation. In other words, the ability of thinking tools to connect one with reality implies that the universe didn't emerge by happenstance.

Most Christians accept that some form of evolution was the means through which life forms emerged on this planet, though some do not. All Christians, however, believe that the universe exists for specific reasons known to its Creator and that human beings are equipped and called to discover these reasons. The ability to do this implies that reason is not merely a habit of the human mind for imposing patterns on random data but is rather an indication that a trained mind recognizes in data an existent underlying order. Furthermore, mind participates in the source of order, which is conscious information.

The quest to discover truths about the universe then is not only a component of human development but of the ongoing development of the entire universe. The human mind in other words, was formed to be a participatory character in the Creator's ultimate design for creation. This means that human beings are not meant to live as passive inhabitants of creation but rather as active agents of their Creator by understanding and caring for God's creation.

In this sense then, science and mathematics are not merely tools for gathering knowledge. They are implements of spiritual discernment. Rational pursuits, such as science and mathematics, are practices consistent with spiritual life, no less so than prayer and study of scripture. That human beings are responsible to their Creator and to one another for discerning the difference between what is true and what is not as they manage all aspects of their earthly life is clearly established in the first chapters of Genesis.

Truth—which means a connection with what actually exists—is not only the gold standard of science and mathematics then, but also of theology, biblical morality, and ethics. Nothing that is not in some sense true can be good or beautiful. For this reason, the three eternal transcendentals—goodness, truth, and beauty—are inseparable. Each of them leads to the others, in all times, and in all places.

Since human beings are fallen and therefore imperfect, all individual perspectives on truth, goodness, and beauty are provisional and incomplete. Discernment, the process through which we evaluate perspectives, is thus necessary for arriving at an ever-clearer grasp of truth. For although human beings are created equal, opinions are not. Some opinions move us closer to reality. Others move us further away. The opinions to which we are most loyal are often the very ones that hinder us the most in our journey toward truth.

Furthermore, some levels of knowledge are beyond us. In the words of the Psalmist, "we cannot attain to it." Nonetheless, because truth is consistent in all times and in all places, even those levels of reality beyond our grasp emanate shadows and figures through which they may be partially discerned.

This feature of reality is the basis of all metaphor, allegory, algorithm, and parable—the instruments through which human beings intuit things they do not yet know fully, or with absolute certainty. In the words of the Epistle to the Hebrews, the deep sense that one has made a connection with such transcendent realities is the "assurance of things hoped for," and an "evidence of things unseen."

The word *universe* expresses the reliable character of reality. It implies that reality is a composite whole, that is to say a carefully ordered and arranged system of amalgamated components. The ancient term that most forcibly express this conviction is the word *cosmos*.

The English word *cosmetics* derives from this Greek term and can help us grasp its meaning. One uses cosmetics to order one's appearance. One orders their appearance because they do not wish to leave their appearance in that unprocessed form in which nature manifests it. A face embellished by cosmetics has been thus purposefully arranged. When we describe the whole of reality as cosmos then, we are implying the same thing: that matter is ordered rather than chaotic.

(Helpful as this analogy is, it will not be altogether healthy for me to say more about cosmetics. Certain writers have wives and daughters, after all!)

Philosophers like Pythagoras wrote extensively about the implications of living within a cosmos. Over the following millennia and a half, others, mostly Greek, expanded those reflections.

For the Hebrews, however, reality didn't begin as cosmos, but as chaos. The Hebrew phrase for that primal state is the strange phrase *tohu wa-bohu*. Although the Bible uses the word "tohu" several times, the first chapter of Genesis is one of only three places where one encounters the word *bohu*. The phrase unites the word *tohu*, meaning "waste or nothingness" with the similar-sounding word *bohu*, meaning emptiness, to drive home its point. We would be doing something like that if we said, "My four-year-old just drew a wiggly-squiggly line and told me it was a picture of my tongue!"

All Bible translators are challenged by how best to render this phrase. The Greek Old Testament translates *tohu wa-bohu* as "unseen and unformed." The KJV famously renders it, "without form and void."

However we translate it, the Bible's first description of reality is of a wiggly-squiggly mess of random chaos.

Genesis 1:1 establishes the starting point of both the Bible and the universe in that simple statement, "In the beginning, God created the heavens and the earth." The text does not delve into how or when chaotic matter had been created. We only know that what follows will be not so much a creation as a formation of a material universe in a state of *tohu wa-bohu*.

By "the earth," the ancient writers of this text likely meant what we would call "the universe." That is to say, the entire, visible "everything-that-exists" was in a state of chaos.

In contrast, St. Augustine believed that the phrase "the heavens" was not in a state of "tohu wa-bohu." For Augustine, "the heavens" did not refer to what we call outer space, but to an immaterial dimension that would become God's means for ordering the material universe. We might say then that it has always been God's intention for things on earth to be as they are "in heaven."

In Augustine's view then, "the earth" and "the heavens" were created as mirror images of one another. Heaven was a realm of matterless form. The primal earth was a realm of formless matter.

Although it has often been rejected by Western theologians throughout the modern era, this interpretation of Genesis—indeed, this view of reality—was common to most Christians during the premodern period, and it remains the view of many Christians outside the West even today.

Since I believe early Christian thought has much to add to our response to a number of contemporary questions, I want to go a bit deeper into Augustine's reading of the creation story here.

Along with other patristic writers, Augustine views reality as a cosmos that has been intentionally shaped and impregnated by logos. If that statement seems obscure, rest assured we will get into its meaning in coming pages. It is enough here to note that although

Claude Shannon proposed a much narrower definition of information[1] than the ancients assigned to the word logos, the two words are, if not synonyms, then certainly analogous terms.

At any rate, since the General Theory of Relativity, Quantum Mechanics, Information Theory, and the discovery of the Human Genome, ancient and medieval reflections on the implications of living in a world created and maintained through logos becomes once more a viable concept. Indeed, those reflections on logos may be a necessary connection for creating a Christian response to those scientific advancements and the philosophical questions they raise.

Until the modern era, all Western thought, not merely or even primarily Christian thought, revolved around the concept of logos. Of course, we have learned a lot about the universe since then. So, we will move on now from how Augustine and other Patristic writers read Genesis. We will revisit that topic, however, as we address the role of pattern, providence, metaphor, and parable in Christian thought.

For this chapter, we will refocus on the Christian claim that human beings live within a universe, a cosmos, an ordered system of integrated parts. From a Christian viewpoint, this is why the laws of physics work everywhere. Few of us believe that we exist within a computer program. We do not seriously think our brains are stored in vats while aliens pacify us with entertaining software. The great majority of human beings are confident that reality is reasonably stable.

Although Christians see hints everywhere that a spiritual realm exerts influence upon (and within) the created order, we infer all we know about that realm from personal experience and a few cryptic and mostly allegorical passages of scripture. This implies that Christians, just like their secular neighbors, believe that human beings are best equipped (and therefore designed) for investigating the visible universe through their natural senses and informed imagination. Although spiritual revelation is for us a type of knowledge, for such knowledge to become of practical use (or communicable to those outside the faith) it must be explained by principles discoverable and demonstrable in the natural world.

Escaping Self Deception

Scientific progress requires us to deal honestly with the material universe. Although most of us try to do that, we naturally notice data that seems to agree with our existing opinions and to overlook data that does not. Thinking tools help us bypass those preconceptions and prejudices responsible for our selective attention. They keep us accountable to the deep structures of reality. It is this honest connection to what is true rather than what we would prefer to be true that leads to scientific, mathematical, and technological advances. This, in turn, promotes human flourishing.

The laptop on which I am writing these words is an example of creative thought held accountable to reality. The plow and the aqueduct were just as startling in their time. Corn, a human engineered species of plant life, was an even older expansion of human engineering. Such developments grow from the stewardship role that God gave to human beings at the beginning of human history.

Surprisingly, the Bible is more cautious about our dealings with the *non*material world than with the material world. For example, scripture urges us to hold visionaries and miracle workers at arm's length and to carefully investigate claims of supernatural phenomenon.

In contrast to Teilhard de Chardin's famous definition of humans as "spiritual beings having an earthly experience," the Bible depicts its heroes as material beings who occasionally have supernatural experiences. Our dealings with God and other persons—material or immaterial—take place within a created, material order, the realm in which we have been placed.

Christianity then defines human beings as mortal, material creatures. That is not the total story of course. Christ and the apostles invite us to become something much more than material creatures. Even so, we remain, in time and eternity, embodied, material beings. We affirm this every time we confess, "I believe in the resurrection of the body."

St. Thomas Aquinas thought that biblical spirituality requires a humble acknowledgement of the material universe as "our appointed realm." This comes from a man whose colleagues swore on their immortal souls had manifested supernatural gifts.

Christians have always believed in miracles, prophetic insight, and other kinds of supernatural phenomena. Even though believers in the modern era sometimes found these things embarrassing, they could not be eliminated from faith without deconstructing it.

Nonetheless, both scripture and Christianity's most respected teachers have urged both respect and caution when it comes to supernatural claims. They ask us to keep in mind that before anyone was ever given a spiritual gift, God had already given all peoples everywhere the greatest supernatural gift imaginable: a universe that operates by dependable processes. Indeed, we often call those processes *the laws of nature*.

When we say that God purposely placed human beings within a material creation, we are assuming that this was where God intended human beings to live. It would not make sense therefore that God would ask human beings to prove their faith by discounting or ignoring the laws of nature. Although some Christians claim that faith lifts one above nature, this defines human life in a way that is at odds with how God created the world. Submission to God thus involves an acknowledgement of (and compliance with) reality as God created it. This includes an awareness of human limitations, one of which is the tendency to believe what we want to believe and to resist developing critical judgement.

The twentieth century philosopher, Karl Popper, expressed this in less religious language: "Rationality essentially consists in openness to rational criticism."

Whether Christian, Marxist, or physicist, if one is committed to keep believing what he already believes, he will become angry when anyone challenges those beliefs. If, on the other hand, one believes what he believes because he has tried to carefully think through the reasons for those beliefs, he will be grateful if someone shows him how he has erred.

New information offers humanity new potential for making a fuller contact with reality. That is why we should be happy when we discover new information. In practice though, most of us find it difficult to process new information. That becomes especially diffi-cult if it challenges our sense of identity. If an opinion gets attached to our identity, we cannot process challenges to that opinion without experiencing anxiety. This is often the source of emotional outbursts and personal attacks on people who offer new information.

The reason that clear thinking is difficult is because we are beset by individual and collective prejudices. These seriously impede learning. Intellectual growth—indeed, growth of any sort—involves a struggle with the fear and pride that protects our ego from anxi-ety-producing information.

There is no more effective weapon against such pride than the biblical reminder, "From dust thou art and to dust shall thou return." The passage reminds us that we are mortals, participants in the glories and limitations of our God-given station within the mate-rial universe.

To understand how Christianity views this role, we must explore a few ways human beings have thought about their transcendent source of existence and how Christians respond.

4

The One Beyond Image

The cosmos is the work of a Single Personal Being who exists both within and outside of time and space.

THOMAS MERTON DESCRIBES HIS FIRST TRANSCENDENT EXPERIENCE in *The Seven Story Mountain.*

Walking into the kitchen of his Pittsburg home just before daybreak, the five-year-old Thomas saw his mother light a gas oven. He watched as the dancing flame cast its shadows against the wall. Merton, the child of agnostic parents, fell on his face.

It is an archetypal depiction of a nearly universal human impulse.

We can interpret the meaning of the story as a child's reaction to fire. Most of us are at least a bit awed by fire, though we do not tend to invest it with spiritual meaning in the way our distant ancestors did. We assume that as the child in this story matures, mystery will give way to reason. That Merton himself recalls the experience as significant—well, even brilliant thinkers have their quirks.

Contemporary people tend not to view worship as a human need. That is odd, historically speaking, for when and where have human beings not worshipped?

Atheism has always been a possible reaction to the world, though it has usually required years of education. Atheists are certainly aware of the ubiquity of religion in human history but rarely offer an explanation beyond that of humans being susceptible to suggestion and superstition. It is not an impossible explanation for religion, though it is sobering to think that only a handful of individuals, possessing the financial wherewithal to acquire high levels of education, can hope to achieve freedom from a form of irrationality that has afflicted nearly the entire human race.

Many of today's professing atheists do not fit this caricature, I hasten to say. Many of them were raised in religious households but claim that their intellectual quest led them to abandon their faith. Some are sad about that because their faith once brought them comfort. Others seem to embrace atheism because of some hurtful or disillusioning experience involving religion. At any rate, I am not trying to portray atheism as a sham. I am merely claiming it has been rare.

If spiritual life has been an illusion, it has been a most powerful and persistent one. Attempts to erase religion from society have been relatively short-lived. The French and Russian revolutions are good examples. Eventually, some substitute—an ideology, a Führer, drugs—something communal and overwhelming, poured into the vacuum.

The accelerating erosion of religious life in contemporary North America seems somewhat different, however. For one thing, it is probably the fruit of apathy and disillusionment more than of anger. This may result in a more enduring kind of atheism than the sort imposed by persecutory governments on an unwilling populace. If that is indeed the case, this is a major change in the historical patterns of religion as a cultural force.

Although not all—or even a majority—of spiritually inclined individuals have believed in the God of the Bible. However, most human beings throughout history have claimed to experience some presence beyond themselves (or perhaps inside themselves) that they believed was more than a projection of their own imagination. This aspect of religious life—the sense of something beyond, what we call the transcendent realm—persists. Even many atheists are willing to acknowledge it.

A. J. Jacob is a good example. He describes a transcendent experience of his own in his Year *of Living Biblically*[1].

Jacobs is known for taking on self-imposed disciplines as performance art, which he then shares in delightful books. One of these was *The Know It All*, in which he describes his experiences of reading through the Encyclopedia Britannica in a year. After that, he dedicated a year to "living biblically," meaning that for a year he would keep all the commands of the Bible. This included stoning an adulterer in Central Park, which didn't go as planned!

Knowing his experiment with keeping commandments should include prayer, Jacobs stood in the middle of his New York apartment one morning and lifted his hands. After mumbling a few nonsense phrases, he ended the prayer with "whoever, whatever you are."

He suddenly had a chill, a deep sense that mockery would not be tolerated. He could either pray or not pray. He was not to blaspheme. In a book filled with amusing stories, this was one that Jacob refused to make into a caricature.

What Jacobs experienced that day was what Jews and Christians define as the ground zero of spiritual life: awe. It is an uncanny awareness of a presence supremely great, a sort of spiritual arousal. Like sexual arousal, awe leads one to focus his entire attention—to behold—until the primal force has released its grip. The Book of Proverbs calls this "the awe of the Lord," and describes it as the foundation of wisdom.

Rabbi Abraham Joshua Heschel choses the word *ineffable* to describe the human reaction to transcendent experience. While reading Heschel's *God in Search of Man*, I became annoyed by how often the rabbi used this word. It struck me at first as a literary tick. Gradually though, I understood that for Rabbi Heschel, ineffability —being struck dumb in the presence of something too great to be expressed—was the very core of an experience with the God of scripture. Indeed, the old English word *dumbstruck* may be even more expressive.

In an age that has so strongly discounted religion as a social good, transcendent experience becomes the common ground upon which to discuss the meaning of spiritual life. Although the religious person may differ from the secular one about the origin and meaning of such experiences, they offer an opportunity to step outside the daily grind. Occasionally, such an experience awakens one to the possibility that there may be more to reality than the material world.

Secular Perspectives on Transcendence

Julian Janes offers a secular explanation for historical accounts of transcendent experience in his work, The *Origin of Consciousness in the Breakdown of the Bicameral Mind.*[2] Janes assumed that many such accounts were written by honest and rational individuals and was especially interested in those in which someone heard the audible voice of a god, demon, or deceased person.

Since Janes didn't believe in the supernatural, he arrived at an intriguing explanation. When such experiences were common, he hypothesized, evolution had not yet fully integrated the cerebral hemispheres into a single sense of self. Noting how often the stories involved a warning or a command to take immediate action, Janes believed the voice came from the hearer's own non-dominant hemisphere. Not knowing that human beings house within themselves two different systems for processing thought, ancient peoples experienced the voice as that of a supernatural being.

The popular 2016 HBO series *Westworld* drew on Janes's theory to develop a believable explanation for android sentience. In the series, a theme park recreates the American West in the not-so-distant future. The park is staffed by intelligent, human-like robots, physically indistinguishable from the tourists, and the tourists fight, joke, and have sex with them. When tortured, which increasingly happens, the android seems to suffer. They even appear to die when shot. Because the tourists know that there are safeguards against harming another tourist, they are free from the moral impediments that might otherwise inhibit them from abusing other humans.

The programmers, meanwhile, keep looking for ways to deepen the android's illusion of consciousness. One method they discover of doing this is to download a "back story" into each android. This creates a perception of recalling fuzzy memories, which provokes unpredictable actions. Sometimes though, the androids experience input from their not-fully-integrated backstories as mysterious, as coming from outside, which they interpret as a supernatural experience.

All of this is a nod to Janes's theory about why so many human beings have had encounters that they experienced as being super-natural.

Whatever we think of the theory, Janes does attempt to explain why spiritual experience has been nearly universal. He does not discount all the accounts of them as a deliberate deception or as proof of madness. He did, however, search for an explanation that would be consistent with his materialist worldview. From his perspective, humanity's experience of the divine, though sincere, has emerged from a faulty understanding of our own brain and central nervous system.

By seeking to understand accounts of the supernatural, Janes represented the kinder side of the modern perspective on religion and spirituality. Sigmund Freud, on the other hand, represented the more common approach of modern intellectuals. The title of his book on the subject, *The Future of an Illusion*[3], is self-explanatory.

In Freud's view, the human mind produces illusions of transcen-dence to meet its own inner needs. A trained therapist should listen respectfully to patients about these illusions, but for the purpose of demystifying the practical message they deliver. However, even the most convincing testimony of a supernatural experience amounts to little more than a reflection in a hall of mirrors.

We see then a common assumption in Freud and Janes, despite the difference in their approach. It is that transcendent experience is an internally generated phenomenon. Stigmata, near-death experi-ence, ghosts, visions, and spontaneous healing are not visitations from somewhere outside the self but rather projections of the unconscious into the conscious.

Postmodern scholars tend to take a different approach. They are often willing to face the emotional consequence of living in a demystified world, focusing on the ways human beings overcome their loss of faith by finding transcendence through sexual experience, the arts, augmented reality, and recreational drugs. These studies are nearly always respectful and complementary. Even so, traditional religion is rarely thought relevant in such studies and is very often depicted as an impediment to healthy transcendence.

An example of this approach is Michael Pollen's *How to Change Your Mind.*[4] The book is a history about psychedelic drug use in the United States and the lost opportunity for exploring the therapeutic potential of psychedelics. He concludes with a moving disclosure about his personal experience with three types of psychedelics: psilocybin, LSD, and DMT.

As the book begins, Pollen describes himself as an agnostic leaning toward atheism. As the story progresses, psychedelic drug use awakens in him a sense of cautious openness to spirituality. Christians will be understandably cautious toward what is for them a potential gateway to the demonic. However, such accounts of transcendence may be the only "god space" left in the contemporary secular world's conceptual framework of many of the individuals we meet.

This has happened before. During Europe's Romantic era, literature often explored ways of maintaining awareness of some sort of spiritual dimension. Although belief in God had been waning for decades in the West, a longing for "something beyond" had persisted. Throughout the 1880's and into the first couple of decades, many European and American intellectuals experimented with the numinous effects of drug use, poetry, art, sex, and music on the human psyche. A few of them walked into faith as a result.

In the contemporary world, discussions about transcendence can likewise serve as a kind of meeting place in which believers and agnostics can explore aspects of the inner life. Such conversations will likely draw upon psychology, anthropology, music, drug use, sexual expression, and the arts. Christians will find it challenging to draw upon their own commitment to scripture, sacrament, and community as the context of spiritual experience in ways that resonate with their secular neighbors. They should keep in mind though that respectful conversation about spiritual hunger and transcendent experience has often been the starting place for seekers moving from agnosticism toward an encounter with Christ.

C. S. Lewis's recount of his journey from atheism is an example of how spiritual experiences, even of a troubling sort, can lead to robust faith. For Lewis, poetry, fantasy literature, and even a brief interest in the occult, all contributed to the opening of first his mind, and then his heart to God.

How Do We Talk About God?

C. S. Lewis's *Mere Christianity* is still a good overview of how Christians can discuss God with others. Lewis begins where modern seekers nearly always began, by asking whether any sort of spiritual beings exist. He then moves to the question of whether these beings or Being are personal or impersonal. He asks whether one can (or should) directly know such beings. Lewis then concludes with the question of whether the personal Creator became a human being.

Mere Christianity is obviously written from a Christian point of view. However, it takes other points of view seriously. Lewis understood that it was dishonest and uncharitable to dismiss atheism and other religious perspectives as utterly unreasonable. The book is not therefore an airtight apologetic that forever ends honest conversation about the existence of God. It is simply a statement of one man's reasons for choosing Christian faith over other options he had encountered.

I will roughly repeat the flow of Lewis's thought here.

The overview is not spiritually warm. Philosophical and anthropological approaches to religion begins with an assumption that piety and practice are components of one's own cultural formation. According to this "view from the outside," experiences of religious transcendence are categorized with patriotic or athletic experiences. From a spiritual point of view, this is woefully inadequate. Rabbi

Abraham Joshua Heschel forcibly makes this point in his writings. Rudolph Otto, in the classic *The Idea of the Holy*, does as well.

However spiritually inadequate though, a philosophical or anthropological approach to religion offers a sort of "town square," a safe common space for religious conversations. So, beginning with the materialist perspective in which there is no room for nonmaterial entities of any sort, let us take a quick look at the main ways human beings have thought about the spiritual world.

Atheism and Agnosticism

Atheism denies the existence of any sort of disembodied intelligence —gods, angels, ghosts, and the like. In this view, the ultimate origin of the universe is still unknown but will likely become clearer in the future. Human consciousness is a feature of evolutionary processes and is dependent on material components. As a result, consciousness does not survive death.

Agnosticism takes a step away from atheism but is sympathetic to it. It retains a degree of curiosity, however, about why many human beings seem so convinced in the reality of a spiritual realm. Agnostics generally assume atheism is probably the most reasonable view of reality but are willing to consider other points of view.

Impersonal Monism

Impersonal monism is "Star Wars theology."

May the Force be with you!

Since before written history, several cultures around the world embraced impersonal monism, and it remains the view of many yet today. Taoism is an obvious example. This view of spiritual life emerges from the conviction that a primal force moves through the universe which wise persons must discern and with which they must cooperate. The Force neither rewards nor punishes but it does operate by deep laws.

We might define monism as an awareness of the Whole within

the parts. Since everything reflects the Whole, one comes to see a river, a tree and a kangaroo as deeply connected to oneself. A belief in the cosmic integration of all things is profoundly spiritual, though it does not necessarily lead to belief in a Creator.

In *fung shui*, an aesthetic philosophy based on impersonal monism, one attempts to discern how the Force manifests at a specific place. For example, a designer will stand on the proposed site of a new building to observe how the shadow of a mountain falls on the landscape or how the river bends as it flows past the site. They will then design the footprint of the building in a way that they believe acknowledges and honors the flow of energy in that place. The shape of the roof and the placement of windows and doors will also align with this information.

This philosophy is prominent in some Asian nations. However, it has influenced Western design as well. Frank Lloyd Wright is an example, as is Christopher Alexander. Alexander wrote a book called *A Timeless Way of Building* influenced by impersonal monism.

One of the ways ancient peoples sought to discern the movement of energy was through oracles. The *I Ching* (Book of Changes), was one of these. The Chinese thought of this text as a spiritual tool through which they could determine the invisible but underlying changes of energy that affected the visible world. By examining the patterns of bamboo sticks or coins tossed on a flat surface and consulting the corresponding pattern in the I Chang, one could decide whether or not to marry, do a business deal, or wait on the underlying energy patterns to change.

Nearly all of the world's peoples have at one time or another used similar techniques for accessing what they believed were deeper layers of reality. Although Hebrew/Christian Scripture forbids fortune telling, both the "casting of lots" described in Acts 1 and the *urim* and *thummin* of the Old Testament, were such spiritual tools. Well-witching is one that is familiar to rural Americans. All such "tools" assume the existence of a discernible force of nature.

Many Buddhists embrace a form of impersonal monism. In Buddhism, there is no personal god. Indeed, there is not a self that might relate to a god. There is only awareness itself, reflecting the ceaseless flow of phenomena. In this Buddhist view, reality is dance that creates temporary dancers called humans, rabbits, and all the other elements of the universe.

This spiritual belief does not require any sort of personal God or gods. It would be possible therefore to encounter atheists and agnostics who embrace it. Because it requires no commitment to a specific doctrine or practice, it is tailor-made for our times. Indeed, the so-called New Age movement and countless movies are examples of its resurging influence.

Pantheism

Aldous Huxley called his book *The Perennial Religion*. It was a great title for describing pantheism, humankind's most traveled spiritual path. We find it in the Canaanite fertility religions that the Hebrew prophets so bitterly denounced. It takes on seemingly infinite forms within Hinduism as well. There have been multiple expressions in every age (and in most of the world's cultures) of the pantheistic impulse.

Pantheism is a form of monism but as a personal, rather than an impersonal force. As with impersonal monism, Pantheists perceive the presence of the whole in everything, in everyone, and everywhere. Pantheists, however, experience the presence of the Whole in all things as a conscious, personal being who takes myriads of forms and observes no boundaries.

Young Merton's spiritual experience with fire is a great example of the pantheistic experience. It grows out of the sense that some Presence other than oneself is observing one. The ancient world was filled with shrines to mark special places where this Presence made itself known. In hopes of receiving guidance or provision from this Presence, people prayed and even slept in these shrines. Sometimes, as in ancient Canaan, people had sex in the shrines as an attempt to direct the procreative force of the Great Cosmic Soul toward their families and fields.

Hindu literature is probably the most eloquently stated form of pantheism. The Hindu canon, if we may call it that, is vast, containing profound philosophical speculations about reality as a manifestation of a single consciousness in which all beings, including the divinities, participate and manifest. The Bhagavad Gita (Song of God) is reasonably accessible to the non-Hindu reader and is a beautiful part of that collection.

While Pantheism may seem alien to contemporary Western culture, the idea of being "spiritual but not religious" is representative of this ancient path. As I said of postmodernism earlier, pantheism also is more of a mood than a philosophy. It is the worshipful attitude toward a conscious universe that makes few demands about how one should think or behave. This makes pantheism a perfect fit for those who long for spiritual experience but dislike dogma or personal restriction.

Many who suspect that pantheism does not describe anything objectively real nonetheless find it attractive. Because it invites one to explore and experience spiritual phenomena without commitment, many well-known Western intellectuals have turned toward this ancient path. Karl Jung and Aldous Huxley are a couple of note. One finds in pantheism a language and a process for spiritual exploration that can validate one's own inner life without endangering one's place within the modern intellectual tradition.

The pantheistic impulse, old as humanity itself, will be with us for as long as there are human beings. Huxley was right, it is humankind's perennial religion.

Animism

Animists assume that all living and nonliving things are conscious. Most of us know, or think we know, when our pets are hungry or want to go outside. Animists take this much further. They believe that all of nature, organic and inorganic, communicates with us. Thus, a shaman under the influence of *ayahuasca* can claim that the forest has told him that it is unhappy, perhaps because the tribe built its village too close to a sacred grove.

For animists, material objects are portals that can channel power and information between the spiritual and the material realms. An animist hunter may lift a small stone from a sacred river and then wear it around his neck. He may then say a prayer to the forest spirits as he tenderly touches the stone. If he is successful in killing an animal, he may touch the stone to the animal's head while chanting a thanksgiving litany.

Shamanism, which is the animistic practice, uses fertility rituals, hallucinogenics, dance, and other trance-induction methods, to commune with the spirits of animals, plants, ancestors, and deities. The focus of animistic practice is not on transcendence, as in Christian or Jewish worship. It is on immanence.

In other words, for an animist, spiritual reality is not something far away or something radically *other* than the worshipper. It is a network of entities that inhabits living and nonliving things. Animists thus approach spiritual life as a guest living within the domain of innumerable intelligences, some seen and others unseen.

We often associate animism with non-literate, non-technological peoples. The truth is, animism is widespread in developed modern cultures as well. For example, Shintoism, the national religion of Japan, is animistic. One notes its influence on all religious life in Japan, especially at the folk level. The same is true of many contemporary cultures.

Christianity is no exception. Animism has often influenced Christian life.

Father Gregory Rasputin is a great example of this. Deeply rooted in the shamanistic culture of his native Siberia, Rasputin amazed the Czarist court with impressive signs and wonders. Many Christian missionaries will not find this surprising. They have often encountered animistic influences within the Christian communities they serve. Indeed, these influences can survive generations after a people have nominally professed the way of Christ. Usually, animistic influence survives within folk traditions. Although the overt spiritual significance of these traditions lessens in time, the primal connection to a culture's ancestral heritage survives.

The use of mistletoe is a good example. Most contemporary

people no longer think of mistletoe as a fertility talisman. Besides, a kiss or two won't hurt anybody! Although we never know where a kiss or two might lead, we rarely attribute any unanticipated erotic reactions to the bit of green over the door. Western people, Christians included, often feel they are beyond such primitive animism.

In contrast, Christians raised in areas where animism has exerted a more recent presence are often more cautious than their Western counterparts. Non-Western Christians are also more likely to be known for having keen spiritual insight or even for having mystical gifts. This is rarely because the Christian in question is a practicing animist. It is usually because he or she has been formed by a culture more alert to spiritual realities than those living in a materialist/secular West.

The worlds' various cultures differ among themselves then about whether an object possesses or exudes a spiritual presence. As a result, if someone claims to experience such a presence, we are left wondering whether their experience is the result of the cultural framework in which they have been raised or is in any way an objective reality. One thing for sure, an account of a supernatural occurrence can quickly lead to rather intense disagreements.

Missionaries, who must learn to live between cultures, discover early in their careers to speak cautiously to friends at home about spiritual experiences abroad. They know Western Christians embrace a more materialist and secular point of view than they usually realize and are more comfortable hearing a miracle story from the Bible than one experienced by a friend.

Even non-Christians working abroad often experience this disconnect.

Daniel Everett, the renown linguist, is an atheist. Nonetheless, in his book, *Don't Sleep, There Are Snakes,* he recounts his own inexplicable experience in an Amazonian village.

One day, he was astounded when the villagers with whom he had lived for years began running around and looking up. He had never experienced these same people being religious or even superstitious in any way before. When he asked what was going on, the villagers pointed up and said, "See, the deities are yelling at us."

Everett saw and heard nothing. In interviews with the villagers later, he was amazed to discover that their accounts were consistent. They had clearly experienced the same thing. That provoked him to ask himself why he had not seen or heard anything. Even more puzzling, the villagers went back to their normal routines the next day and had no interest in pursuing the matter further.

While this experience does not clearly fit into the category of animism (in that it did not involve animals or material objects), it helps us to understand the ground of animistic and shamanistic culture. Animism is a human enmeshment in a natural environment. Unlike in a city, there is no mediation between the human psyche and the natural world. An animist thus enters the realm of nature as a citizen among non-human citizens. He senses without evaluating. He understands without reflection. He looks at the world through a vastly different lens.

Everett observes that were those villagers to experience the same event in an American city, believers and unbelievers alike would dismiss their report as simply a hallucination. In such case, the villagers would be the outliers in a culture that long ago eliminated such experiences as a possibility for healthy, sober people. What are we to do then, Everett asks, if the opposite occurs: if a Westerner, living within a culture, does not experience the same mystical phenomena shared by everyone else in that culture?

Everett asks us to consider whether the reasons for which he did not share his neighbors experience was due to a sort of spiritual blindness caused by his own cultural formation. Or, on the other hand, was it because the Western world has replaced superstition with science. Everett, an anthropologist and linguist, insists that a serious encounter with an alien culture will raise such questions and that they are far more difficult to answer than we usually suppose.

A person living within a single culture rarely finds Everett's question existentially threatening. It may be interesting but does not rock his world. Everett is a decidedly non-mystical person. He may have been uninterested in discussing the incident he recorded had he heard it from someone else. Like many missionaries, anthropologists, and Peace Corps workers though, Everett was confronted by an experience for which he had no explanation. In an era in which the world's peoples are on the move, an increasing number of Westerners will discover that animism is not as easy to dismiss as their grandparents thought.

Shamanistic practice has become especially interesting for many contemporary people, either as an anthropological curiosity or as an opportunity for one's own spiritual experimentation. Indeed, a growing interest in psychedelic drug experiences, even for therapeutic purposes, intentionally draws on animistic experience and worldview to give such experiences context.

Polytheism

Polytheism means "belief in many gods." Depending on the form, this belief has assumed in each time or place, gods and goddesses may either be imagined as separate beings or as the multiple ways in which the Cosmic Soul manifests itself to humanity. Although polytheism has fueled the world's earliest oral and written literature, it has rarely bothered itself with theological speculation. As a result, polytheistic expression accommodates itself to local needs.

The great Greek, Roman, and Nordic myths of pre-Christian Europe were all products of polytheistic cultures. These myths have exerted enormous influence on Western literature and, as Karl Jung insisted, live on within the collective consciousness of Western peoples. In most Western languages, even the days of the week and the months of the year point toward the gods and goddesses of our distant but still influential pagan ancestors.

Hinduism, which we listed above as an example of pantheism, could also be categorized as polytheistic. As with most religions, there is a gap between what Hindu literature theorizes and what its worshippers practice. Other than Hinduism, none of the world's other major religions are truly polytheistic.

Monotheism

Monotheism is the belief in a single personal Deity who created and sustains the universe.

Major examples of monotheism are Judaism, Zoroastrianism, Christianity, Islam, Sikhism, and the Baha'i Faith. All but two of these, Zoroastrianism and Sikhism, claim Abraham as their spiritual father.

The three major Abrahamic faiths, Judaism, Christianity, and Islam, confess as their central premise that there is but One God. Each of these profess beliefs unique to itself. All of them reject idolatry or the worship of nature. In the Abrahamic perspective, the worship of created things obscures and misrepresents the character of God. Furthermore, idolatry diminishes the role of human beings in the created order.

While most older expressions of Christianity allow for symbolic representation of God and the saints, these are (officially) subject to restrictions. Eastern Orthodoxy, for example, uses icons, which are stylized symbols rather than realistic depictions of biblical stories or spiritual entities. (St. Athanasius's work, *On Divine Images*, articulates the Orthodox position on this.) Roman Catholicism has been the most lenient among Christian communities in the use of statuary as sacred symbol. Since Vatican II, however, Roman Catholics have become more cautious in their use of statuary.

All Abrahamic faiths reject the worship of nature. A human being may become aware of God's existence because of an experience with nature. Scripture is full of such instances. However, as is the case with consecrated objects, one looks *through* rather than *at* the natural environment for spiritual connections. Judaism and Islam tend to be even more iconoclastic than Christianity in this regard.

Monotheism also seeks to solve an issue that has plagued Western culture from the beginning of recorded history: the question of "the one or the many." Philosophers wanted to know whether things in the universe emerged from a single source or from separate sources. Did the many things of the universe somehow cohere into a cosmic unity, or was it better to say that a Cosmic Unity has manifested within the world as many things?

Although such questions are rarely of interest to contemporary people, they go to the heart of how one views reality. Monotheism thus remains an important voice in the postmodern era, not only as a religious expression but as a philosophical one.

Religious Conversation in the Contemporary World

Honest and healthy conversations about God become possible when we keep a few things in mind.

Most people would like to know *if* God, gods, or a universal mind exists.

They want to know whether God, gods, or a universal mind cares anything about humanity.

They want to know if God, gods, or a universal mind communicates and if so, how.

Christians answer all three questions in the affirmative.

Christians believe that God exists.

They believe that God desires to meet with every individual in all times and in all places.

Christians should not deny the challenging nature of such claims, especially in the contemporary world. Since conversations between Christians and non-Christians require each to honestly consider the fundamental assumptions assumed by each partner in that conversation, philosophy can play a mediating role. Conversation partners need not be philosophers in the formal sense. They must, however, become consciously aware of their own foundational beliefs and learn to communicate those beliefs in a way that others can understand and evaluate.

Christians believe in God; atheists do not. Christians do not worship nature; pantheists and animists do. Christians believe in One God; polytheists do not. Christians believe God became a human being; other kinds of monotheists do not.

Despite such differences, meaningful discussion is possible and desirable.

The reason Christians should always engage with the opinions of others is that they have much to learn as well as things to teach. Unfortunately, Christians have not always done well with either learning or teaching. We have failed with this even in our relationships with Jews, our nearest spiritual kin.

However, there is one place Christians can always find a peaceful connection with others: the human longing for meaning. As we shall soon see, Jewish writers especially have had much to say about that.

5

Discovering Personal and Cosmic Meaning

Creation has not only a purposeful origin but a purposeful process and a purposeful end.

"GIVE ME YOUR WEDDING BAND!" THE GUARD SHOUTED.

The naked man before him had just been deloused. Other guards had shaved the man's body hair and had tattooed the number on his arm that he would carry for the rest of his life. As a respected neurologist and psychiatrist, this prisoner had served the people of Vienna, arguably the intellectual center of Western Civilization at that time.

To the guard, none of this mattered. The naked man before him was just another Jew.

This man, whom the people of Vienna knew as Dr. Viktor Frankl, looked into the guard's eyes. For a second, Frankl thought about refusing. The guard would shoot him, of course. Then he would take Frankl's ring anyway. Still, the prisoner thought, the guard will be taking a ring off the finger of a dead man. He'll have the ring, but he will not have my submission. Perhaps that is important enough to me to refuse his request.

"I have a choice!" Frankl realized.

"I can decide for myself about whether I choose to give up my ring. The guard cannot force this choice. That means I am a human being, made in God's own image and likeness. My human worth is inalienable!"

Empowered by this realization of the vital importance of choice, Dr. Frankl pulled off his ring. He then gently handed it to the guard.

The guard now had what he had asked for. He was not pleased, however. The guard knew he did not own this prisoner. The prisoner knew it too.

So, Dr. Victor Frankl, naked and tattooed but clothed with human dignity, walked to his barracks. Shivering both from the cold and from the discovery of his own significance, Frankl knew he would survive.

He was a son of Abraham, the son of Adam. He had been called to bear witness to the inalienable purpose of human life. God had given him an assignment: to observe his own experience in this camp as an experienced psychologist. He would be called upon to give his testimony about why it is important to keep on living when the worst happens.

After being released from the camp, Frankl wrote his testimony in less than a week. More accurately, he rewrote it. For he had already written it once on scraps of toilet paper. That copy, the guards had confiscated. Fortunately, Frankl had maintained a daily practice during which he mentally rehearsed what he had written. During his first days of freedom, he simply wrote what he had been mentally constructing.

Frankl called his meditation *Man's Search for Meaning*.

It is short. One can read it in a few hours. Nothing in it refers to the author's prior fame or erudition. It is simply a man's account about how faith in one's purpose can keep one alive and even cause one to flourish as one walks through hell.

Frankl encourages us to recover a concept that much of the contemporary world finds unhelpful. The fancy word for this concept is *teleology*, the belief that the universe, including one's own life, has purpose and meaning. The term is formed from two Greek words: *telos*, meaning "end," and *logos*, meaning "reason." A teleological view is thus one that envisions a thing, an event, a situation, or a person as inclined toward a discernible purpose.

Purpose and Meaning

Teleology was a central element of Aristotle's teaching. He believed that every object carried within itself a reason (or a cause) for its existence, which he explained manifests itself in four different ways:

1. A **material cause**, what a thing is made from
2. An **efficient cause**, the processes that make something possible
3. A **formal cause**, that which gives a thing its individual identity
4. A **final cause**, the ultimate reason for the existence of a thing, what we call its "bottom line."

The *material cause* of an automobile is metal, plastic, glass, and leather.

Its *efficient cause* is its design and assembly.

Its *formal cause* are the workers and robots who transform raw material into a car.

Its *final cause* (from the perspective of the manufacturer) is the financial profit made from automotive sales.

In a previous chapter, we looked at how Hebrew scripture begins with God speaking order and purpose into undifferentiated, purposeless matter.

Leon Kass, in what I consider the best contemporary book on Genesis, bludgeons his readers with the phrase "difference and distinction." He intends for the reader to notice that creation is the process through which God instructs meaningless matter to individuate and specialize. Kass describes primal undifferentiated matter as something similar to fetal stem cells. (My own analogy.) Stem cells are ones that have not yet specialized, found most abundantly in early fetal development. After these undifferentiated cells become bone, hair, muscle, and blood cells, they appear to be quite distinct from one another, though they derive from the same substance.

Like stem cells, primal, undifferentiated matter, was pure potential, capable of becoming anything. For primal matter to become something specific, it had to be *in*formed with particular purpose. It had to become "this' rather than "that." Unformed matter, in other words, had to exchange potential to become anything in order to become something specific, or *individuated*.

Page after page, Kass wears the reader out with this principle. Light is not darkness, he says. Water is neither sky nor land. Nature is not God. Human beings both belong to and are separated from the rest of nature.

Individuation, however, is not the entire story. For although God differentiates the whole of the unformed universe into individuated parts, God then reassembles the differentiated parts into a systemic whole. From the Hebrew perspective, Kass says, this creative act of individuation followed by systemic unity is what constitutes reality.

Contrary to monism then, Hebrew cosmology views reality as a systemic whole comprised of individuated components. However, like the cells of a body, the individuated components, regardless of how distinct they appear from one another, carry within themselves the information that connects them to the whole. Furthermore, the whole has been aimed toward the Creator's objective. Human beings can partially discern this objective through scripture and investigation of the natural world.

We are not far into Genesis then before we sense that an intentional plan of some sort is unfolding. We are not entirely certain where things are headed, but we do perceive that nothing is occurring by happenstance. Even the names of places, things, and people are significant. Everything in the stories seem to point toward something beyond themselves. This becomes true throughout scripture, concluding with *The Book of Revelation*, in which the writer throws layers of symbol and allegory into our heads and hearts for describing the various forces that aim human history toward God's ultimate purpose.

The teleological view that Kass describes, and which most

Jewish and Christian writers share, was not common in the ancient world. Most people imagined history as cyclical, as repeating the patterns of the past. For the Hebrews, however, history had a distinct beginning and would have a distinct ending. Time was thus an orderly and purposeful sequence in which effects emerged from causes. Finally, time would culminate in the good ends that the Creator had chosen before Creation.

In the final centuries of Greco-Roman civilization, the Hebrew concept of time as linear and purposeful was stamped deeply into the Western soul. Although this may be changing, it remains the way most Western people experience and imagine time.

The Hebrew view of time is best known today through a secularized concept called *progress*. The word literally means "moving forward." When we say that something is progressing then, we mean that it is moving toward an intended direction. Although the secular West has grown increasingly unsure about what exactly it is that we are moving toward, we retain the notion that impeding society's movement forward is a malicious act. To attempt to move society in the opposite direction—to regress—is downright evil.

When we look at what the secular concept of progress actually says, however, we see that it is a pale and inadequate version of the Hebrew (or even the ancient Greek) notion of teleology. Progress without a discernible goal is literally meaningless.

C. S. Lewis points out that the secular notion of progress means nothing more than "the next thing." If we are expected to keep moving toward the next thing, however, we have a right to know what the next thing is. Lewis insists that if we discern that "the next thing" is undesirable—jumping off a cliff, for example—then *re*gress becomes a sensible rather than a reprehensible action.

So where are we headed?

The ancient Hebrews believed they knew the answer to that question. They believed God had aimed human history toward justice. Martin Luther King expressed that idea when he reminded us that in a struggle for justice, we align ourselves to "the long arc of history."

The exemplary picture of M. L. King and Abraham Joshua

Heschel walking side by side across the Edmund Pettus bridge illustrates the way the Christian view of time roots itself in Hebrew soil. Like its parent religion, Christianity views itself as a vehicle through which knowledge of the Lord fills the earth, the sea, and the sky.

Biblical teleology then does not envision God as standing at the beginning of history, thrusting creation toward an uncertain future. It sees God rather at the end of history, or the *eschaton*, pulling creation toward the purpose for which it exists. Between creation and the eschaton, human beings are called to discern the way their own individual lives are meant to fit into the Creator's narrative. To do this, they learn what occurred before they were born and (more importantly) reflect on what is to come.

That is the essence of biblical teleology.

Prophesy then, rather than history, is the most formative element of human flourishing. It is not therefore where we have come from that contributes the most to who we are; it is where we believe ourselves to be headed. This was what the Hebrew prophets taught the world and what the New Testament writers affirmed and developed.

Unlike other ancient cultures, the Hebrews focused more on their descendants than on their ancestors. It was an anticipated future rather than an idealized past that formed their values and goals. "A good man lays up treasure for his children's children," the scripture says. "One generation shall inform the next of the Lord's marvelous deeds." "Let it not be said that the fathers ate sour grapes and so the children's teeth are set on edge."

Although the details of the eschaton remain unclear, scriptural metaphor, symbol, and poetry point the imagination toward it. The wolf shall lay down beside the lamb. Everyone will be at peace under his own fig tree.

As I write these words, I hear Jessie Dixon's musical rendition of Job's promise: "the wicked shall cease their troubling and the weary shall be at rest." Adlai Stevenson once summarized it as "the day where no one wears a sword, and no one carries a chain."

The Apostle Paul, ecstatic rather than exasperated, admits that "eye has not seen, nor ear heard, nor has it yet entered into the heart of anyone, all that God has prepared for us." This is the divine goal that pulls the children of Abraham toward the supreme good that lies ahead. It is the "blessed hope" that enlightens the long dark stretches of history in which bitter trials, stagnation, and catastrophic loss threaten to kill, steal, and destroy all that is true, good, and beautiful.

Is This All for Me?

In 1986, Oxford University Press released a massive philosophical work called *The Anthropic Cosmological Principle*[1]. It addressed what had been unmentionable throughout the modern era: the fact that the universe seemed fine-tuned to support human consciousness.

John D. Barrow and Frank J. Tipler, the authors of this work, knew that teleology—they called it *whiggism*—had been used by some to challenge solid science. To distance themselves especially from religious arguments, they challenged traditional ways of thinking about purpose and design. They also denied that they were motivated by any ideological commitment. The work, they insisted, was evidence-based data gathered from multiple scientific and mathematical disciplines. It showed that layers of unlikely coincidence and synchronistic pattern had made the emergence and maintenance of conscious life possible.

The word *anthropic* derives from the Greek word *antropos*, which means "man." The title of the work thus implies that the cosmos is fine-tuned for the emergence of human life. Because many scientists found such a claim repulsive, Barrow and Tipler were thrust into an intellectual maelstrom.

In hindsight, the reaction seems extreme. Barrow and Tipler did not believe their research pointed to any kind of creationism. Even today, scientists who reflect on the anthropic principle deny that the concept has religious implications. It simply expresses what is still a reasonable conclusion: that the universe seems "set up" for human life.

From the size and age of the universe to the uncanny conditions necessary for the formation of carbon; from the uncertainty principle of quantum physics to the "goldilocks location" of our planet, multiple conditions have produced the very sort of environment that makes life possible.

There is general agreement that the universe is indeed "fine-tuned" in just the way Barrow and Tipler describe. A few hours on the internet though reveals how scientists and mathematicians have argued about what the fine-tuning implies. Reactions fall into two major camps: so-called weak and strong perspectives on the anthropic principle.

The weak position says, "Well, yeah. Any creature with a capacity to understand its environment will sooner or later discover the conditions that made its existence possible. That doesn't imply that those conditions were aimed toward that eventuality."

The strong position says, "Although we do not have yet all the facts, the material universe seems to contain a chain of extraordinary coincidences without which conscious life as we know it would not exist."

Either take on the anthropic principle offers an opportunity for Christians interested in what, if anything, the structures of reality imply about ultimate meaning. While most scientists do not believe that the universe is purposefully designed, they do acknowledge that a remarkable cosmic order has somehow emerged. Agreement on this point does not lead irrefutably to belief in God, though it has led to a belief that matter may be structured by non-material processes.

For a growing number of scientists, mathematicians, and philosophers, that non-material source of cosmic order is information.

6

A Universe Formed by Word

The ordering of the cosmos is carried out through systematized patterns that exist at every level of reality, from the cosmic to the subatomic. The cosmos is thus a mystery, which arouses the human intellect and so demands our thoughtful, thorough observation and investigation.

ST. JOHN'S GOSPEL BEGINS WITH ONE OF HISTORY'S MOST IMPORTANT statements: "In the beginning was the Word." It is arguably the very foundation of Christian theology. Until now, few believed it had much relevance outside the theological context. During the last twelve decades though, a similar concept emerged from physics, cybernetics, and computer science. In that secular form, the notion that material reality emerges from information is rapidly reorganizing both all we know and how we know what we know.

Earlier we noted how Claude Shannon submitted *A Mathematical Theory of Communication* to The Bell System Technical Journal in 1948. We saw how this technical paper was about how entropy ("noise") affects communication and what that implied. Few of its early readers would have predicted how far-reaching its insights would prove to be.

Shannon's particular genius was in the way he synthesizes the work of others. A hundred years before Shannon, George Boole (1815-1864) had developed an algebraic system for communicating numerical, alphabetical, and pictorial information. Alan Touring had built a highly sophisticated computational machine as World War II was raging. Shannon connected them, along with and other advances, into a coherent, unified system that, perhaps more any other single contribution, set the stage for digital computers, the internet, and artificial intelligence.

Despite his protests then, we rightfully honor Shannon as the father of Information Theory. Whatever his aim for publishing *A Mathematical Theory of Communication*, his contribution changed the world, making possible not only digital information, but the emergence of new fields of study such as cognitive psychology. The new fields, in turn, have led to advances in neurology and genetics. Indeed, some are asking whether the implications of the information revolution should lead to a radical reworking in how we think about reality itself.

There are several opinions about what such a reworking would look like. One is that that we would begin to think of the universe as a simulation. The notion that we live within a simulation remains for most scientists an unlikely hypothesis. However, many of them do not dismiss it as total nonsense.

It is not difficult to understand why such a "crazy" idea has found a following.

Gamers and other programmers routinely create digital worlds that are increasingly sophisticated. They know that such computer programs can do utterly unanticipated things. A growing number of scientists and mathematicians have spent untold hours playing with such programs before they entered graduate school. So, the universe-as-simulation idea, along with many other forms of scientific idealism, will continue to spread.

Did Early Christians Anticipate the Computer Era?

During the modern era, few Western theologians reflected on the nature of reality. In most cases, they either shared the assumptions of the Enlightenment or retreated into various forms of escapism. Theology tended to divide into voices for either social nostalgia or progressive utopianism. Millions of believers opted out of serious reflection altogether, experiencing faith as something largely separate from "non-spiritual" things. In a postmodern world, that sort of escapism will be increasingly difficult. Technology alone will force believers to wrestle with what, if anything, their faith has to say about contemporary life and thought.

Earlier, I claimed that premodern Christians can help us form a response to our own times. We should not try to dust off ancient ideas and pass them off as relevant, of course. What we can do is reflect on the process through which the formative ideas of Christianity developed. By taking seriously the writings of key patristic and medieval believers, we can understand more fully how and why the faith as we inherited it was shaped—sometimes in unhelpful ways—by the long centuries of modernism. That alone can help us escape the liberal/conservative polarization that has been in large part the fruit of the modern era.

It may seem strange at first to think that premodern thinkers may be more helpful than modern ones for forming a response to our times. However, the postmodern era asks questions of our faith that differ substantially from those of the modern era. If we continue answering modern questions to a world that has moved on, we will find ourselves without an audience. The premodern thinkers understood their times. They also knew how their faith seemed either compatible or incompatible with those times.

If we could resurrect a few of the greatest thinkers of the late Roman Empire, they would doubtlessly be surprised by contemporary technology. They would not be surprised by contemporary questions. Most intellectuals of late antiquity assumed that that the visible universe rests upon an invisible substructure. It is not too much therefore to claim that educated believers, from the time of Christ to the fall of Byzantium (1453 AD), would have found it relatively easy to engage with contemporary discussions about the nature of reality. In fact, ancient thinkers would probably find it easier than the scientists and theologians from a hundred years ago.

The intellectual world of late Greco-Roman antiquity, although lacking much of the scientific understanding of our times, nonetheless arrived at similar beliefs about the nature of reality. Although the underlying reasons for those beliefs are different, many of the conclusions are strikingly similar.

The Apostle John, for example, who was neither an idealist nor a materialist, was nonetheless aware of his intellectual environment. He knew how his Gospel would come across to the Greek-speaking peoples of the Eastern Mediterranean. In fact, he tailored his introduction of the work to bridge the gap between Greek and Hebrew thought. Deeply rooted in (and thoroughly committed to) Hebrew Scripture, St. John's presentation of Jesus did not require a reader's familiarity with Jewish thought. His aim was to connect Christ to Hellenists, most specifically the Greek-speaking Jewish intellectual community.

As we have seen, John begins his Gospel with a literary allusion to Genesis. However, unlike Genesis, John's focus would not be the origins of the physical universe. John's attention was on the spiritual realm. For intellectuals in John's time, whether Jew or Gentile, "the heavens" would not have referred to a realm spatially above the earth. Heaven was not located in any sort of physical space, in fact. It was rather a realm coexisting with (but distinct from) the natural world, the dwelling place of spiritual beings and ideas.

To introduce his readers to Christ's cosmic significance, John used words like *arche* and *logos*. These philosophical terms implied that Christ was a bridge that now linked the heavens and the earth, spirit and matter, the visible and invisible realms of reality. This bridge, he claimed, came from the spiritual realm but had become fully human in Jesus of Nazareth.

In What Sort of Beginning?

For his Gospel's first phrase, "*In the beginning,*" St. John uses the word *arche*. It means beginning but carried metaphysical implications as well.

The Septuagint (the Greek Old Testament) used this word to

translate the Hebrew *barishit* in Genesis 1. When translating the Bible into English, we usually render both *arche* and *barishit* as "beginning." Barishit precisely means that. However, when encountering the Greek word *arche*, we are not always sure if a writer means "a beginning in time," "the beginning *of* time," "the cosmological foundation," or even "the first principle." All these translations are possible, though "in the beginning" is surely the best, since one can read any or all of these possibilities into that simple English word.

That said, English words like archaic, architect, and arch all derive from *arche* (pronounced *àrk-kay*), a hint of that spectrum of meanings contained within the "parent" word.

Imagine crossing a bridge. We are unlikely to notice the arch beneath that gives the bridge its structural integrity. Neither are we likely to think about the *arch*itect who designed the bridge. Were we to we take a moment though to think about the arch and the architect, we would realize that this visible bridge on which we cross is merely the tip of an iceberg. For the visible bridge emerges from a network of materials and processes, both visible and invisible.

The word *arche* thus refers to the "roots" of things. The Greek philosophers imagined everything as having a beginning not only in time and space but also in purpose. They assumed that like humans, the gods also carried out their intentions through seen and unseen processes. The apostle John's readers would have known therefore that this phrase, "in arche," or "in the beginning," referred to the many ways visible things are nested within elements known and unknown, seen and unseen. Time is one of those elements of course, which rightfully is the first thing we think of when we hear the phrase "in the beginning."

The writer to the Hebrews clearly refers to the way we are expanding the implications of John's opening phrase. "By faith we understand that the visible world emerged from invisible causes," the Epistle says. In past generations, the reader hardly knew what to think about this sentence. Though Christians accepted the passage as inspired, they had only a vague notion of what it meant. Today, however, we know that the material universe—indeed time and space, from which the universe emerges—rests upon a network of subatomic particles that are continually zipping in and out of existence. We know that subatomic particles interact across great distances and even across time itself, which makes our universe both possible and mysterious.

While astrophysics and quantum mechanics seem far removed from the world known by the early writers of the New Testament, these contemporary disciplines envision reality in ways that first century people, including the Apostle John, would not have found terribly difficult to grasp. In fact, a contemporary educated person would find it easier to discuss physics with the writer of the Epistle to the Hebrews than with his great-grandmother.

To make sense of that statement, we should review a few things we know that our great-grandmother did not, things we have learned only in the last hundred and twenty years. We know subatomic particles are infinitesimally small, much smaller as compared to an atom than an atom to a bowling ball. In fact, whether it even makes sense to think of subatomic particles as "objects" is debatable. Sub-atomic particles are more like mathematical probabilities than like things. Nonetheless, these shadowy "things" are the building blocks of our material world. They form the atoms that form molecules. Molecules in turn, are the basic units of all the elements on the chart that hung on the walls of our high school science class.

Subatomic and atomic material—quarks, atoms, molecules and so forth—all came into existence during the first seconds of time. For reasons yet unknown, time and space began then, together with all the elements that make the universe possible. We call that primal event "the Big Bang."

Scientists can describe what our universe looked like the .0005 *after* the Big Bang. They know what elements existed and in what quantities. What scientists cannot say, however, is how things looked a second *before* the Big Bang. They reason they cannot do this is because the Big Bang is the birth of time itself. Before that, physics is unimaginable. There are fascinating theories that try to explain this, such as the universe having emerged from a black hole. Of course, such theories, even if true, always lead one back to the same question: why or how does anything exist? Presumably, any black hole from which our universe would have emerged would have had a beginning as well.

So far then—for both materialists and idealists and for Christians, atheists, and everyone else—the starting line of everything that exists is simply "the beginning." Everything that exists, including the time and space in which things exist, emerges from and rests upon something else, the mysterious "nest" that the ancient Greeks called "arche."

So, our knowledge of the natural world is profoundly vaster than that of the most informed ancient person. Our terminology is more precise and clearer. Nonetheless, there is a sense in which we have returned to many of the questions that preoccupied the people of late antiquity. They too understood that the visible world emerged from a single point in time and space, a point witnessed by God alone.

Logos

It would be difficult to overestimate the impact of another word St. John uses in his Gospel, a word that would preoccupy the greatest minds of the Christian faith for centuries. *Logos.*

Depending on the era, dialect, or context of a Greek text, one can translate logos as "word," "speech," "reason," or even "blueprint." By the time the Apostle John wrote his Gospel, logos may have been the densest concept in the Greek language, containing far more than the simple, original meaning of speech. By John's time, the word had been used (and misused) to express endless metaphysical theories, which would remain the case for another thousand years. Theologians and philosophers even today, whether in admiration or frustration, contend with the ways this single word influenced Western thought.

To capture the way a first century reader might have heard the opening words of St. John's Gospel, I offer the following paraphrase. I hasten to add that I do not believe our translators have gotten this passage wrong. Nor do I think contemporary readers naturally read the passage as I paraphrase it. I am merely trying to help us imagine how St. John's contemporaries might have read it.

The Logos was with God (indeed, the Logos was God) at the beginning. Logos is thus the blueprint for existence itself. Everything that exists or has ever existed came into being through the agency of the Logos. Nothing that has ever come into being has done so through any other means.

paraphrase of John 1:1

Testing the reader's patience for long quotes, let us compare way Ovid expresses creation in the *Metamorphosis*. The pagan reference can help us imagine how readers in the late Roman empire might have understood the opening lines of both Genesis and St. John's Gospel.

At first, the sea, the earth, and the heaven, which covers all things, were the only face of nature throughout the whole universe, which men have named Chaos; a rude and undigested mass, and nothing *more* than an inert weight, and the discordant atoms of things not harmonizing, heaped together in the same spot. No Sun as yet gave light to the world; nor did the Moon, by increasing, recover her horns anew. The Earth did not *as yet* hang in the surrounding air, balanced by its own weight, nor had Amphitrite stretched out her arms along the lengthened margin of the coasts. Wherever, too, was the land, there also was the sea and the air; *and* thus was the earth without firmness, the sea unnavigable, the air void of light; in no one *of them* did its *present* form exist. And one was *ever* obstructing the other; because in the same body the cold was striving with the hot, the moist with the dry, the soft with the hard, things having weight with *those* devoid of weight.

To this discord God and bounteous Nature put an end; for he separated the earth from the heavens, and the waters from the earth, and distinguished the clear heavens from the gross atmosphere. And after he had unraveled these *elements*, and released them from *that* confused heap, he combined them, *thus* disjoined, in harmonious unison, *each* in *its proper* place.[1]

Both liberal and conservative Christians in the contemporary West have often expressed their frustration at any hint of the debt Christian theology owes to Hellenism (the ancient Greek culture of the Eastern Mediterranean.) One of my seminary professors even asked us to avoid quoting from either The Gospel of St John or the Epistle to the Hebrews because he was put off by their Hellenized content.

What I find suspicious is the attempt to rewrite history.

If we ought to acknowledge and respect the Hebrew foundations of scripture, one wonders why Greek influences on the New Testament are unworthy of that same respect. We can't settle that question here, but we can make this strange quirk of Western Christianity visible. Most Christians of other times and places have not shared this anti-Greek sentiment of modern Western theology. We should be aware of the incompatibilities between ancient Greek thought and scripture, as even the most Hellenized Patristic writers emphasized. However, Greek influences abound in the New Testament, beginning of course with the sheer fact that the text is written in that language.

Judaism, like Christianity, has been ever on the move. Contemporary Judaism in all its forms differs considerably from the Judaism practiced in New-Testament times. Judaism then was different than the religious life of the Hebrews in the Old Testament. One observes within scripture itself the evolution of religious practice and thought especially after the Babylonian captivity. In the Jewish texts usually omitted from modern Protestant Bibles, the evolution becomes even more evident, including, incidentally, from the very language of the text, which changes first from Hebrew to Aramaic, and then from Aramaic to Greek.

A clear continuity undergirds all the changes, of course. The relative stability of core belief and practice though is counterbalanced by dynamic changes in popular piety, linguistic shifts that transformed Hebrew into a classical and liturgical language rather than the spoken tongue of most Jews, and a continual interaction with Persian and Greek influences. The Jews and Christians of the first century CE were shaped by such influences.

Even when writing *in opposition to pagan* assumptions about the universe then, Jews and Christians were reacting as fellow citizens. They usually were writing in Greek, for example, so their very vocabulary carried connotations that they either quietly accepted or were forced to deliberately reject.

Contemporary English speakers can identify.

Imagine inviting a group of immigrants to a Christmas party. The invitation includes the phrase "be sure to wear your gay apparel!" Native English speakers will recognize this as a reference to a well-known English carol. Speakers of Contemporary International English on the other hand, a group that includes those for whom English is a second language, will likely misunderstand the phrase.

That is roughly the same situation we face when reading Greek, a language spoken and written for over three thousand years in various dialects by people from every walk of life. Furthermore, most Greek speakers in New Testament times were not Greek natives. They were Hellenes, citizens of an international order in which Greek language and culture served as a meeting place for all kinds of social exchange.

We can assume then, that the Apostle John deliberately chose the word Logos, knowing full well the metaphysical baggage it carried. Had the apostle intended to narrow the meaning of the word to exclude those metaphysical associations, he would have done so. Since he did not, the Beloved Apostle was opening the door, quite deliberately I think, to the kinds of theological and philosophical speculation that followed after the publication of his Gospel.

The great Dutch Reformed writer, Abraham Kyper (1837-1920) pointed to the logos doctrine as the basis for any Christian perspective on contemporary science. He explored the implications of this claim in *De Gemeene Gratie in Wetenschap en Kunst*, a work partially translated into contemporary English by Nelson D. Kloosterman under the title *Wisdom and Wonder: Common Grace in Sciences and Art*[2].

Kuyper was certainly not arguing for a full embrace of Neo-Platonism. In fact, he would have been even more cautious about than the Patristic writers. Nonetheless, one cannot access the wisdom of early Christians, including the New Testament writers, without some knowledge of the worldview through which they and their contemporaries thought and wrote.

It is well worth our effort to enter the mindset of late antiquity because writers of that era confronted many of the questions now surfacing in the postmodern, informational society. For example, the writers of antiquity discussed whether reality could be reduced to matter, to information, or to something else. Early Christian writers participated in that discussion. Such issues were of little interest to most people in the modern era but have been reemerging in the last few decades. Christians are affected by this development and will be forced to respond.

Logos and the Language of Life

Shortly after we learned that all information could be represented by ones and zeros, the Genome Project (2003) demonstrated that all known life forms on our planet share a common genetic code. Together, these two twentieth-century breakthroughs, one from computer science and the other from genetics, pointed to language as a basic element of nature. This implies that information is not only the core of social life, but of biological life as well.

Indeed, information seems to be foundational to everything. Our bodies, for example, are produced and managed by an "alphabet" that consists of twenty amino acids. Every function of one's body is written within every cell by the means of this alphabet. This organic coding is different than computer code, of course. However, the operational heart of both computers and organisms is information processed through symbol. The simple word for this is "language."

The scientific name for the language of life is the *Canonical Genetic Code*. Every cell of every known plant and animal contains detailed instructions written in this code, or genome.

The Genome Project (1990-2003) focused on mapping the Human Genome. The result was what we might call a Genetic Code/English dictionary. The colossal breakthrough immediately began pushing medical science into a different way of imagining health and disease. During the global Covid pandemic of 2019-2022, for example, the world's nations focused enormous resources for responding to the viral pathogen. Although theoretical knowledge for producing a genomic defense against viruses had existed for a couple of decades, the global crisis seriously accelerated the timeline, resulting in mRNA vaccines.

Many people were stunned. Since most had no idea that such medical technology existed, they were understandably shaken. Perhaps though they were shaken by something even more alarming than a new kind of vaccine.

The very possibility of genomic coding exposed a radical shift in how we defined our own humanity and, indeed, reality itself. The existence of mRNA vaccines implied that organic processes are simply the movement of biological information. This means that the material carriers of life—blood, bone, brain and so forth—are simply the way biological information travels and manifests.

A couple of decades ago, not many people would have seen a connection between Information Theory and the Genome Project. In the aftermath of mRNA vaccines, however, most of us are aware that information is always involved in the fundamental ordering of reality. Matter, whether organic or inorganic, doesn't do anything and doesn't become anything on its own. All things and all processes thus involve information. Without information, matter is mere potential.

DNA and RNA function in organic beings similar to how ones and zeros function in computers operations: they carry information. This implies that information is not merely something material objects manifest but is at the heart of what a material object is.

Viewing information in this way leads us to understand processes as diverse as the stock market, human conception, tides, actuary tables, photographs, and telepresence as simply information on the move. It is no wonder then that an increasing number of humanity's most brilliant thinkers are asking whether the universe itself is not more like an information system than a collection of material things.

This may be shocking to those of us raised in the modern age. It requires a radical shift in how one understands reality. Early Christians would have had no problem with it though. They assumed as much. For them it was obvious that information proceeds matter and energy.

History professors will rant about the sin of anachronism, seeing in the past influences that were not yet in existence. I listened carefully to the lectures that warned us of committing such a sin. So, I am not claiming the Church Fathers invented the Internet or predicted the uncertainty principle. I am saying that a degree of interesting compatibility exists between ancient and contemporary thought. That is why I insist that the Apostolic and Patristic writers have much to add to contemporary discussions.

The Apostle John used the word "logos" to introduce Jesus Christ to the Greek-speaking world. He knew that earlier Jewish literature—the Book of Proverbs and the Book of Sirach specifically —leaned toward the view of reality his Gospel would openly embrace. He was headed for even deeper waters, however. He intended to claim that the Logos, what a secular person might call Cosmic Information, had become a human being.

The Word Made Flesh

Eric Bazilian's song *One of Us* (made famous by Joan Osborn), captures the essence of St. John's view of the incarnation. It was, and is still, a revolutionary statement. That is why every Christian throughout history has wrestled with its implications.

Four hundred years after the death of the Apostle John, St. Augustine was still startled by St. John's words. It was not the early words of the Gospel's introduction that had so profoundly affected him. Augustine was a respected professor of rhetoric in the University of Milan. He had heard countless pagan lecturers say similar things. What so moved Augustine was what became the 16th verse of the first chapter: "The Logos became flesh and dwelt among us, and we beheld his glory."

"That," said Augustine, "stopped me in my tracks."

Most of the New Testament and Patristic writers worked to develop the implications of the Logos as human being. The Apostle Paul, for example, said in the Epistle to the Colossians, that Christ is the cohesive principle that holds all things together.

According to Christianity's earliest writers, this is the very heart of a Christian view of reality.

The Code of Creation

The philosophers of late antiquity believed that the universe was permeated with discernible patterns, called providence, through which the cosmos was managed. The total effect of this was economia, a word that literally meant household management. The ability to bring one's goods and actions into harmony with providence was called prudence. Christians adapted these values into their own definition of moral excellence, as we see in passages such as 2 Peter 1: 5-8.

The Protestant Reformers (1517- 1600) were concerned about any hint of the involvement of the human will or effort in the work of sanctification. They nonetheless retained the classical notions that the universe was ordered through divinely instituted patterns and that wisdom involved aligning oneself with them. We see that in colonial North America, where providence was a popular name for people and places.

Today, the word providence is nearly an antiquated term, recognized but rarely used. An exception is its use as an adjective. We may describe a fortunate turn of events as being providential, as in "it was *providential* that it began to rain shortly after the fire broke out." Used this way, the word becomes a poetic synonym, roughly meaning "coincidence."

Those who believe in providence in its original sense, experience phenomena, situations, and patterns in the natural world as possible forms of communication. It is the belief that natural entities and processes may contain lessons about values and meaning, or even personal guidance. Christians have always believed that such providential information was accessible to all discerning human beings. Ancient literature, from Aesop's Fables to the Tao Te Ching, is full of examples. From the Christian perspective though, even the wisest humans have often misinterpreted the lessons of the natural world. As the Book of Judge demonstrates, bad things happen when "everyone does that which is good in his own eyes."

Christians and Jews believe that this is the very reason God gave us the Holy Scripture.

Christians do not mean by this that scripture is meant to replace, but rather clarify and complete nature. Fallen human beings have constantly attempted to inappropriately transcend nature and to act as lords over it. That is the central lesson of the Tower of Babel story. This hubristic impulse leads to a gross misunderstandings and misuses of nature. At its worse, it leads to sheer evil.

By continually reminding us that the world is the Lord's and all it contains, Scripture cleanses the doors of our perception, to use William Blake's phrase. Shakespeare expresses a biblical sentiment when he says, "the fault is not in the stars but in ourselves." The Apostle Peter, recalling a supernatural experience of his own, remarked "now we have a surer word of prophesy to which we must give heed." Both are reminders that the human soul in its present state not only misunderstands the lessons of nature but even the lessons of supernatural events.

Such warnings notwithstanding, Christians have maintained a cautious belief that the natural world is more than a machine. It also serves as a form of communication. Thus, Galileo, defending natural science as a Christian vocation, quotes Tertullian (AD 155-220) in his letter to the Grand Duchess of Tuscany.

We conclude that God is known first through Nature, and then again, more particularly, by doctrine, by Nature in His works, and by doctrine in His revealed word.

— Galileo

By the late medieval era, belief that providence embodies Divine intention led to new approaches to the study of nature. In hindsight, we can justifiably label those approaches as scientific, though at the time, they were often experienced as forms of spiritual practice. This spiritualized view of science continued well into the seventeenth century, at which time science, then called natural philosophy, gradually lost its connection to piety.

Despite the secularized nature of scientific work today though, science remains a legitimate Christian vocation. I use the word vocation here in its original sense, a calling. St. Maximus the Confessor among many other have made a clear case for this. Maximus insisted that everything in creation contained logos— patterned information that reflects God's character and intention. If one believes this and possesses the intellectual ability and the desire to understand those patterns, science and math, like music and other arts, become fields in which a believer loves and glorifies God.

Although we cannot know our Creator's full intentions for the universe, or even for ourselves for that matter, we can discern what is knowable by carefully observing those parts of reality available for examination. Such a quest furthers human knowledge and often awakens the soul. That is why Francis Collins entitled his history of the Genome Project, *The Language of God*, and why hymn writer Maltbie D. Babcock penned the lines, "in the rustling grass I hear Him pass."

7

Reason, Reality, and Faith

Nature proves itself to have been made for the sake of consciousness, not consciousness for the sake of nature. Nature shows itself as a rationality that has been molded materially, and that can, in principle, be molded endlessly by consciousness.[1]

WHILE WALKING LEISURELY THROUGH THE DESERT IN ARIZONA several years ago, I suddenly began to walk backwards. Alarmed, since I had not intended to walk backwards, I scanned the area. That is when I saw the rattlesnake! Right where I had just been, it was raised, coiled, and ready for action.

I then watched the snake uncoil and go on its way.

It was years before I learned that monkeys who have never lived in the wild react that way to even a rubber snake. When there is not enough time to consciously react to a life-threatening situation, we react unconsciously. In fact, recent experiments indicate that even when we reach what we believe to be a carefully considered decision, we are actually becoming aware of a decision already made by our unconscious.

In other words, we are not fully in charge of ourselves. Most of our convictions and choices are unconscious reactions to our environment. For the most part, we may prefer fried chicken to tofu, love Bach but not rap, or be passionate about liberal or conservative politics because our brains have been programed to react in just those ways. Unconscious "programs" can be overturned through long, patient, and consistent effort. However, that requires great effort and emotional distress.[2] We are rarely interested enough in deep personal change to face such inner pressures. People *convert* (embrace a new way of interpreting and responding to the world) only when they are facing an overwhelming sort of threat or opportunity.

William James offers a helpful description of conversion in his *Varieties of Religious Experience*. James realized that a religious conversion was a restructuring of one's being, which was also true of other kinds of conversion. Radical personal change was rarely the result of cool-headed, rational thought. It is nearly always the result of an existential threat.

"Mr. Jones, if you don't stop smoking, you will be dead in three years!"

"Fred, I am not living with a hoarder. If all this crap is not gone in a month, I'm moving out."

"No one speaks English on this island, Billy Bob. No one is coming from home to get you. If you don't develop a taste for seaweed and learn to speak the language of this island, you're going to starve."

In these examples, someone faces a serious threat to life as they have known it. They have two choices: a personal or a relational death on one hand, and radical personal change on the other. Both choices throw one into a severe personal crisis.

Early in life, our genetic heritage, culture, and family relationships form what we perceive as normal. By young adulthood, this personalized definition of "normal" becomes a part of how we perceive our own self. As a result, we become highly resistant to change. For example, although we acquire our family's language with little effort, acquiring a language as an adult requires great effort. Our brain must be intentionally led, kicking and screaming, to say words and sounds that do not exist in our mother tongue.

Adopting the word order of another language is not only difficult but feels perverse. The same sort of internal resistance arises when we are exposed to any new information that threatens our current view about religion, philosophy, politics, or the economy.

We all like what we like the way we like it.

Nonetheless, in times of existential threat, radical change may occur quickly. We can learn a new language, form an appetite for disgusting things, and transform our views of morality. In other words, despite our unconscious programing, we all have a potential to convert.

In the encounter with the snake, my unconscious mind perceived something threatening in my environment. That is why I reacted before thinking. This implies that there is more to oneself than what one consciously knows.

It was a good thing my unconscious mind acted without my conscious permission when it saw the snake. Unfortunately, the same unconscious causes me to gag at unfamiliar foods or become enraged at an opinion I do not share. The reason it does these things is that one's brain learns to identify potential danger, opportunity, arousal, pleasure, and discomfort in the social environment, just as it does in the natural environment. What it learns over time becomes second nature, provoking the unconscious mind what to notice and what to ignore, what to tolerate and what to resist. When it comes to this body of personal knowledge, we mostly operate on automatic pilot.

It is possible to go through life without ever updating those unconscious programs that run one's life. The unconscious believes that just as I need to feel safe from a tiger in the woods, I also need to feel safe from persons and situations it has decided threatens my life, income, or identity. This sense of social safety comes at a price, however: a deep-seated resistance to anything or anyone that seems to threaten (or even alter) our identity.

At some point in life, most of us become aware that untrue beliefs and unhelpful behaviors may be hindering our ability to flourish. Sometimes, we see this in our friends and family members before we see it in ourselves. We know that Uncle Fred is a hoarder, though he claims to collect rare bottle caps. We know that our sister Sally is an alcoholic, though she says she merely enjoys a drink now and then. Observing denial at work in our friends may—though often it does not—provoke us to question whether we might be hiding parts of ourselves from ourselves.

Even if we get that far, the self-evaluation usually stops there. This is why learning about psychological theory does not usually lead to gut level work. Unfortunately, even many knowledgeable therapists are terrified of doing that. The vulnerability required for examining one's beliefs, emotions, and relationships is just too scary. It's much easier to learn about concepts or just take medication. Unless, that is, we face an existential threat.

If Fred's beloved wife says, "Fred, it's either all this crap or me," Fred may finally find enough courage to challenge those parts of his self that threatens his marriage. Even if he accepts his wife's intervention as an act of love though, it may feel like death at first. Of course, that is what conversion is, bring an end to one sort of self-identity and embracing a new one. When Christians talk about conversion, they mean more than what William James meant by the term. However, conversion, even in a spiritual context must include this sort of radical shift.

The point here is that human beings, both as individuals and as groups, tend to hold on to false beliefs and unhelpful behaviors even when there is strong evidence against them. As we have seen, the sort of conditions that force us to reevaluate our loyalty to our own unfounded opinions usually come from outside ourselves. However, it is possible to form habits of mind that force our own opinions to defend themselves. These habits of mind are tools for clear thinking. Like tools that help our hands lift heavy objects, thinking tools help us process challenging data.

Thinking Tools

Over the centuries, humanity has developed a number of important tools to help us overcome our natural resistance toward new information. Our ancestors learned that without such help, one inevitably keeps believing what one wants to believe, even if the facts lead elsewhere. They knew that one's opinions are often lodged deep in the psyche. Without a lever and a fulcrum—thinking tools— the individual is not wise enough, honest enough, or courageous enough to overcome or even edit those opinions.

No human mind makes full contact with raw reality. We all experience reality through our individual personality and opinions we have been accumulating since we were born. Our unconscious evaluates everything in the light of our memories and our deepest held values. It honors our phobias, interests, and prejudices. Before we ever become conscious of anything, the unconscious has already observed it, evaluated it, and passed on its finding to our conscious mind. It is the unconscious that decides what we notice and what we ignore. Sometimes, as with the snake in Phoenix, the unconscious even decides to act before getting our conscious consent.

Most of the time, the unconscious makes good decisions. Life comes at us too quickly for us to make conscious decisions about everything we think or do. That's why we must run our tongue over our teeth to remember whether we have already brushed them. However, these automatic programs that keep us safe and efficient, also hinder us from noticing or honestly evaluating new information. That's why we need tools that enable the brain to process new data and, when warranted, to form new conclusions about reality and our place in it.

Even our most brilliant scientists and philosophers need thinking tools. They too, just like the rest of us, tend to remain within the safe confines of familiar opinions.

One of the oldest thinking tools is called *Logic*, a term derived from the word logos.

Ancient philosophers like Aristotle developed this tool for keeping our thoughts focused and moving from a premise to a conclusion. For example, if I offer the premise that all horses are black, logic accepts the statement, but reminds me that the discovery of a single brown or white horse will falsify my premise. My premise in this case doesn't make it very far into the process.

If, on the other hand, I claim that all animals breathe oxygen and further claim that horses are animals, logic allows me to keep moving through the process. Since we have not yet found any animal that does not breathe oxygen, and if horses are indeed, animals, it is reasonable to conclude that horses breathe oxygen. If at some date we discover some animal that breathes cyanide or ammonia instead of oxygen, the premise, "all animals breathe oxygen," will be invalidated, though it may remain true to say that all horses breathe oxygen.

That's the simple version.

We can use logic to inform ourselves about things we know nothing about. For example, if I have learned in school that all *samakata* eat *ooka* and discover a previously unknown subspecies of samakata, I will conclude that this subspecies probably eats ooka. I do not need to know anything else about either samakatas or ooka to arrive at that conclusion.

I just made all that up, by the way. Samakata and ooka erupted from a rather twisted imagination. My conclusion is nonetheless correct because the logic is sound. Logic doesn't prove that samakata exists. It simply tells me that if samakata did exist, a subspecies could most likely eat ooka.

Logic can even process information about nothing in particular. For example, if X is a subset of Y and Y is a subset of Q, we know that Q contains X.

Logic gets very complicated. But you get the idea.

Even though logic was developed many centuries before Christ, people continue to expand it. Scientists and mathematicians use it every day, clarifying their theories and evaluating their data.

So yay, for logic!

In some eras of history, scholars forgot that logic has a few serious limitations. They were so impressed that logic could expand one's understanding of a premise that they failed to notice that one can use it to develop an impressive system even if the premise is false. The medieval era produced intellectual giants, people who developed systems of thought that still amaze us. Generations of scholars refined those systems until they were nearly airtight. Still today, we struggle to find internal inconsistencies in these systems. They were, nonetheless, false.

During the medieval age, most educated people assumed their job was to discover and correct any internal inconsistencies in the systems they had inherited. It rarely occurred to them to step outside of the paradigm altogether and examine the original premises of those systems. Who were they, after all, to argue with the venerable saints and scholars who had proceeded them?

As the medieval era ended, however, some began to suspect that their culture's most elaborate systems of thought could be resting on concepts that lacked connections to observable reality. They made the shocking discovery that logic could only clarify the implications of a premise. It could not evaluate the premise itself. The premise was a "given," provisionally accepted for determining what follows if one assumes it to be true.

The modern age reacted to medieval misuse of logic by developing another thinking tool: the *scientific method*. Like other tools, the scientific method had to be consciously learned and deliberately practiced. When early scientists began to do that, they began making new discoveries about how the world works.

One of the individuals most responsible for developing the scientific method was Francis Bacon (1561–1626) who describes the method in his delightfully readable classic, *Novum Organum*. Alluding to the failure of medieval thinkers to notice logic's limitations, Bacon reminded his readers that a spider weaves an impressive web from just three stable points. In the same way, an intelligent person may weave an impressive system of thought, *regardless of whether its premises are true*. That is why, Bacon says, we must test the validity of a system's premise rather than be prematurely impressed by a system's internal consistencies.

Imagine we are at a conference, hearing a man claim there are intelligent beings under the surface of the moon. We are surprised. The man seems intelligent and speaks with such conviction. So, we listen to his presentation, noticing that each point he makes leads logically to the next.

The more we listen, the more we know that we are in the presence of a gifted and original thinker. He is also kind. He's not offended by our skepticism and responds respectfully to each question. He's not at all like another lecturer we heard earlier, the one who mercilessly ridiculed this kind man. We decide that we like him. By the end of his presentation, we hope he's right about the moon people, but even if not, we are determined that his point of view will be respected.

By the time we reach this point, acknowledging that this man's ideas about moon people is simply false will be emotionally difficult to do. It will be even more difficult to admit that the jerk who ridiculed those who believe in moon people is correct. What we want to be true, and who we want to win the argument, cannot survive a cool-headed analysis of the moon-people premise.

Science fiction readers will understand. We would love to believe that the creatures described in *Project Hail Mary* exist. And why not? Andy Wier describes them so beautifully. Why can't his story be true? His plot makes sense. He keeps our attention. The details of his story remain consistent with its premise. But for all of that, it's unlikely that a creature exists anywhere that breathes ammonia. Furthermore, even if such a creature exists, it's even more unlikely that it communicates in musical tones like Wier's alien.

A sci-fi reader must accept a writer's premise to enjoy how a story unfolds. As with fiction, so with science. A plausible theory will motivate scientists to think through its implications. At some point though, a way must be found to test the theory's foundational claims. For example, throughout the twentieth century, the theories of relativity and quantum mechanics were repeatedly tested. Scientists and mathematicians had believed the theories were plausible and had continued to refine them. However, it was only as tests were developed and then carried out that certainty grew that the theories were grounded in what is really real.

Thinking tools are not important merely to scientists and mathematicians. An architect must be certain that a new material is capable of supporting a structure they have designed. Even though the drawing and the model of the structure are exciting, the engineers must be convinced that the project is sound. Indeed, everyone who desires to discover the truth about anything must develop strategies for confronting his or her own biases. Even religious and political life requires this sort of critical thought.

I am attempting to convince you that the ideas in this book are sound. I am trying to present them with integrity. That said, I am an Anglican priest. I am committed to what I believe to be "the faith once and for all delivered to the saints." That is a bias. It is an openly stated rather than a hidden bias, but is a bias, nonetheless.

Secular materialism is also a bias. Since there is no such thing as a perspective from nowhere, every assumption of every writer, scientist, priest, accountant, and king is a kind of a premise. Conclusions drawn from it may therefore be reasonable but do not prove the validity of the premise itself.

The takeaway point of this section is that an embrace of a system of thought should require more than an eloquent presentation or even proof of its internal consistency. For us to embrace a system of thought, we should be convinced that its foundational premises are likely true. The word "likely" is important, since there are many important theories in every field that cannot be proven beyond all doubt, but which serve humanity well as we continue to explore alternatives. Euclidean geometry comes to mind as an example.

Rejecting a system of thought should also require more of us than simply our distaste for it. Einstein hated quantum mechanics. He worked long and hard to disprove it. So far though, neither Einstein's passion nor his reputation has undermined quantum mechanics. Experiment after experiment—including some which Einstein developed—have only confirmed it.

What does any of this have to do with Christianity?

Father Dumitru Staniloae, who spent fifteen years in prison because of his faith, believed that scientific investigation is a type of spiritual discernment. Sanctification, he said, involves both a liberation from delusion and a commitment to follow the truth, wherever it leads. In his view then, it is not only secular science that advances in that way, but even faith in God.

Father Staniloae knew firsthand that examining what one

believes requires serious effort, perhaps even suffering. However, it is the path that an honest, humble, and wise person will choose to walk. It is the way of Abraham, who made of his life a pilgrimage.

A Christian with the sort of intellectual gifts that Staniloae possessed is compelled to find "an answer for the faith that lies within us." This includes developing one's understanding of the natural world as well as the acquisition of critical thinking skills for discerning the implications of what one has learned. In father Staniloae's words:

"As a consciously rational being whose knowledge of the rationality of nature and its meaning keeps on improving, only the human person himself becomes more rational through nature, that is, he actualizes his reason to a greater and greater degree."[3]

Reason, in other words, is part of our spiritual, as well as our natural discernment. Mystery and miracles may occasionally confound our reason, provoking our worshipful awe. Nonetheless, when rain falls inside a church, it is usually due to a leaky roof rather than a sign of divine disapproval.

Natural explanations in other words, are usually correct, though not always sufficient. A leaky roof may point to something beyond the obvious, but we need compelling reasons for entertaining that possibility. This way of understanding the world is one of the blessings of modernity, for which we should be grateful and from which we should continually learn.

Thought Experiments and Contemporary Science

When Benjamin Franklin wanted to know whether lightning was a form of electricity, he did not conduct a thought experiment. Franklin had read Bacon and would have had little patience with clever speculations about nature that didn't involve experiments. So, he didn't tweak an existing theory. He didn't write a moving essay. He flew a kite during a storm!

Franklin learned his theory was sound when the lightening connected to his central nervous system. We learned that Franklin's theory was sound because he survived the experiment.

Early scientists insisted on the need for direct observation and experimentation. Bacon, for example, died from pneumonia while learning how to freeze meat. It would have alarmed those early scientists to know that some of the most important theories of the twentieth century emerged from thought experiments. Einstein imagined riding a light beam and daydreamed about standing in a falling elevator that never crashes.

In some ways, such thought experiments were a return to earlier ways of investigating reality. The difference now was that theory had to be tested. Medieval philosophers had treated the insights of Aristotle and Ptolemy as dogma. Modern science, in contrast, urges us to avoid such loyalty. It doesn't always happen. Chomsky bitterly opposed Daniel Everett for challenging sacrosanct linguistic theories, for example. Still, science proceeds by either proving disproving the theories proposed by its practitioners.

This is the reason that scientists worked throughout the twentieth century to develop experiments for testing the theories of relativity and quantum mechanics. Most scientists believed the theories were accurate, but they still needed proof.

Staniloae believed that all systems of thought, including Christian dogma, develop in this same way—by being put to the test. As an Orthodox priest, he represented a Christian expression with roots deep into the apostolic and post-apostolic centuries. Nonetheless, Staniloae didn't define orthodoxy as frozen tradition. He saw it rather as piety, thought, and behavior consistent with—but not imprisoned by—our spiritual ancestors. He therefore assumed that any Christian claim about the nature of either the material or the spiritual realm, should be demonstrable. Although faith involves respect for mystery, it is not a commitment to irrationality. Reason is simply a formal process for recognizing reality. It is an intellectual submission to the Creator's management of the universe.

At the heart of an honest faith then is a pursuit of truth, tempered by an awareness of human frailty. Thinking tools therefore—such as logic and the scientific method—are part of the yoke the believer accepts for making full contact with reality. As the Apostle Peter put it, we avoid committing ourselves to "cleverly devised fables."

Occasionally, this commitment provokes in us a crisis of faith, as it did with Job, Jeremiah, and many others throughout history. The faith *as one has understood it* can give way, leading the believer to reexamine what and why he believes. In such times, faith often reorganizes itself around the new information that caused the crisis.

Fresh discoveries of the patterns that form and maintain creation move and mold the soul. When we believe that our Creator's presence may be discerned everywhere and in everything, the quest for truth and the discoveries that result from it, become a sacramental means for individual and collective transformation.

Science and Public Skepticism

The growth of human knowledge over the last hundred years has come at a serious cost: the growing alienation of the public from the scientific community.

An alarming percentage of people deny that the sciences are truth-revealing disciplines, which exposes our culture to a passionate embrace of the irrational. The internet, a stunning achievement of abstract science, thus has become a haven for flat-earth theorists and medical quackery.

Although the public constantly uses conveniences and life-saving procedures procured by scientific advance, a growing percentage of contemporary people, including many Christians, are suspicious about what science is up to.

The lack of trust in science is alarming but understandable. Western Civilization is in the middle of a major shift in how we evaluate truth and meaning. This has provoked a paralysis of judgement in which truth about anything becomes a matter of personal opinion. It is an important change in how the public processes scientific knowledge.

Our great-grandparents tended to believe that despite the frailty of human perception, it was possible to arrive at objective, shared conclusions about the natural world. Contemporary people, in contrast, tend to believe in the sovereignty of an individual perception, making them suspicious about claims of objectivity. A shared sense of reality thus becomes challenging to maintain.

In *Contact with Reality*, Esther Lightcap Meeks, reflecting on the work of Michael Polanyi, writes this:

"Truth is not made or invented, but rather discovered. Discovery then is the paradigm of all scientific knowledge, making the acquisition of knowledge a product of one's submission to the real."

Meeks assumes that scientific investigation may lead to verifiable fact. In that case, an honest person submits independent judgement to what is learned through the scientific process. That is what she means by "knowledge achieved by submission to the real."

Let's consider a historical example.

From the beginning of human history, people assumed that maggots spontaneously emerged from rotten meat. It had been a commonly held belief supported by history's great thinkers. Aristotle believed this, for example.

Louis Pasteur overturned that opinion, proving through an experiment that maggots emerge from tiny eggs. Rotten meat, he discovered, was merely the source of food for infant maggots. That meant the "common sense" opinion about spontaneous generation of maggots was false. Ancient opinion, in this case at least, had not made contact with reality.

Pasteur's experiment thus led to an amendment of our common (or shared) sense.

Our great-grandparents, learning the truth about the origin of maggots, gradually accepted Pasteur's conclusions. After his experiment, people who insisted on believing in the spontaneous generation of maggots were viewed as uneducated. That sort of trust in scientific experimentation is more challenging to achieve in our times. Today, scientists can arrive at a near united position on a matter only to encounter skepticism or even hostility from the general public. This is due not only in a widespread distrust in objective truth, but because of misuse of scientific data on the part of industry, government, and marketers.

The American government once sterilized members of unsuspecting minority groups in the name of research. Early forms of psychotherapy made naïve and harmful claims about gender, spirituality, and child-rearing. Neurologists performed crude lobotomies on unsuspecting people. Nuclear science taught us how to incinerate the unarmed civilians of an entire city. Such misuse of science over the last many decades seriously eroded the public's trust.

Alexander Solzhenitsyn documented how the Soviet regime combined a view of dialectical materialism with psychiatry to justify diagnosing religion as a mental illness. That made it justifiable to imprison and torture believers as "wards of the state." Similarly, American academic communities sometimes withhold employment from otherwise qualified persons because of their religious convictions.

In light of such abuses, we cannot dismiss the dangers of scientific overreach. Throughout history, scientific advances have often outrun a society's moral and ethical convictions. Nazi Germany's industrial sophistication enabled the regime to efficiently murder millions of people. However, an awareness that nefarious things have been done in the name of science does not justify the dismissal of truth.

Although all people are created equal, all opinions are not.

When we know that a passionately held opinion is false, pretending it is otherwise is neither virtuous nor kind. A parent who belongs to the flat-earth society does not have the right therefore to silence a public-school teacher from talking about Galileo. When we argue that all such opinions must be treated equally and are entitled to protection against reasonable pushback, we destroy our ability to distinguish fact from fiction. A society that embraces that sort of intellectual anarchy will not survive.

A person has a right to not believe in germs. If he is willing, we can show him the germs through a microscope. We can share with him all we have learned about germs and how they behave. We can show him that responding appropriately to germs increases his odds of living healthier and longer. If he's uninterested in learning about germs, he can continue to believe what he wants to believe. If, however, we stop teaching about germs because he and his friends do not believe in germs, we will be unraveling medical science.

People will die from that sort of intolerant tolerance.

If, as Esther Meeks insists, truth is not made or invented but only discovered, it follows that one's submission to facts, once these are determined, becomes the necessary foundation for intellectual growth. Such growth requires humility because none of us are specialists in everything. One who instead values personal opinion over verifiable fact fails to increase his connection to reality. By becoming the final arbitrator of what is true, he willfully embraces ignorance. The Book of Proverbs calls such a person a fool. The second Psalm in fact, warns us that an entire community can choose foolishness over wisdom.

It is a sobering possibility that our culture may be playing with that very choice.

Providence and Personal Growth

Belief in providence leads not only to knowledge about the universe but to the growth of one's inner life. That means that scientific pursuit can be an instrument of spiritual discernment. Christians are accustomed to using the word discernment in discussions about faith. However, if the earth and all it contains truly is God's handiwork, then the attempt to understand nature is a necessary spiritual quest.

True Christian piety certainly cannot not lead one to reject an honest inquiry into nature. Because God created human beings as material creatures, we can conclude that the material environment has something to do with how God intends us to live our lives.

Spirituality then is not a disembodied experience but is rather connected to how we interact with money, how we express our sexuality, how we eat, and how we play. In fact, nothing human is outside what it means to be a "spiritual person."

The acceptance of human mortality, meaning not only the awareness that we all die but also the fact that we live within material limitations, is called humility. In fact, the word humility derives from the Latin adjective *humilis*, "grounded," or "related to earth" (*humus*).

In its very first story about human beings, the Bible stresses this very point. God makes human beings from the earth and tells them, "To earth thou shalt return." Soil is the literal and figurative ground of our earthly lives.

The Greco-Roman tradition is rarely in agreement with this core Christian value, seeing humility as the mark of a servile, weak individual. This means that Western Christians have always been forced to see the model for greatness in either Nimrod or Abraham, either Caesar or Christ. Another way of saying this is that we aim for either humility or hubris.

Although we do not often associate humility with the acquisition of knowledge, humility is the essential ground of learning. Ungrounded people remain "up in the air," unable to descend to the earth where instruction occurs. Awe of creation on the other hand, coupled with a curiosity about the structure and function of the universe, leads to continual change in one's character.

Humility restrains one's arrogant inclination to resist other points of view. It forces one to hold their perceptions lightly. Humility motivates us to adopt systems of evaluation—such as logic and the scientific method—to help us separate what we wished were true from what can be demonstrated to be truly true.

Humility does not require the surrender of good judgment. Although we always should remain open to new information and should resist our desire to be right about everything, we can nonetheless arrive at a reasonable level of certainty about some things.

Respect for others does not require us to suppress what we know to be true.

A man once introduced himself to me as Elijah the Tishbite and said that he had a message from God. I didn't believe he was Elijah. I believed he struggled with mental illness. Nonetheless, he was a human being, made in God's own image and likeness. Besides, I have learned that some mentally ill persons become incredibly wise. Of course, since Christians believe in the communion of saints, it was not impossible that Elijah the Tishbite might make an appearance. Even then, scripture teaches me to be cautious even of angelic visitors. The real Elijah would know that.

Dysfunctional families, gurus, and cults have this in common: they convince us to surrender our judgement. Once we do, we will begin suppressing valid questions about the people and systems who claim to be above such accountability. Neither healthy faith nor authentic humility requires our slothful stupefaction.

Christian humility then is not self-humiliation but rather a hospitable, humble, and wise life of discernment.

The way to truth moves us toward what can be proven, even if uncomfortable. It moves us away from our preferred opinions, however comforting, if we learn that we are mistaken. This requires humility and courage.

The development of Western science is an example of how humility, honesty, and courage can connect us to reality. In discussions with non-Christians about contemporary discoveries therefore, we must remain aware of our own inclination to pretentiousness and hubris. We must remember that humility rarely erodes a relationship. It never erodes genuine faith.

Contemporary science seems to continually presses Christians to explain their faith. This is not always, or even usually due to any intentional hostility on the part of secular people. It is rather a form of intellectual accountability. We need not fear it because the scientific quest is consistent with belief in a universe governed by God's providential structures. Although a secular person may disagree with that statement, he does so from a philosophical rather than a scientific commitment.

Throughout this chapter, I have pressed the point that respect for creation is a necessary component of spiritual growth. Indeed, the Apostle Paul claimed if were we to understand all that nature reveals, we would know everything we need to know about everything, even God's power and godhead! Paul went on to say that our issue is not with the failure of creation to communicate. It is with our ability to read nature's divine message.

Nature nonetheless reveals the glory of God. Discerning its patterns and seeking to align ourselves with what is real, results in the quality of life we call wisdom.

8

Aligning With Reality
THE QUEST FOR WISDOM AND JUSTICE

Providence can be discerned by those who seek to align their thoughts and behaviors to the patterns embedded within creation.

SOMETIME IN THE SIXTH CENTURY BCE, AN OLD MAN TRIED TO cross the Chinese border. The guards had recognized him as the wisest man alive and so had blocked his way. The frustrated man plead with the guards to let him pass.

Finally, the guards agreed. He could cross, they said, if he would agree to write down everything he knew. For the next few weeks, the old man did just that, birthing one of the world's most treasured books: *The Tao Te Ching.*

The old man's name was Li. History honored him with the title Lao Tzu, "the old master."

The theme of Lao's book is "the Tao," (pronounced as "dowl") which literally means "the way" or "path." Lao Tzu expanded the meaning of this common word as a reference to existence itself, which he believed could be experienced.

The Tao, Lao Tzu explained, is the grain of the universe. It is a discernible presence that upholds everything and moves through everything. Wise people learn the way of the Tao and conform their thoughts and actions to it.

Western scholars have compared Lao's use of the word *Tao* to Plato's use of the word *logos*. That helps a Western person reading the Tao Te Ching for the first time, but it is a rough analogy. For Lao Tzu, the Tao is something felt more than thought. It is a fuzzy awareness more than a clear concept, a right-brain "sense" rather than a left-brain analysis.

After a few readings of the Tao Te Ching, one begins to grasp the reasons for the enormous influence Taoist philosophy has exerted throughout Asia and does now in the contemporary West.

Lao Tsu admits that the meaning of the Tao is difficult to express. The Tao Te Ching begins with that admission:

> *"Those who know the Tao do not name it; those who name it do not know it."*

Lao follows this with numerous metaphors explaining how one experiences life, meaning, and reality as expressions of Tao.

"I saw a wheel," the old Master says, "and observed how its spokes connected the rim to the hub. I saw that the wheel's usefulness was not due to the rim because the rim was held in place by the spokes. Neither was the wheel's usefulness due to the spokes because they were supported by the rim. I realized then that the wheel's usefulness came from the hole at the hub's center. That emptiness was an essence around which the hub revolved and from which the wheel emerges."

Lao Tsu continues, "I saw a beautiful cup and sensed that its usefulness was not due to its material substance. The cup's material merely manifested the emptiness into which liquid could be poured. It was emptiness then, and not the material, that was the essence of the cup.

For many Western people, an exposure to Zen Buddhism opens up this way of viewing reality. There is a simple reason for that. Zen emerged in China, where Buddhism was influenced by the Taoist tradition it encountered there. This Taoist influenced Buddhism is what the Japanese embraced and then developed into the Buddhist expression we call Zen. Much of Japanese culture thus reflects the Taoist influence, particularly in the arts.

When a Japanese designer encourages us to imagine a room as space punctured by objects rather than as objects surrounded by space, we hear echoes of the Tao Te Ching. That perspective extends beyond interior design, however.

Many influential Western thinkers in several fields have been impacted by the soulful minimalism of this aesthetic philosophy. Two notable examples are Frank Lloyd Wright and Steve Jobs. When Apple requires engineers and programmers to pay attention to how their work will look and feel to a customer, they are expressing Steve Job's Zen-Taoist convictions.

Taoism has also influenced contemporary Western philosophy and religion, including one well-known Christian writer. C. S. Lewis refers to the Tao in *Mere Christianity*, as the sense of a rightness or wrongness of a thing. The Tao is, Lewis insisted, the ground of all spiritual perception. It is the human yearning to harmonize one's soul with the deep structures of reality. It is a longing for something we cannot name. It is what we sense pouring through a thing, but which does not come from it.

Lewis developed a Christian apologetic around the concept of Tao, arguing that all human beings intuit that there is "an ought-ness" around the choices we make. It is for this reason that a thief becomes outraged when someone steals from him. It is why people arguing with one another not only want to win the argument but to be right. We quarrel, Lewis said, because we passionately believe that a right conclusion exists that should be embraced. We usually have that conviction even before we are certain of what the right conclusion is.

Lewis believed Lao Tzu had identified something true that transcends religions, eras, and cultures: the hazy perception that some sort of wholeness undergirds everything. It is a barely perceptible quality but if attended to, will evoke a conviction about how one ought to live. The Tao is thus a kind of moral gravity.

Tao in other words, is a soul's perception of a universal integrity.

Wise people pay attention and adjust their lives accordingly. From a Christian point of view, that perception does not make one righteous. It may, however, awaken a person to the discord of his own soul. Learning that one is at odds with the grain of the universe can ignite a hunger for righteousness and initiate a journey Godward. The journey itself is the path of wisdom, which attempts to reject illusion and respond to reality.

When we say that a person is wise, we mean that he attempts to align himself with the way things work. We express a far different thing when we say that someone is crafty. Craftiness is also an awareness of how the world works. However, craftiness aims at manipulating reality to one's advantage. Craftiness, therefore, need not involve virtue. Wisdom does.

A crafty person perceives the Tao and learns to use it. A wise person submits to the Tao and is shaped by it. Although the world's many cultures have defined wisdom differently and have proposed different ways to obtain it, most have described it as a kind of harmony with the natural world. Lao Tzu certainly thought so.

Unfortunately, this is something easier said than done for contemporary people!

Most of us live in large cities. The clock, rather than the sun, manages our daily rhythm. For us, chicken is not a flightless bird running around a barn. It is a slab of meat wrapped in cellophane. Water flows from a pipe, not from a creek. Our feet do not touch grass. Our children do not touch a lamb. Nature is a stranger, and so we either exploit it or worship it.

If Lao Tzu was correct about how to find wisdom, what hope can contemporary people have to obtain it? Can one find wisdom in a concrete jungle? Or in cyberspace? How can we "consider the lily" if we do not know what a lily looks like? How can we know why one should not pour new wine into old wineskins? What is the social significance of the village well to those who have never drank from a well? How can we know what it is like to sleep on a threshing floor during barley harvest? Having no experience of the things our ancestors took for granted, how can ancient wisdom even reach us?

In other words, what sort of relevance does the world's accumulated wisdom, including the Bible, have for contemporary people?

Can one find the Tao at Starbucks? In a microbrewery?

Christianity has something important to say about this apparent scarcity of wisdom. It claims that wisdom is available to everyone, everywhere. For although wisdom shines through nature, it comes from beyond nature. One does not need to search for wisdom; wisdom will come looking for us. A wise person is one who has been apprehended by Wisdom and has joyfully submitted the chaos of his unformed soul to its transforming tutelage.

The Book of Proverbs says that Wisdom is a person. Wisdom was God's master craftsman in creation. Wisdom roams the streets searching for anyone who is weary of his own foolishness. Wisdom, says Sirach, searches for a nation that will welcome instruction. Wisdom, says St. Paul, became a Jewish child. Neither borders nor bars can obstruct wisdom, and neither wealth nor poverty offers an advantage to those who are weary from resisting the Tao's moral gravity.

Wisdom Requires Humility

Wisdom requires one to acknowledge his place in the universe. Although we are each unique, we are here but for a short time. We have a few gifts. We have many weaknesses. We can do a few things but cannot do everything. One must, therefore, learn why one is here, what one should do, and how one should live.

We are responsible, in other words, to live our lives intentionally. We must not drift about wherever the tides of time toss us. Furthermore, we must not only discover our limitations, but we must also discover our agency. And, most of all, we must know our Creator.

Science is one of the ways contemporary people can discover both their limitations and their sense of agency. A seasoned scientist knows there is more to know than anyone can know. Like those of all professions, scientists squabble. They fuss about theories, discoveries, and who should get recognition. Nonetheless, because science is a moving target, it offers less opportunities than many other disciplines for fooling oneself. A scientist may work his entire life to prove some theory only to learn that he has been pursuing a false lead. He has to be content with having closed off a dead end for others.

The discipline required to make even a small contribution to science thus makes a deep mark on one's personality and character.

Take Albert Einstein, for example.

The young Einstein was not what we would call an upright person. He treated his first wife abominably. He so thoroughly neglected his children that one of them spent his last days alone, in an asylum. And yet, as the world became aware of Einstein's genius and began wrestling with what he had discovered, he grew ever more concerned about human suffering. Although he had broken with Judaism early in life, as he aged, he began to publicly identify as a Jew. He also began to speak, though in unorthodox terms, about the mind of the Creator, whom, he believed, had ordered creation in ways that the human mind could grasp.

Atheism and agnosticism are widespread in the scientific disciplines. Even so, if one listens deeply to those who have wrestled with the meaning of what we have discovered, one will often detect a sense of awe. Awe, in turn, develops humility, ground zero for spiritual awareness. That is why it is not unusual for an aging scientist to grow increasingly involved in some spiritual quest.

A scientist can reach the limits of his own field, a moment in which one becomes willing to explore insights from other disciplines. This is important for scientists because the scope of science is limited. It exists to answer the question "what?" It cannot answer the question "what for?" And it is this "what for?" that opens the door to the humanities, philosophy, and religion. These disciplines explore the human experience itself, about which science has little to say.

Discovering the limits of one's own discipline is a humbling experience. For example, many theologians fail to reach this point. Paradoxically though, the discovery of one's limitations is the very thing that leads to wisdom. For wisdom leads one into the cloud of unknowing. The role of this unknowing is not a veneration of ignorance but an acknowledgement of the boundaries of one's intellectual capacity. Reaching that point makes it possible to worship, for worship is the opening of one's soul to that which may be perceived but which cannot be grasped.

A person who delights in knowledge becomes wise but is also aware of its limitations. Wisdom is greater than knowledge because it is aware of an integrity, a wholeness, that it cannot fully articulate. Without a hunger for knowledge therefore, one does not discover the limits of knowledge. Without wisdom, one will not long for what lies beyond knowledge.

Wisdom, which is the alignment with providence, creates the state of human flourishing that the ancient Hebrews called *shalom*. Jesus most likely had this state of human flourishing in mind when he said, "I have come that you might have life and have it in abundance." (John 10:10).

Shalom is peace, not in the sense of an absence of conflict, but rather a deep connection to the way things are.

Science, which teaches us much, cannot calm our souls. Neither can it bring peace to the world nor teach us how to love. Science without shalom is therefore soulless, the meaningless quest for more information about a universe that has no meaning. The postmodern denial of metanarrative, that is to say a narrative that pulls all the pieces of knowledge together into a meaningful whole, is the dismissal of wisdom. It is the use of knowledge to erode knowledge. It is, therefore, an evisceration, not only of worship, but of science.

Wisdom and Spiritual Life

In his *Handbook of Rabbinic Theology*, Rabbi Neusner says that one of the central assumptions Jews make about scripture is that "the data of Torah" corresponds with "the data of nature." What he means is this: if God is both the Creator of nature and the Author of scripture, then the contents of each reflect the contents of the other.

That's an important statement, worth considerable reflection.

It explains why most contemporary believers, even quite conservative ones, reading that the sun once stood still in the Valley of Aijalon, understand it as a poetic description. Although contemporary believers, like those of all times and places, believe God directed the event on Israel's behalf, they do not assume it occurred literally as Joshua describes it. The reason we read the story this way is because Galileo, a believer who lived centuries after Joshua, discovered that the earth moves around the sun. That is something Joshua didn't know.

Many church leaders in Galileo's time refused to look through a telescope because they were afraid of disagreeing with Joshua. Nonetheless, educated people, even pious ones, came to accept that we live in a heliocentric solar system. The sun does not move around the earth. Nonetheless, in answer to Joshua's prayer, one memorable day in the Valley of Aijalon, daylight lasted much longer than normal.

Christians believe that unexplainable, supernatural events still occur. God offers guidance, provision, deliverance, and healing through means that are sometimes inexplicable. If, a week after praying for $10,000, I receive a letter about a long-forgotten investment I made years ago, is that a miracle? Do I refuse to call it a miracle because the money did not materialize from nothing in the middle of my living room? On the other hand, scripture tells us to carefully evaluate such occurrences.

I have received information and provision through an unlikely chain of circumstances many times in my life. I recall those times with gratitude and believe they were answers to prayer. However, it is not an act of impiety to acknowledge that those experiences did not overturn the laws of nature. And why should they if, as Christians claim, nature is the handiwork of the very God who answers prayer?

Even in the Bible, supernatural events rarely conflict with the natural order. In fact, the Bible warns us about becoming enthralled with people who claim they or their actions transcend the natural order.

The Book of Numbers tells the story of a prophet-for-hire named Balaam. People believed he was a great seer and a spokesman for God. We can understand why they thought so because Ballam's words are among some of the Old Testament's most beautiful. And yet, circumstance showed that Ballam lacked a moral constitution. Scripture ridicules him as "dumber than an ass."

The Bible is not as nearly as impressed with wonderworkers like Balaam as with men and women of character. The heroes of scripture, even if occasionally blessed with supernatural dreams or miracles, plod through life with everyone else. They endure famines, wars, and pestilence. They struggle with family quarrels. They run out of money. They are in every way participants in the human condition. In fact, it is the different ways they face the challenges of their lives and their calling that defines them as heroes. In those rare moments when God does wonders through or around them, they are as awestruck as everyone else.

An angel greets the Mother of the Lord with the title "full of grace." Soon after this, Mary visits John the Baptist's mother, Elizabeth, who is overcome. "Who am I that the Mother of the Lord should come to me?" she asks. As both women are seized by the Spirit, Mary prophesies that she is "blessed among women."

For all of that, the highly favored one did not find a sanitary place for giving birth to the incarnate God.

The apostles wrote scripture. Some of them performed miracles. They were also flogged, shipwrecked, humiliated, and killed. They were mortals, subject to the laws of nature, as indeed are we all.

Some of the miracles recorded in the Bible certainly seem to transcend natural explanation. Creation, the exodus, the incarnation, the transfiguration, and the resurrection are a few examples. Not all of these completely exclude a natural explanation, however. For example, the creation story is not affected by calling it the Big Bang. Our belief that the cosmos is a divine creation does not suffer from learning about thermonuclear, chemical, and astronomical details of the universe's beginning.

Many of the miracles connected to the person and work of Christ do transcend natural explanation. That is not surprising, though. If Christ is indeed God, we might expect that how he arrives and leaves the earth will be difficult to explain.

Even so, Jesus gets hungry and tired. He grieves a friend's death. He is disappointed because a man decides not to become a disciple.

Furthermore, Jesus grounds spirituality in the natural world. He teaches about heavenly things by telling stories from farming, fishing, and commerce. He doesn't levitate. He doesn't change Pharisees into lizards. He doesn't call ten thousand angels to overthrow Caesar. No supernaturally obtained knowledge nor miraculous action replaces the Lord's hard work of growing in stature, in wisdom, and in favor with God and with people.

Jesus, along with all the Bible's characters, lived within the material world, in what St. Thomas Aquinas called "our appointed realm."

There is a difference then between biblical spirituality and shamanism. The apostle Peter falls into a trance and has a vision. He must nonetheless explain himself to the suspicious counsel in Jerusalem. The trance cannot serve as a sufficient defense for his actions.

The prophet Agabus prophesies that Paul should not go to Jerusalem. Paul listens respectfully and goes anyway. Throughout scripture, supernatural grace empowers, restores, and completes nature. It does not deny nor replace it.

We become wise then through natural means infused with grace. The reading of scripture, our experiences of life, our relationships with others, and our studies of nature weave together to become the means of our spiritual formation. Though we may long for supernatural deliverance from our natural state, most of the time Christians will walk through the same sorts of things as everyone else. It is in this crucible of the ordinary where one's cognitive, emotional, relational, and practical life slowly leans toward wisdom. The sign of spiritual growth is that one gradually learns to do justly, to love mercy, and to walk humbly with God.

Justice

Kong Fuzi, better known in the West as Confucius (552-479 BCE), wanted to lead his nation to become a just society. He is thus a counterbalance to Lao Tzu's focus on the individual. After his death, the Chinese revered the venerable sage and sought to internalize his vision of what constitutes an ethical and just society. A collection of his sayings, *The Analects*, was, until recent times, the basis for an extensive examination given to those entering government service.

The Western World has also produced remarkable works about creating a just society. Plato's *Republic* is probably the best-known of these, though most of his readers say, "No, thanks!" *The Communist Manifesto* by Marx and Engels is another. St. Augustine, in *The City of God*, imagines how a healthy Christian society should work.

Each of these define justice in a specific way. Marx believed the core value of a just community is the economic equality of its citizens. Plato believed knowledge is the most important value of a just society. Jefferson believed it was the pursuit of happiness.

According to the Bible, a just nation is one that honors God by honoring its inhabitants, by treating them as creatures made in God's own image and likeness.

Unlike Marx, a biblical definition of justice does not assume economic equality. It does, however, rebuke greed, exploitation, and the miserly stockpiling of goods needed by others. Unlike Plato, the biblical prophets demand that knowledge be made assessable to all, rather than be confined to the nation's elite. Most importantly, the Hebrew view of justice insists that kings, royalty, and even God are bound by the same ethics and morals as the nation's citizens.

A just society accepts the responsibility to live out the moral and ethical commitments it professes. The question then becomes, "What morals and ethics?" Is it Marx, Confucius, Jefferson, Plato, or someone else who defines this? Making an informed oligarchy (rule by a few) the standard for justice, as Plato suggested, hasn't worked out. An educated king doesn't work either. Nor priests. It is far too easy for democracy to become mob rule. Anarchy is the denial of any common good. Libertarianism is simply "every man for himself."

What then?

The New Testament writers deny that human beings, whether as individuals or as societies, possess the necessary wisdom, righteousness, or justice to achieve and maintain a state of flourishing.

Indeed, humanity cannot even agree on how to define these

qualities. The New Testament writers, especially St. Paul, locates them in God alone. A society reaches for justice, knowing that we never fully reach it. It must be *semper reformata*, to use the language of the reformation, "always in the process of reform."

From a Christian standpoint then, the standard of justice toward which a community reaches, is God—as scripture defines God. But what do we mean when we say that God is just?

Do we mean that God is just simply because God is the One who defines justice? That is how Louis IV defined justice. "The state is myself," the king said. In this view, justice is simply whatever the king, or God in this case, decides is just.

Is this what we have in mind when we say that God is just?

"No," Rabbi Neusner says. Justice is a quality that God embodies, and toward which God points us. God models justice. God IS justice.

We learn this, Neusner says, in the story of Abraham's intercession for Sodom. God tells Abraham he is fed up with the sinful city and intends to destroy it.

Abraham is shocked. He doesn't reply, "Good for you!" Abraham instead pleads with God to act justly. "Far be it from you to do this thing," Abraham says, "to destroy the innocent with the guilty." Abraham finally expresses his growing frustration: "Will not the judge of the entire earth do what is right?"

God does not rebuke Abraham for insubordination, Rabbi Neusner points out. God is pleased with Abraham's reply. This, says Neusner, implies that scripture defines justice as derived from God's character and not merely from God's sovereignty.

Of course, human beings will not always understand God's ways. We can nonetheless count on God to be consistent. He will do what is required of us. God will rest on the seventh day, just as He asks us to do. God will judge wrongdoing, sometimes severely, but He "takes no delight in the death of the wicked." God "is not willing that any should perish." God gives to the nations "the gift of repentance." And so forth.

The idea that justice emerges from God's character rather than from God's sovereignty has a number of political implications that help us define a just society.

Here are a few of them:

- Kings are subject to the laws of the nations they rule.
- Pastors are subject to the policies of the church they govern.
- Business leaders are subject to the procedures and ethics of the companies they lead.

Justice, in other words, is not merely an exercise of power. It is a manifestation of the community's values. When a nation professes biblical values, it will attempt to apply its stated ethical and moral standards to everyone, ruler and subject alike.

Although no human society, including Israel (ancient or modern) has ever fully embodied biblical justice, it is important that communities that claim to honor justice keep stretching toward it. In those societies that do—whether families, churches, corporations, or nations—individuals will feel drawn toward wisdom and goodness, and will, as a result, flourish.

Does Christianity Create Just Societies?

The Bible teaches that covenant with God leads to a radically transformed community. Contemporary non-Christians doubt this. So, before responding defensively, Christians should ask themselves whether there are compelling reasons for claiming that the Gospel transforms a community.

Some Christians claim that if they were in charge of the nation, that it would become a better place. Many go so far as to hope for theocracy, a government in which Christians establish the nation's ethical and moral standards. Unfortunately, when we look honestly at how Christians govern their houses of worship, their denominations, and their parachurch institutions, it is difficult to back up that assumption.

What Christians can reasonably claim is that a belief in human imperfection—including the awareness that Christians are themselves imperfect—leads them (or ought to lead them) to submit to structures of accountability.

So, while Christians should long for a just society and continually work toward such a society, limiting and restraining human depravity (including our own) is where we must start. Moreover, Christians should begin by demonstrating that such structures of accountability actually work in the institutions they control.

For decades, religious organizations have carried out massive coverups of sexual and financial abuse. Some have cultivated a culture of unaccountability for their leaders. We have witnessed the church's naked political entanglement with public figures known for fraud, exploitation, and cruelty. In the light of such abuse, it has become challenging to believe that imposing Christian ethical and moral values on non-Christians would lead to a more wholesome society. No group can export something it does not have. As the Apostle Peter said, "Let judgment begin in the house of God."

What Christians can legitimately claim is that a hunger for righteousness does transform individuals. Transformed individuals, in turn, offer models of justice and integrity to the society they serve.

Christians can also claim that nations that have recognized both the inalienable dignity of human beings *and* human imperfection, have usually developed more wholesome, though far-from-perfect, communities than nations without such values. Of course, it is possible to passionately profess a Christian ethic while publicly ignoring social ills. Nonetheless, we can confidently say that Christian ethic, when actually embraced by Christians, leads to a considerable alleviation of hunger, sickness, ignorance, and poverty within those nations influenced by it.

These are modest rather than grandiose claims and do not incline people to reject the imperfect good in a quixotic quest for the unobtainable perfect. Wisdom leads us to define justice in this way, acknowledging the reality of the human condition as both flawed and infinitely valuable.

In short, Christianity does indeed lead indirectly to a more just society when Christians actually practice the faith they profess and discover ways to serve, rather than rule, their neighbors. Goodness enters a society through influence earned by service, not through the imposition of authority. The model of this is Christ, "who came not to be served, but to serve, and to give himself a ransom for many."

The Wisdom of Hospitality and Grace

In the past, people rarely thought about why they believed or behaved as they did. They rarely imagined that things could be different than how they experienced them.

A polygamist, hearing about a country where men are permitted only one wife, would have laughed. "They must be very poor in that country," he may have thought. Upon learning that in some future countries a person would be permitted to hunt animals only a few weeks of the year, a man living in the jungle would have wondered how people in such a country eat. People of the past would have expressed bewilderment had they known how their descendants would deal with sex and dying, war and commerce, and who would be obligated to bow to whom.

Only a few decades ago, if Americans living in a rural area or small town heard someone talking about how Japanese, Hopis, or Samoans live, eat and worship, a typical reaction might have been, "Wow, that sure is strange."

Today, in contrast, most people are exposed constantly to other cultures. Looking for a restaurant involves choosing between Mexican, Thai, Ethiopian, or something else.

Most contemporary people do not automatically assume that one should continue believing or behaving as he was raised. We also realize that had we been born in India we might be Hindu. Had we been born in Sweden we likely would have a more secular viewpoint. Experiencing the vastly different ways in which human beings think, eat, worship, and organize themselves has eroded the idea that there is a single cultural standard toward which everyone should reach. Even categories like race and gender no longer seem as permanent as we thought a decade or two ago.

This growing awareness of how people understand the world

differently can be a source of stress. Our grandparents worried about the weather and war; they were rarely anxious about which kind of food to eat, whether they should affirm or challenge their biological gender, or whether they should go to church. For our grandparents, these things had been settled at birth.

Earlier, I stressed the importance of thinking tools in helping us connect with reality. The postmodern era insists that we must also take into consideration the person using these tools.

Research from several disciplines have made us aware that however clear-thinking we are, we are always looking at our world through layers of assumptions, memories, values, and emotions. Furthermore, much of what feels to us like personal choice is actually the values of our community. A postmodern culture forces us to look *at* what we are accustomed to looking *through*.

Christians too have a culture. Our faith is not merely a set of beliefs and experiences. That means a believer looks at reality through scripture, creeds (whether formally or informally affirmed), hymns, liturgy (either formal or informal), and the seemingly endless regional/denominational/ethnic expressions through which Christianity presents itself to the world. The way things look through these layers of social conditioning feel normal and self-evident to Christians. That is why it can be challenging for Christians to understand why the Sermon on the Mount, or the Ten Commandments, may not make sense to non-Christians.

Although we can be perplexed by the continual clash of perspectives around us, we also have much greater freedom than our ancestors for making personal change. In the contemporary world, one's tribe does not have the final word. That means we have more responsibility than those in the past for making conscious, deliberate decisions about our identity, values, and philosophy of life.

Most people do not welcome this responsibility. They would rather live their lives without ever questioning the values they were taught. Most people in fact, would prefer that their neighbors live by those same values.

In the contemporary world, Christians are free to love according to the values they profess, but they are expected to give their neighbor that same right. As for choosing the best path for one's community, Christians can weigh in on that as well. However, when we attempt to force non-Christians to accept biblical morality, we face the record of history. Like communism, dictatorship, and monarchy, Christian theocracies have a track record. We can expect unbelievers to ask how well our faith has performed when it has governed nations.

Many Christian rulers have governed honestly and effectively. Unfortunately, others have used faith to justify great atrocities. Some of the worst offenders saw themselves as God's instrument for imposing order on the heathen. Christians seem to govern best when they serve the entire population well, regardless of creed. Daniel the prophet is a good example of this, willing to suffer for his faith but unwilling to impose suffering on others in the name of his faith.

Christian witness in the contemporary world requires believers to not only to act and speak in ways consistent with their faith. It also requires Christians to respect their neighbors by manifesting a hospitable curiosity about how the world looks through their neighbor's perspective. In the contemporary world, "sharing one's faith" cannot be a one-way street.

Wisdom In the Contemporary World

I reread Durant's *The Age of Greece* and *Caesar and Christ* while writing this chapter. I realized as I read how close the ancient world came to developing modern science and technology. By the late Roman and early Byzantine eras, steam engines, pumps, advances in anatomy and astronomy, an accurate measurement of the size of the earth, and the distance to the moon had all come into view.

In 1901, fishermen discovered an ancient ship in the Mediterranean, which archeologists were able to recover. It contained a most unusual instrument. The archeologists called it the *Antikythera Mechanism*. After studying the instrument for decades, no one could figure out its purpose. Then, in 2008, computer-enhanced scanning revealed the mechanism to have been a complex navigational system. Its purpose was to combine the changes of tide, the position of the stars, and the phases of the moon to determine the ship's location and trajectory. Nothing remotely like it would exist for another sixteen hundred years.

The ancient world was not undone by a lack of science and technology. It unraveled from its bitter class conflicts; the debauchery and indifferences of its upper classes toward the suffering of the masses; and from a general rot of ethical and moral norms.

When the people of a society begin to ignore knowledge; when they dismiss the importance of wisdom and ethics; when they aim their energies toward wishful thinking, never-ending amusement, and an inordinate love of wealth, the society begins to crumble. Increasing scientific knowledge, even if accompanied by a flowering in the arts, cannot protect such a society from the ancient evils of factionalism, theft, violence, and fraud.

Acquisition and the impartation of knowledge becomes increasingly difficult in a society that has lost its respect for learning. Learning must therefore involve more than knowledge. It must include a respect for wisdom, for wisdom is what connects our diverse fields of knowledge into a meaningful and purposeful whole.

Maintaining a society's accumulated knowledge also requires social stability. A society must have enough faith and patience to tolerate diverse ideas, including those that disturb its rulers. Ideas must have the freedom to clash. A society must therefore protect both those who articulate unpopular ideas and those who question them.

Because of human frailty, ethical and moral principles are always in danger of eroding. A society must therefore acknowledge both the importance of its stated values and its inability to perfectly live them out.

For example, equality before the law is a professed value that is often violated. Wealthy and powerful people can hire clever lawyers; the poor cannot. Nonetheless, because it offers an imperfect guardrail to contain human behavior, the principle should be professed. Sometimes, a society becomes ashamed of the gap between what it professes and how it behaves. In such times, reforms are enacted that usher in a season of improved well-being.

The Roman government became too cynical to keep up even the appearance of virtue. When its leaders stopped giving even lip service to the responsibility for maintaining the common good, the suffering masses began siding with the barbarians at the gate.

When the ancient civilization collapsed, it took sixteen centuries for the Western World to recover its knowledge of sewage management, arithmetic, medicine, library science, postal service, and the thousand more moving parts required to sustain a well-ordered society. By the time the American Republic was founded, only those living in the largest cities of Europe and North America enjoyed the same standard of living as St. Paul.

Civilization is fragile. It is more difficult to construct than to destroy. Knowledge alone does not keep us reminded us of that. That is why a civilization requires wisdom. It is wisdom that turns the insights of a people into social, scientific, and spiritual progress. Without wisdom, knowledge decays. Indeed, only wisdom reminds us about the importance of knowledge.

The border guards that detained Lao Tzu were right. Had they allowed him to cross the border without writing his book, China, and the rest of the world, would have lost his profound perspective. By detaining Lao Tzu, the border guards offer us a valuable lesson: societies do not survive the loss of wisdom.

Neither do individuals.

9

Reality's Reflection
WHAT METAPHOR REVEALS ABOUT THE UNIVERSE

The patterns and processes that permeate creation make possible, indeed make inevitable, simile, metaphor, and allegory, not merely as communication tools but as meaning-generating structures. These reoccurring patterns make scientific discovery imaginable, compelling, and possible.

MANY YEARS AGO, A PASTOR FRIEND'S MOM GAVE ME THE DVD OF *Chocolat*, starring Juliette Binoche and Johnny Depp.

In the film, a Mexican woman moves to a tiny French village to set up a pastry shop. The devout village mayor watches Binoche arrange her pastries in the shop window and becomes alarmed. Lent is coming. The delicious pastries, perhaps even the pastry chef, will be a source of temptation for weak believers.

We see the mayor's sincerity. We also realize that something deeper is at work when someone gets this worked up about pastries.

"Why can't the mayor see what is going on?" we ask ourselves.

After watching the movie, I thanked the pastor's mother for the gift.

"I don't think the movie was really about chocolate," I said.

Cocking her head to one side, she responded, "You think?"

Twenty-five years later, I am asking myself why the pastor's mother thought I should watch this movie!

"Hey," I tell myself. "I am nothing like the mayor of that town!

I'm not!

I'm not!"

Pilgrim's Progress is much less subtle than *Chocolat*. John Bunyan's characters are not real persons. His characters are as he intended, one dimensional symbols, representing qualities and values one meets along the spiritual journey. Bunyan hopes the reader will identify with Christian, the central character and, like Christian, begin the walk toward the Celestial city. Evangelist, who first convinces Christian to think about his soul, likely represents Bunyan himself. Christian's neighbor Obstinate, who is opposed to Christian's pilgrimage, represents all those who will oppose one's pilgrimage.

You get the idea.

Allegories were popular in past centuries, which most of us find difficult to understand.

The film *Pleasantville* is an example of a contemporary allegory. It is the story of a teenage brother and sister upset by their parents' divorce. We first meet them as they are busy fighting over who will control the television. The brother is obsessed with old black and white sitcoms. His sister loathes them. She wants to watch something new and edgy. As the siblings fight over the remote, the TV suddenly sucks them into a Mayberry-like village where everyone, including the siblings, are black and white.

We watch as these young people adjust to their black-and-white world. As the story continues, we begin forming our opinions what this film is about. Well, more or less. Perhaps it's a movie about theology. It features an apple and a flood, after all. Then again, it may be a social commentary on late twentieth-century America. The town does divide between those who turn color and those who remain black and white. The movie may even be about psychology. The characters transform into full technicolor as they express their repressed desires.

Pleasantville is about all these things, perhaps it is about much more. Even after watching it many times, I always see something new. Good allegory is like that. The deeper we look, and the more we revisit it, the meaning expands.

Jesus's parables, which are short allegories, work in this same way. The parables frustrated his followers. They continually asked Jesus to teach in plain, unadorned speech.

But Jesus wasn't speaking in parables because he was unsure of what he wanted to say. He used parables because he could embed them with multiple layers of meaning. That is why they have been so effective in so many contexts. Even after a reader is certain he has exhausted a parable's meaning, he discovers something new in it.

Western art is full of references to Jesus's parables. Rembrandt painted them. Tolstoy fashioned them into short stories. Our music and iconography are fill with allusions to them. The parables appeal to children and to the elderly. The barely literate enjoy them and they intrigue the highly educated. They strike us at times as bewildering and at other times boundless.

At the first hearing, one can usually grasp a parable's surface message. However, since one rarely forgets a parable, it may reemerge years later to offer fresh insight into some difficult situation we are facing. Because the parables transcend culture and generational taste, they have been at work for two thousand years, shining their timeless light into diverse cultures and into unique situations.

Prose struggles to achieve that level of meaning. That is why Plato is easier to read than Aristotle. Plato tells stories. It is also why other parts of the New Testament seem more complex than Jesus's simple parables; it is the parable that becomes ever more intriguing with each reading.

In my opinion, the Bible is best understood when its prose is read as a commentary on its poetry, narrative, and parable. In this view, the Epistles, are reflections on the Bible's narrative, Psalms, and other poetic writing. The prose transposes the dense material of biblical allegory and metaphor into a more linear medium, though often at the cost of subtlety and applicability.

Allegory utilizes surface-level backdrops, characters, and plot to pull the reader into a soul-transforming experience. The allegory may be brief and simple, as with the Lord's story about the Good Samaritan. It can also be rather complicated, as with the movie *Pleasantville*. An allegory can even be visual, as when Picasso uses bicycle handles to create the image of a bull.

Great teachers often use simile, metaphor, and allegory to convey new information. For example, a science teacher may use a simile to explain how atoms are structured. "It's something like a small solar system," a teacher says. The student then forms a somewhat mistaken but nonetheless helpful mental image of atomic structure.

Metaphor dispenses with the words "is like." However, it is nearly the same thing.

If a teacher says, "These miniature solar systems called atoms were unknown through much of human history," they become even less precise than the example above. However, the metaphor provokes more delight than a simile, thus capturing the student's attention long enough for them to process (and perhaps retain) the new information.

I will not differentiate between types of symbolic language here. Just keep in mind that by "metaphor" I will be referring to the ways human beings use patterns from one situation to explain something in a different context. Even *algorithm* fits roughly into this definition. This is not precise enough for some contexts, but I trust the reader will tolerate the use of this single term "metaphor" to refer the many ways we use patterns to understand and communicate new information.

The reader will also notice that I follow this chapter on metaphor with another on the same subject. There is thus considerable overlap between these two chapters. However, they deal with the subject from different perspectives. That can be helpful when dealing with something as "slippery" as metaphor, which as you surely notice, is a metaphor of its own!

Metaphors, Mathematics, and Anatomy

In 1202, Leonard of Pisa, better known as Fibonacci, calculated how many rabbits would be born from an original pair over a specific period of time.

To arrive at his answer, Fibonacci used a mathematical sequence that had fascinated scholars in ancient India. It is a sequence of numbers that are the sum of the two numbers preceding it. Thus, we get 1, 2, 3, 5, 8, 13, . . .

The pattern occurs often in nature. In fact, since Fibonacci, all sorts of examples have been discovered, in flowers, water currents, seashells, and even computer coding.

The golden ratio is a sequence in which the sum of two numbers (a, b) is divided by the larger (a). The result is called Φ (phi) and stands for 1.618033988749895 . . . Phi is a so-called irrational number, meaning it has no final resolution.

Everywhere in nature one finds such sequences.

My wife and I lived in Montréal several years ago. We marveled at how patterns that looked like tiny jungles appeared on our ice-coated windows. I once decided to look at them through a magnifying glass and was amazed to see tiny "leaves" on the miniature trees. I pondered several times about where these tree-like and flower-like patterns came from.

Years later, I learned about fractals, self-propagating patterns that develop from simple repeating sequences. This can result in complex structures. Today, we use fractals in computer programing to model dynamic, natural processes like ocean currents and climate change.

The contemporary study of fractals is in many ways a continuation of our long fascination with reoccurring pattern. The Ancient Greeks discovered long ago that the use of the golden ratio in architectural design was aesthetically pleasing. It is, in fact, one of the reasons we so admire ancient ruins. Though the buildings long ago lost their practical utility, they remain a kind of visual music.

Numerical sequences reoccur in widely diverging contexts. While they are not metaphors, they do reveal what a metaphor is and why they are so compelling. We do not impose numerical patterns upon nature, as when we imagine a cloud to look like Micky Mouse. It would be much more accurate to say that they impose themselves on our mind. Once they do, we notice their reoccurrence in many contexts. Metaphors are like that. Once we notice some similarity of function between different domains, we begin inferring from our knowledge of the domain with which we are most familiar what may lurk undiscovered in the domain with which we are less familiar.

If the president says in his State of the Union speech that the ship of state has weathered another storm, we will understand that the president believes the nation has recently emerged from a significant crisis. Although the nation is not a ship, a picture forms in our minds of a vessel, which though afloat, may need repair. This picture is pregnant with implications, both warranted and not.

The word "metaphor" literally means "carrying across," and what a metaphor carries across is information. The human mind carries information gathered in one domain to access and understand another. As in the example of "the ship of state," the domains may be apparently far apart. Nonetheless, we perceive an underlying similarity within them, which allows us to carry information from one across to the other.

When a musician transposes a melody from one key to another, they maintain the same ratios and rests between notes. When we use a metaphor, we likewise "transpose" a pattern from one domain into another. Unlike transposing music, however, metaphor rarely results in an exact duplication. Nonetheless, the use of metaphor alters the way we perceive the domains connected by it. If we say, "Charlie Jones is a bear of a man," the metaphor changes how we think about both Charlie and bears.

A metaphor is the acknowledgment of a repetitious structure. A particularly useful metaphor therefore deepens not only our understanding of the specific situation we wish to address, but our perception of reality itself. The remark about Charlie Jones reminds us that humans and bears do, after all, have much in common.

When human beings began understanding electricity, they

needed terms for describing its behavior. They settled on describing electricity as a "current." It wouldn't be the only time our knowledge of water would be used to understand energy. We refer to most kinds of energy as flowing, being stored, creating waves, and so forth.

Water metaphors are so pervasive in so many fields that we rarely notice them as metaphors. For example, we use a water metaphor to describe the economy. The tangible symbol of economic energy is "currency." Coins and dollar bills thus serve as an interface between economic movement (a current) and the visible, tangible world. A coin or a bill is a faucet that controls the economic current. A bank is a dam, restraining and releasing currency. In times of inflation, currency floods the society. In times of recession, currency recedes. Like water in canals, currency can be directed to specific places. We can liquidate an asset, which means to release the economic energy stored in an object or an account. A bank or court can also freeze one's assets, which means prohibiting the release of economic energy. And we could go on.

We also use water metaphors to describe light and sound.

When Einstein began imagining light as a wave, which is how people in his day thought about light, he discovered several inconsistencies. While the metaphor had helped scientists form several correct conclusions about light, Einstein noticed that light didn't always behave like a wave. It sometimes behaved like a particle. The water metaphor had led to a somewhat true, but imprecise, view of light.

Quantum mechanics returned to the wave metaphor. Subatomic particles, as small in comparison to atoms as atoms are to a speck of dust, do indeed behave like waves. Light is both wave and particle, the embodiment of something our high school English teachers deplored: the dreaded mixed metaphor.

Our growing knowledge of light, discovered in part from musings about how water metaphors both reveal and obscure the true nature of light, led to serious questions about the nature of reality itself. If the building blocks of everything we see and touch are more like waves than things, what exactly is "waving?" The answer is information.

So, how should we describe information? Making full circle, we describe information as something that flows, can be stored, and moves everything it touches.

As we can see, imagining any part of reality that is too large, too small, or too abstract to directly experience, requires the extensive use of metaphor.

It is important to say that metaphors can send us on a wild goose chase. Most of the time, however, a metaphor, even when imprecise, helps us acquire knowledge.

Electricity and light do not behave exactly like water. As Einstein discovered, these forms of energy are quite different than water, in many ways. Nonetheless, Einstein would not have discovered that had he not first imagined electricity and light as behaving like water.

We can say then that metaphors offer fuzzy rather than precise information. This too has implications for how we imagine and describe reality. It is why the modern era, which began with such a resounding rejection of metaphor, found itself stretched beyond recovery by the rediscovery of metaphor. The result is Postmodernism, which ping-pongs between a near mystical affirmation of metaphor and a rejection of any claim to truth as something more than metaphor.

How did we get here?

A Modern History of Metaphor

When Europe emerged from the premodern era, Western intellectuals, particularly Protestants, developed an intense distaste for metaphor. Educated people were reacting to the abuse of metaphor during the medieval era, when some theologians had seemed to interpret scripture to say whatever they wished it to say. There were several reasons for this misuse.

For one thing, medieval writers tended to treat any ancient text as sacred. Aware that a large percentage of ancient literature had not survived, they treasured every existing text. This high respect for ancient books led medieval people to synthesize their contents. The synthesis included much that was incompatible. The project thus required an abundant use of allegory and metaphor. Since the medieval synthesis included the biblical canon, allegorical interpretations of scripture were required for synthesizing it with other texts. This came at the cost of sometimes stretching the obvious meaning of scripture to a breaking point.

The recovery of scripture required reformers to dismantle the synthesizing impulse, which led not only to isolating scripture from Plato, Aristotle, and Euripides, but ultimately to an insistence that Isaiah should be isolated from Genesis or Romans. For Protestants, the war on metaphor and allegory led to a suspicion of the Patristic writers as well, which became even more intense among modern Evangelicals.

The rejection of metaphor was not merely a theological reaction though. It became a feature of intellectual life throughout the modern period. As the modern era began to end, some scholars began to overuse metaphor in just the way the early reformers deplored.

Sigmund Freud and Karl Jung for example, were probably overly ambitious in the way they allegorized folk tales, myths, and even the personal dreams of their patients. That is why Freud was once forced to admit that "sometimes a cigar is just a cigar." He had to make that clarification because . . . well, Freud often suggested that too much talk about a cigar was really talk about a body part that reminded him of a cigar.

Unfortunately, many of the well-known photographs of Freud depict him holding a rather prominent cigar! When people began pointing this out, Freud realized that his metaphor had been stretched too far!

In 1929, Megré Magritte painted a picture of a pipe. Underneath it, he included these words: *"Ceci n'est pas une pipe"* (this is not a pipe).

Well, that is confusing since it was a pipe.

Wasn't it?

No. It wasn't. That was Magritte's point.

Magritte's painting was a *picture* of a pipe. A picture of a pipe is not a pipe. Assembling the letters p-i-p-e also do not create a pipe. For that matter, the spoken word "pipe" is not a pipe either.

Magritte's painting, p-i-p-e, and the spoken word "pipe" are all symbols. Symbols enable the mind to form models of reality, which in turn makes communication between minds possible. Our mental models are not reality itself, however.

At the end of the modern period then, intellectuals became aware of the difference between mental modeling and experienced reality. This soon gave rise to phenomenology, a discipline for analyzing the contents of one's own consciousness. The aim of phenomenology, however, was to encourage full contact with the reality outside one's head, separated from one's private interpretation. We might describe phenomenology as a kind of Western Zen.

Magritte was expressing this late modern anxiety about language, its slippery hold on meaning, and its habit of intruding between an object and our direct perception of it. In his painting, we see the modern era transitioning into what will soon become the postmodern age.

Peter Watson describes this transition in his book, *The Modern Mind*. He describes the most important discoveries of the twentieth century by the year in which they occurred. One of Watson's most important insights is the ever-expanding chasm that began to develop within Western Civilization during that century. On one side were those cheering the century's writers, artists, and scientists as liberators. On the other side were those who denounced the Western intelligentsia as cultural assassins.

Watson begins his account with Freud's 1901 publication of the *Interpretation of Dreams*. The literary public quickly affirmed Freud's claim that Europe's stated ethics and morals were a thin veneer, stretched over a vast, largely unconscious, swamp. Meanwhile, experiments in electrical engineering called into question Newton's orderly universe. By 1916, Albert Einstein proved that the speed of light was the only constant feature of the universe.

By the end of the first quarter of the century, populous reaction to discoveries like these intensified. As opinions hardened about how to respond to what seemed to many as the dismantling of common sense, the peoples of the Western World found it increasingly difficult to relate to one another.

For Watson, a single event, on the evening of May 29th, 1913, epitomized the severing of the West into liberal and conservative camps. Igor Stravinsky's debut of his *Rite of Spring* in a Paris theatre moved some of the audience to ecstatic praise and others to enraged protest. The police were called to break up the fight. The divided character of the Western World was on full display that evening in a single room!

As the twentieth century continued to move through its turbulent decades, Western art, physics, and politics reflected and reacted to the new vision of reality that had emerged from physics.

Magritte's painting of the pipe was thus an insistence that we should make a difference between symbol and reality. It forced one to acknowledge that a canvas contained no pipe. Indeed, while there were millions of pipes held in millions of hands, no Universal Pipe existed anywhere. Images conjured in our heads by the word pipe are therefore as different as those held by millions of pipe smokers. Furthermore, those mental images only potentially pointed toward real objects in the real world.

Intentionally or not, Magritte was also demonstrating the final break of the Western World from the ancient view that an image participates in the reality it depicts. It had become possible for a symbolic world to exist that claimed no connection to anything outside itself.

As Watson claims, the inner life of Western peoples kept changing throughout the twentieth century. As human beings walked on the moon and learned to fit vast libraries on the head of a pin, our philosophers, psychologists, and physicists were busy deconstructing much of what the Western World had taken for granted since the Modern Age had begun.

Magritte's insistence that a picture of a pipe was not a pipe alerts us to how the language of deconstruction leads down the rabbit hole. If language is indeed an artificial construct and does not actually participate in what it describes, then any shared meaning, or at least precise shared meaning, becomes next to impossible. In that case, we are all prisoners, locked inside our own heads. All of our thoughts and opinions are cultural constructs that represent nothing substantial.

The modern era's assumption that calculation and rational process is the bedrock of reality had come to seem unbearably empty by the late 20th century. Its long banishment of intuition, collective memory, myth, and spiritual practice as generators of cultural meaning had pushed the Western World into a collective depression.

In the words of Kansas, it suddenly seemed that all we are is dust in the wind.

The author of the Old Testament Book of Ecclesiastes had understood where the slippery slope leads.

"It's all smoke!" he shouted.

Well, it is mostly smoke. That is unless some ground exists from which all meaning is derived. Until very recently, Western Civilization assumed there was such a ground. Our ancestors had taken for granted that meaning was the quality of a universe whose parts purposefully interpenetrate to form repetitive patterns. They were able to discover, study, artistically depict, and employ those patterns to enhance their lives. Indeed, that is how they defined civilization.

The center of meaning was thus the interpenetrating character of image, symbol, thought, language, idea, mind, and matter.

Understanding the role of metaphor is thus an important component for restoring any sense of an individual and cultural meaning in our times. Innumerable fundamentalisms—most of them non-religious—are the harbingers of the many kinds of authoritarian darkness that overtakes a people when they plunge into a world where it is always winter but never Christmas.

Many Jews and Christians have known this all along. A growing number of postmodern secularists believe it as well.

Secular Use of Metaphor

Mark Johnson, professor of Liberal Arts and Sciences at the University of Oregon, is a passionate advocate for the importance of metaphor. He has written extensively on the subject, but most of my reflections here are reactions to his 2017 work, *Embodied Mind, Meaning, and Reason.*[1]

Johnson's interest in metaphor has nothing to do with Neoplatonism, much less with Christianity. Johnson sees metaphor as an evolutionary development that emerges from human bodies embedded within a constantly changing environment. Metaphor is thus crucial, probably even foundational, to human thought. It enables the mind to adapt what it has learned to different conditions and situations.

This fact, that what one knows must be altered to fit new contexts (including abstract contexts) is, Johnson believes, the basis of metaphor. When I say, "Let me put it this way," I am drawing on the experience of placing objects in a container. Although I may be referring to an abstract concept, which cannot literally be placed anywhere because it doesn't exist as an object in the material world, I nonetheless imagine "placing" in into the mind of the person with whom I am speaking.

A remark like "I see what you are saying," has no literal meaning. Literally, I am not seeing anything because there is nothing to see! The statement nonetheless draws on our experience of observing a material object coming into view.

"Up there," I say, while I point. "That's a plane, isn't it?"

"I think I see what you are seeing," my friend replies.

"Now," says my nerdy friend, "think about what Karl Marx meant by the alienation of capital. A carriage maker had pride in what he made with his own hands. However, a worker in a modern automobile factory is disconnected to the final product of his work because all he does is screw wheels on axles!"

"Ahh," I reply. "I think I see what you are saying."

Johnson insists that human communication is nearly impossible without using metaphors. He offers examples of this from writers who raged against using them. They are funny because the rants are full of metaphors. They demonstrate that we cannot even express our rage at a metaphor without using metaphor. Think about the word "full" in the phrase "full of metaphors." The phrase is literally meaningless. So even our explanations of metaphor are necessarily metaphors.

Johnson claims that it is more reasonable to say that language emerges from metaphor than to say that metaphor emerges from language. After many centuries of dismissing metaphor as a lazy and inexact form of communication, Johnson demonstrates—conclusively in my mind—that metaphor is foundational not only to communication but to thought itself.

"I will not be using 'metaphor' in the traditional sense as merely a figure of speech; rather, I shall identify it as a pervasive, indispensable structure of human understanding by means of which we figuratively comprehend our world."[2]

I do not know if Johnson believes that the existence of metaphor points to the multi-layered nature of reality or that the existence of metaphor suggests the human mind participates in and influences those levels of reality. As a Christian, I do draw such conclusions. I believe they are critical elements of what our faith offers contemporary secularists.

Postmodernism "giveth and it taketh away." One of the things it had taken away is the conviction that an objective reality exists—truth, in other words. From a Christian standpoint this is tragic. However, postmodernism also acknowledges, as modern thinkers did not, that the human mind interprets reality "as in a glass, darkly."

Postmodernism makes room for metaphor but as a suggestion that reality is slippery. Christianity, in contrast, uses metaphor not because we believe reality is imprecise but because the reflection of reality in our mind's mirror contains too much information to express otherwise.

Postmodernism and Metaphor

Postmodernism is both a continuation of and a rebellion against modernity. As the twentieth century unfolded, the modern perception of reality as a material machine led Western peoples to doubt their own significance. Throughout the modern period there had been considerable resistance to this mechanistic view. As the twentieth century began winding down, however, it became obvious that either something was amiss in the way Western peoples had been viewing the world or human beings really were dust in the wind. This anxiety only increased as our culture began moving into the postmodern era.

We have noted that postmodernism isn't so much a philosophy as it is a reactive mood, clearer about what rejects than about what it affirms. That notwithstanding, the Western World has acknowledged that the modern era, which began with such great optimism, has hit a dead end. We were unable to fit Hiroshima and Auschwitz into the secular millennia promised by the early modernist thinkers.

Postmodernism has not only rejected the modern myth of progress but has also rejected any view of reality that claims to clearly explain much of anything. Postmodernism's famous dictum says as much: *there is no metanarrative.*

By dismissing the possibility of metanarrative, postmodernism assumes that human beings create meaning rather than discover it. This postmodernist belief first emerged in neo-Marxist forms of literary criticism. It is founded in the assumption that an appeal to truth or objectivity is a power-play by those who stand to profit from a particular definition of truth.

For postmoderns, the great narratives that offered a sense of significance in past centuries, were cruel and oppressive. Marxism gave us the Gulag. Fascism gave us Bergen-Belsen. Christianity, despite its talk of love and brotherhood, failed to confront racism, slavery, genocide, and many other inequities. Capitalism lifted multitudes out of poverty but at the cost of eroding the structures of kith and kin that made life meaningful. Science has expanded our understanding but has in the process eroded our conviction that any of it matters.

Postmoderns seem to say, "We are disillusioned by all big claims. We have discovered the truth: there is no TRUTH; there is only one damned thing after another."

All this may seem new. However, Western Civilization has been struggling for centuries over what is really real. The debate rarely reached the palace or the marketplace, but people have been engaged with it for a long time. In fact, Arthur Herman insists that the Western World has been in a tug-of-war about reality since Plato and Aristotle walked the streets of ancient Athens.

In *The Cave and the Light*,[3] Herman explains how our culture has continually see-sawed between the two ancient giants. Plato taught that qualities exist apart from the objects in which we encounter them. Goodness, Truth, Justice, and Beauty are not merely qualities of things, they merely shine through things. Things, according to Plato, are less significant than these qualities (or forms). In fact, things derive their significance because they participate in such forms.

Reality, Plato says, is best understood by looking at the big picture before breaking it up into details. We must know what Beauty is before we ask whether a particular thing is beautiful. We must first ask the meaning of Justice before we can discern whether a specific situation is just. Aiming at maintaining a healthy society is more important than trying to make individuals happy because individuals are components of a society. One should take in a wide-angle perspective before zooming in on the details.

Aristotle disagrees. He insists that we arrive at accurate views of reality by studying concrete particulars. Only then can we speculate about a larger narrative. Abstract principles are not real, in the sense that material things are real. Categories are only useful short-cuts created by our imagination for organizing data. The wider our angle of vision, the less certainty we can have that what we are seeing is real.

As one would expect, the Platonic part of the Western heritage is systemic. It looks at the components of a system in light of the whole. Platonists also believe that reality embodies and reflects eternal principles, which exist independently from any specific thing or event. Platonic discourse thus makes frequent use of metaphor because it assumes the universe as a whole is reflected in all its parts.

The Aristotelian tradition, in contrast, prefers straightforward prose. For Aristotelians, an item reveals information only about itself. It therefore uses metaphor sparingly, viewing it at best as a blunt communication tool for explaining something challenging to understand.

Western civilization has always swung between these two ancient poles of thought. However, the Judeo-Christian influence on Western culture found in each philosopher things to admire and things to reject. This ambivalent use of both Aristotle and Plato mitigated the division between them. As the West has grown ever more secular, the corresponding loss of this mitigating influence has exposed the culture to an increasing danger of extreme polarization.

Dr. Iain McGilchrist, member of the Royal College of Psychiatrists, argues that metaphor was largely dismissed during the modern era because the West became guilty of a rational overreach. In his view, the left cerebral hemisphere experiences reality in a computer-like manner. It is more efficient at dealing with details and objects than its right counterpart but is challenged in grasping the value of subjective experiences involving relationships, art, and spirituality. The modern era, which tended to envision reality as a machine, increasingly privileged the left cerebral hemisphere perspective. This led to a mistrust of the messier, emotionally entangled, intuitive view of reality favored by the right cerebral hemisphere.

The privileging of the left cerebral hemisphere for so long in the West, McGilchrist believes, has provoked several serious reactions against rationality. As a left-hemisphere dominant culture pushed our culture to become ever more mechanized, measured, streamlined, and focused on immediate results, a growing percentage of Western peoples became willing to tolerate irrationality as perhaps a necessary price for recovering their meaning and dignity. In McGilchrist's view, metaphor thus serves as not merely an intuitive means for acquiring new knowledge but as a means for confirming and communicating whatever view one finds comforting.

Platonic allegorizing has a long history of being misused to justify ecstatic leaps into irrationality. When a culture swings too far toward this right-brain tendency, it becomes easy to neglect the importance of empirical verification of creative insights.

Numbers of our great scientists and philosophers are warning us that Western Civilization is at risk of this very thing. If they are right, then the scientific disciplines that led to the polio vaccine, space travel, and iPads will erode, plunging us back into the sort of scientific unraveling that occurred in late antiquity.

A positive aspect of our movement beyond modernism is that an increasing number of scientists and mathematicians are willing to entertain questions long ignored by our culture. For example, if information is, as it appears to be, a non-reducible component of reality, does this not legitimately raise the question of whether information precedes rather than emerges from matter? And doesn't such a question raise legitimate questions about who we are, why we are here, and what the universe means?

Because postmodernism allows such questions to be taken seriously in ways that modernism did not, we have new possibilities for respectful communication between the sciences, humanities, religion, and philosophy. In a best-case scenario, science becomes a privileged participant of such conversation rather than the final word on human and cosmic meaning.

The role of metaphor in human thought and language is a promising topic of such a conversation. By its very nature, metaphor unites and synergizes. If we remain vigilant about what can and cannot be synergistically combined, metaphor becomes a playful and speculative way for those of different fields and interests to share insights and concerns.

As it turns out, a few Christian writers have left us helpful advice about how to proceed with such a discussion.

C. S. Lewis's contrarian friend, Owen Barfield, was one of them.

Owen Barfield, C. S. Lewis, and the Responsible Use of Metaphor

According to those who knew him, Barfield was a brilliant and provocative presence. Like the other contrarian voices in this book, he is not easy to categorize. Some of his conclusions were not theologically orthodox; at least Barfield did not express them in orthodox language. Nonetheless, Barfield was one of the first Christian writers of the late modern era to wrestle with the spiritual implications of what we now call postmodernism.

Christians encountering Barfield will understand why he and Lewis often argued. They will also understand why Lewis kept coming back for more.

In his best-known book, *Saving the Appearances*,[4] Barfield muses about how a community's words and metaphors affect the way its inhabitants experience the world. While Johnson and Lakoff's research explores how metaphor emerges from an individual's encounter with an environment, Barfield was interested in how a community's metaphors shape the individual's interpretation of an environment. For Barfield, in other words, an individual encounters an environment predisposed (by his community) to experience it in a certain way.

Barfield claimed that communities create a simulacrum, that is to say a mental representation of its natural and social environment. People born into the community thus experience their world through that simulacrum. Some contemporary philosophers call this communal perspective a *plausibility structure*, which is the phrase we will use here. Barfield claimed it is important to understand a community's plausibility structure because raw reality lies beyond anyone's direct perception. As we noted earlier, every human being looks *through* something and *at* everything else.

Barfield was particularly interested in the plausibility structures of past cultures. History is a record of how various people have lived, died, worshipped, and mated. Looking back, we can reflect on why their belief systems developed as they did and how those systems served them. Barfield's interest was in how the various peoples of the past had perceived reality and about the conditions in which that perception changed.

Barfield believed that societies periodically reassess their plausibility structure. At such times, the people of that society must either defend or reject their traditional way of experiencing and explaining reality. Since most people do not explain, even to themselves, why they perceive reality as they do, being forced to think about this creates a season of unrest. Barfield (who wrote through most of the decades of the twentieth century), believed that the Western World had entered just such a season, feeling forced to look *at* what their ancestors simply had looked *through*.

Barfield begins *Saving the Appearances* by asking what we mean when we say that a rainbow *exists*. He notes that we can share our personal perception of a rainbow with others. We know that they are seeing the same rainbow because they can describe its colors, its brilliance, its size, and so forth. For all of that, we're not certain that a rainbow is "a thing." Perhaps it helps to categorize the rainbow as a phenomenon, though that doesn't quite clarify why exactly we experience a rainbow as different than a thing. On further thought, we may not know exactly what we mean by "thing" either!

In the end, says Barfield, there is no universal agreement about what we mean when we say that a rainbow *exists*.

Defining a rainbow requires us to define reality itself. This, in turn, forces us to examine the structures through which we experience and explain reality. Although it is entirely reasonable to say that rainbows are phenomena rather than things, it is just as possible to categorize chairs, rocks, and human beings as phenomena. Indeed, some cultures do.

The discussion about rainbows reveals that what we generally experience as "things" exist on a spectrum. The entities we perceive as more substantial are on one end of that spectrum and those we experience as less substantial are at the other end. There is no clear line within that spectrum that divides what we perceive as substantial from that which we perceive as insubstantial. Material things, which we experience as substantial, are made of molecules. The molecules are made of atoms. Atoms consist of subatomic particles, which are not really things at all but more like mathematical possibilities. Between those infinitesimal building blocks of particles is empty space. What is true of rainbows, therefore, is true of everything.

Everything is phenomenon.

Some phenomena—rocks, for example—endure much longer than human beings, which leads us to perceive rocks as permanent and unchanging. Other phenomena, such as rainbows, endure for a very short time. We watch them come into existence and then fade away in a matter of minutes. It is the duration of experience therefore that leads us to categorize something as either a thing or a phenomenon. Things, in Barfield's view, are simply phenomena that endure for a long time.

If everything is phenomena, we cannot say that reality is material. The interaction of the human mind with the natural and social environment involves the recognition of patterns. Communities assign names and categories to these patterns, including descriptions of their likely duration, function, and relationship to other patterns.

This is precisely what metaphor is: the perception of a pattern. Metaphor is thus a foundational component of how human beings interact with reality. A metaphor can lead to wrong conclusions or to a deeper understanding of the world. In either case, metaphors shape how we think and behave. A human culture is thus a network of shared metaphors.

As we have seen, this view of metaphor, though ancient, was not common in the West during the modern era. In the postmodern era, however, both religious and secular thinkers are reassessing the function of metaphor in the formation of thought, speech, and human culture. We are relearning something the premodern era took for granted: metaphor enables us to both recognize and participate in reality's deep reoccurring patterns. Furthermore, this is what makes scientific discovery, indeed all discovery, imaginable, compelling, and possible.

10

More on Metaphor

Metaphor applies a pattern of information observed in one situation for understanding an entirely different situation.

IT WAS A WARM ECUADORIAN DAY IN DECEMBER 1970. MY FATHER and I had been visiting friends in Machala.

We had just concluded the evening service when three men approached, asking us to accompany them to the wharf. When we arrived, they pointed to a long primitive boat, outfitted with home-made sails.

"Please go with us to our island," one of the men said. "We have people there to baptize."

"Where is it?" my dad asked.

"Just over there a ways." The man pointed.

"We should go now while it's still cool," the man said. "You can celebrate the baptisms in the morning. Then we'll bring you back."

We stepped into the boat.

Since it was near midnight, the waves soon rocked me to sleep.

When I opened my eyes, it was dawn. As far as I could see, there was only ocean.

"Holy cow!" I sat up. "Have we missed the island?"

The men laughed.

"No," one man said. "It's just over there."

I saw only water.

It was an hour or so later before I saw the faint outline of land.

In the years since, I have often marveled at how those men, without instruments or radio, located their island. I was also impressed about that at the time, though I was mostly focused on getting back home!

Not long ago, I reminded my father about that trip. He confessed that he too had found it unsettling to wake up in a small boat on an endless sea. We remember it now as a grand adventure and found some pictures to prove we were not exaggerating.

Our story doesn't compare to another excursion that occurred five years later though. Micronesian navigator Mau Pialug also sailed a primitive vessel without instruments on the Pacific Ocean. However, Pialug took his craft from Hawaii to Tahiti. That is more than 2,500 miles across open seas!

Pialung made this voyage to settle a dispute between Western anthropologists and Polynesians. He wanted to prove that his ancestors had, just as his people's oral tradition claimed, navigated the Pacific Ocean. Knowing he was one of the last living links to an ancient navigational system, Pialung was determined to set the record straight.

The navigational system contained hundreds of terms describing the environment of the open seas: the temperature, color, and movement of the water; the force of the wind; how light from the moon and stars reflect on the ocean's surface; the positions of stars at various seasons of the year; and other such data. The ancient Polynesians had woven the terms into a mythology that was memorized by their descendants. Each voyage added more content, allowing newer generations to repeat the journeys, sometimes centuries later.

Anthropologists at the time believed old Polynesian tales about navigating the Pacific were legends. Mau Pialug revised their theories by reaching his intended destination days before schedule. It was an astounding demonstration of how ancient peoples used myth not only to express spiritual beliefs but to embody lessons in what we now call sociology, psychology, medicine and, at least in Pialug's case, navigation.

Professor Emeritus at New York University Mary Carruthers spent years researching how ancient cultures encoded and transmitted such information. In her book *The Book of Memory*[1], she claims that ancient Mediterranean peoples used the Zodiac for encoding navigational knowledge. Before movable type, texts were expensive and rare, so people used all sorts of strategies for remembering vast amounts of data. Students learned these strategies, or mnemonics, as part of their early training. Even the countless shrines beside their roads, rivers, and sea were not only places to pray, Carruthers claims, but they served as mnemonic devices for helping them recall the data they needed for travel.

Owen Barfield adds an important addition to our understanding of ancient mnemonics: the peoples of the past didn't organize their mental lives into categories such as concrete, abstract, symbolic, mythological, or common-sense knowledge. They also rarely separated prose from poetry or religion from science. Ancient peoples probably halfway believed the planets were gods who exerted their influence on the universe, but they also understood that gods or not, the planets moved in predictable patterns and at predictable times. Myth, therefore, was entertaining and morally instructive. It taught the young about the yearly drama that unfolded in the sky, the fields, and oceans. One learned from these ancient stories how to find his way across great distances and then home again.

Mythology was about much more than navigation, though. Barfield reminds us that preliterate cultures embedded their knowledge about farming, war, psychology, art, and governance within seamless, interrelated systems that they expressed through mythological language.

An example from early modernity demonstrates how these premodern systems worked. Johannes Kepler (1571-1630) made one of the greatest breakthroughs in modern astronomy when he calculated the orbits of the planets in our solar system. How he made his discovery continues to intrigue us because he based much of his work on the writings of Pythagoras.

Pythagoras, who lived from 570 to 490 BCE, developed the first known system of musical notation. That would have been a major achievement. However, from his musical discoveries he developed several mathematical ones as well. We call one of these discoveries the Pythagorean theorem. You may have learned it in a high school geometry class.

Pythagoras's musical and mathematical discoveries intertwined with mysticism and philosophy. So, modern scholars have found it challenging to decide whether he was a genius or a nutcase. Ancient and medieval scholars, however, didn't share our opinion. In fact, the ancient Greeks were certain Pythagoras descended from a god. Humble man that he was, Pythagoras neither affirmed nor denied the story.

If you begin reading about Pythagoras, you'll be very impressed. The history of western science, math, and music would look quite different had he not lived. Nonetheless, the way Pythagoras explained his discoveries will strike any contemporary person as bizarre. He embeds his knowledge of math, music, and mysticism into a word salad that can seem nearly insane. Nonetheless, Kepler, like many scholars in the early modern period, was still connected to medieval forms of thought. The writings of antiquity, not yet confined to the academic silos they would soon inhabit, were still known and debated by educated people. That is why many early modern works, especially in the arts, were still influenced by the preceding age. Kepler's three laws of planetary motion are unique though because they were a scientific rather than an artistic accomplishment.

Here is how he did it.

One of Pythagoras's central ideas was the significance of shapes as the building blocks of the universe. The circle, in his view, was the primal and perfect shape. The triangle then emerges from the circle. From the triangle comes a square. From the square a pentagon. From the pentagon a hexagon. Viewed as nested within one another, their ratios yield numerical sequences. The structures and sequences can be expressed as either musical or mathematical notations. From these shapes and sequences emerges the overall pattern of reality. You might say that the universe is a symphony.

Kepler had studied Pythagoras, as well as John Scotus Eriugina and Nicholas of Cusa. While agreeing with Galileo and Copernicus that the earth was not the center of the solar system, Kepler was not ready to discard ancient and medieval thought. In his *Mysterium Cosmographicum*, Kepler describes how his studies of Pythagoras led to his breakthrough in astronomy. He had assigned Pythagoras's shapes to the five planets known at the time and then calculated the ratios. The only alteration Kepler made to Pythagoras was assigning an elliptical, rather than circular, orbit to each planet.

In two other works, *Harmonice Mundi* and *Astronomia Nova*, Kepler describes that he checked his discovery by expressing the numbers musically, assigning specific tones for each planet and rests for the ratios! He thus arrived at his discovery in two different ways, mathematically and musically.

Nonsense, surely!

Well, sure. Except that Kepler's calculations were accurate. Naturally, contemporary measurements of these orbits are much more precise than Kepler's original figures. That is because we have better tools than he had. Our calculations are nonetheless consistent with his.

Surely then Kepler's accomplishment requires *some* sort of explanation! He might have gotten one of the orbits right through a lucky guess. Getting all five of them right suggests that his schema was not utterly irrational. One of the things we expect from a good theory is that it yields dependable results in the real world. In this case at least, Pythagoras wins his case.

Perhaps the best explanation for Kepler's discovery is this: what we tend to dismiss as the unscientific, irrational mystical schema of premodern thinkers, is more accurately described as webs of interrelated metaphors. Some of what the premoderns wove into their cognitive webs was indeed inaccurate, even imaginary. Nonetheless, those webs contained observations gathered over the previous centuries and made possible the commerce, architecture, navigation, and astronomical predictions of vast empires. So, we can hardly dismiss them as utter foolishness.

We should judge the premodern systems of thought then as containing considerable scientific, mathematical, and philosophical insight, though mixed with numerous inaccuracies. These systems differ from ours, however, in a way we have rarely noticed: they did not specialize and categorize knowledge as we do.

Their tendency was to synthesize rather than dissect, to view knowledge as a system rather than as a collection of facts. Kepler was able to access the gifts of the premodern plausibility structure because he avoided both gullibility and cynicism.

Memory Palaces

Earlier, I mentioned Mary Carruthers, who was for many decades a professor of literature at New York University. We have already noted her work on the role of memory in premodern culture and how our ancestors used buildings as a way to communicate their culture's memories. Museums and archives still serve that purpose, though by safeguarding objects rather than by symbolizing text.

Medieval cathedrals are an excellent example of the way premodern peoples turned their ideas into stone, hoping their descendants would, from the stone, reconstruct the ideas.

The word cathedral derives from the Latin word for "chair," referring to the bishop's seat. A cathedral is therefore the heart of a diocese. The building itself can be a hut, a tent, or a castle. That the word cathedral has come to suggest an imposing structure in the center of a city is due to the broader significance cathedrals came to play in Western culture. Indeed, they still play some of that role, even for non-religious people.

Medieval cathedrals were nearly always larger than necessary for most worship services. Not only did they need to accommodate occasional gatherings of the entire diocese, but they also communicated, through their structure and décor, biblical, spiritual, and cultural information. Even their proportions preached, since numerology was an important aspect of the stories, practices, and doctrines of the faith. Covered within and without by sculpture, symbol, and color, they connected spiritual life to the earthly city. Both external and internal sources of light illuminated the cathedral's furnishings, which generated a symphony of sensation to those who entered. The aim was to draw the worshipper into a sacred environment where he would be catechized and enraptured.

Carruthers explains that for premodern peoples, texts were not primarily written documents. Books and scrolls merely supported a culture that was embodied within rituals, traditions, art, and monuments. The most important "texts" were the countless chiseled and sculpted models that daily evoked the culture's values and memories.

Carruthers two best known works, *The Book of Memory* and *The Craft of Thought* [2], are invaluable for anyone who wants to understand the function of ancient literature. For example, she explains how ancient readers (or, more accurately, ancient *hearers*, since text was nearly always read aloud) would have understood a document like the *Book of Revelation*. In her view, the book was a carefully constructed collage of images drawn from the entire biblical canon, retelling the central themes of scripture in a symbolic form. The powerful images made it possible for believers to memorize these themes and recall them at those times when the written text was unavailable.

Carruthers claims that every component of premodern culture —documents, buildings, ceremonies, clothing, scent, numbers, melodies, and dramas—served as communication devices. Each cultural artifact was a component embedded within a web of interconnected metaphors through which premodern peoples understood and lived out their lives.

With a bit of imagination, we can see something similar in contemporary culture.

Imagine a video depicting a July 4th celebration on the Washington Mall. It begins with a birds-eye view of the thousands of people assembled between the Lincoln Memorial and the Washington Monument. A sea of flags is backlit by fireworks. An orchestra and a choir underscore the pageantry. As the crowd sings of the nation's glorious birth, they sway as though directed by a choreographer. Viewing this, we too are gripped by waves of patriotism and pride.

In such movements, a crowd is not so much a collection of individuals as it is a manifestation of the nation itself. The human participants have momentarily surrendered their personal identities and have entered a shared, sacred space that gathers the citizens of past and present into the mystical moment.

In the premodern world, the sort of impersonal connectedness we have just described was a way of life. Shrines, pietistic habits, family practice, and endless daily rituals formed the individual's sense of being. One lived out one's life in the bosom of kith and kin. One threw salt over one's shoulders when making an oath. One spit into the fire if someone mentioned the devil. One planted crops three days after a new moon. One boiled birch bark when someone had a fever and rubbed garlic on the chest of a newborn child. The constant mumbo-jumbo contained much which was false and some which was true. As a system, however, it offered individuals a place and a purpose.

The modern era worked hard to purposefully unravel such habits of communal life. Through a process of ceaseless demystification, Western peoples became much more comfortable celebrating their personal identities than their collective one. As the modern period unfolded, each successive generation freed itself from yet another layer of their ancestors' world. As a result, Western peoples came to imagine the premodern era as a veritable swamp of superstition and mystification.

Monuments are like books we can no longer read. A building can be beautiful, but its purpose is practical functionality. Contemporary Christians find it bewildering that their ancestors spent so much time and energy studying the materials and the measurements of Moses's Tabernacle. Experiencing spatial dimensions as a means of communication doesn't make any sense to us. Ceremony and protocol increasingly strike us as silly. Although the dead still speak through yesterday's artifacts, we have become too smart to understand.

Imagine the *quipu*, strands of knotted rope used by the Incan government for recording taxes. For centuries, skill in using quipu was passed from mentor to apprentice. After the interpretive key was lost, the quipu became useless rope.

The vases, robes, pyramids, melodies, and chants that survived from the premodern world were once living texts, filled with information gathered over millennia. Today, like the quipu, they are interesting snapshots from a destroyed world.

No wonder we characterize someone like Pythagoras as a bit crazy. Yes, he was a brilliant mathematician and musician. However, because he was also a mystic and a poet, we can hardly stomach to see him as a scientist. Mysticism and science are incompatible to us and should not coexist in the same person, perhaps not even in the same culture.

We understand premoderns like Pythagoras only by remembering that in the ancient world, math and music were perceived as surface-level manifestations of a single underlying reality.

Perhaps at this point we can begin to imagine then how metaphor functioned in the premodern world: not as a cute way to communicate but rather an awareness of patterns undergirding reality. In such a view, things are experienced as only apparently differentiated. Just as one's hair, liver, bone, and blood all carry the information that identifies them as parts of a single individual, so all apparently separated things embody the information of the cosmos to which all belong.

As William Blake might have put it, premodern peoples experienced the entire world in a grain of sand. That is something worth knowing as the postmodern world retreats from treating written text as the privileged form of cultural communication. We are not returning to the premodern world, but where we are headed has much in common with it.

Metaphor and Scientific Discovery

Life may not really be like a box of chocolates, but believing it certainly helped Forrest Gump walk through life.

A good metaphor does that for us.

It sometimes works in science too.

Sometime in the mid to late fifteenth century, Leonardo da Vinci was painting an eddy. Leonardo, who had been recently dissecting cadavers, watched as the stream of water flowed against the current of the river. Suddenly, he had an insight about something that had puzzled him. Blood flow within the human heart must work like this!

What Leonardo had done was apply a principle of fluid mechanics to anatomy. Heart valves, he decided, keep an eddy from occurring within the human heart. He made several detailed drawings to explain his insight. He might not have bothered. The discovery would not be deemed medically significant until 1969, the year researchers discovered the function of heart valves. It was a medical breakthrough that would save countless lives.

There was one reason why it took so many centuries for medical science to take Leonardo's discovery seriously. The modern era had made it difficult to imagine an artist as having any significant contribution to make to medical science. Besides, the modern mind was no longer wired to see the connection between an eddy and a human heart. The contexts were just too different. So, even a Leonardo could not overcome this way of perceiving the world.

The Leonardo story is an example of how the radical segregation of our fields of knowledge has eroded the pathways that we once used to transfer knowledge from one field to the next. Most of us carry out our careers in a kind of intellectual apartheid where we do well to keep up with the literature of our own specialized field, much less become familiar with the goings-on in other fields.

Since Leonardo's time, specialization of knowledge into ever-narrower fields has continually intensified. Today, a practicing psychiatrist may not know of recent breakthroughs in neurology. A neurologist may be unaware of recent innovations in physical therapy. A brain surgeon may not consider what computer science may have to say about human cognition. As for considering what a cardiologist, artist, or philosopher might contribute to the knowledge of the human brain—well, that seems even less promising.

Even though all these fields focus directly or indirectly on the human brain, the practical demands on those who work in them leave little time for keeping up with what is occurring even in these closely associated fields. This is especially the case after one completes his or her formal education.

Unrelenting specialization has trained most of us to learn more and more about less and less. In this sense at least, the intellectual culture of late antiquity and the medieval era offer certain advantages. Fortunately, those advantages can be recovered without sacrificing the progress we have made during the modern era.

Such a recovery will involve a better grasp of how metaphors work—and why they work.

Music and Math Again

Cardinal Nicholas of Cusa (1401-1464) was a man many find too brilliant to ignore and too quirky to embrace. Like Eriugina, Maximus, and Barfield, Nicholas seemed to view things from another dimension. Not surprising, his focus was mostly on theological issues. However, those interests led to profound insights in other fields.

As with Leonardo da Vinci and Pythagoras, Nicholas de Cusa assumed that a discovery of a pattern in one context is suggestive of a similar pattern in a different context.

Nicholas once asked the astronomer and mathematician Paolo dal Pozzo Proscanelli to explore what Palestrina's music implied about mathematics. People were saying at the time that Palestrina's polyphony was a supernatural gift. Some believed Palestrina had acquired it from angels while in an ecstatic state. Nicholas, in contrast, believed Palestrina had intuited an underlying pattern of nature and had expressed that pattern musically. If that were the case, it should be possible to express Palestrina's discovery through mathematics.

Proscanelli agreed, thus preparing the way for the discovery of calculus a few decades later.

We could cite numerous examples from all eras of history of

people applying information learned in one context to a very different context. This may be in fact, the most common feature of creativity in any field. That brings us to consider an important question: what are the implications of living in a universe in which metaphor, allegory, and logarithm are possible?

Both Maximus and Eriugina offer the same response: we can make these kinds of intuitive leaps because the human mind participates in the very structures we intuit. The universe is "catholic" in the sense that the whole is something more than the collection of its constituted parts. Indeed, the parts reflect the whole. However, no part of the universe reflects the whole as clearly as the human mind.

Summarizing John Scotus Eriugina, Deidre Carabine notes:

There is an interlocking relationship in Eriugina's thought between reality and how the human mind structures reality.[3]

The idea here is that however weird reality turns out to be, the human mind will be able to comprehend it. Unlike other animals, human beings possess a mental faculty that participates in a level of reality beyond our natural environment. "Common sense," the accumulated day-today perceptions of human beings over untold millennia, never has the last word. We are made aware of this every time we hear a physicist talk about multiple dimensions or the non-locality of subatomic particles.

Common sense would not have led to the insights of an Einstein or a Johannes Kepler. Mathematicians have repeatedly uncovered the deep structures of reality because they had developed their minds to consider what might lie beyond our everyday world. The same is true of other disciplines.

Knowledge rarely remains the plaything of nerdy people covered in chalk dust though. The internet is an example of that! Nerdy fun and games with abstract thought often leads to practical innovations that change our everyday world. Mind can leap out of its everyday context because it participates in levels of reality beyond that everyday context.

However, because mind remains embedded in the material world, it must always return from its flights of imagination and abstraction. When it does, it sometimes brings information into our everyday world that seriously alters it—and us.

Eriugina would go further. He claimed that because we are made in the image and likeness of God, we are the Creator's model for the entire universe. Carabine sums up Eriugina's view of humanity in this particularly insightful sentence.

It is in his understanding (*Eriugina*) that it is within the human nature that the whole of creation is brought together in an ineffable harmony.[4]

Eriugina here echoes Maximus the Confessor who had written "the human being is a container for all creation."[5]

These are some of the reasons that early and medieval Christians viewed metaphor as a foundational rather than as a peripheral aspect of human thought. The Church Fathers might have expressed it this way: we don't make metaphors to be cute; we make metaphors to discover and transmit truth. We don't find metaphors delightful because we are incapable of clear and unambiguous thought; we find metaphors delightful because they so often carry great amounts of information.

Once we acknowledge the importance of metaphor, it becomes possible to repair the broken connection between our age and previous ones. We can recover past concepts that were once impossible to prove or adapt because either some essential piece of information was missing, or new technology was needed to prove the concept's practicality. Leonardo's flying machine design was generally correct. However, neither human nor animal power was sufficient to achieve lift. The concept needed an internal combustion engine.

Likewise, some past ideas, expressed at a time in the only terminology available—theology or some other nonscientific discipline—may be reconsidered in the light of more recent scientific discoveries and technological advances.

For decades, psychological writers enjoyed laughing at their ancestors for talking about the *homunculus* (Latin for "little man") inside our heads. Today, we know there is a strip at the top of our brains (just behind the place an old earphone set would rest), that reconstructs our entire body. It is there where we feel sensation because this *sensory homunculus* nearly always succeeds in assigning sensations to the body part in contact with the environment. That is why the pain I felt after stepping on my grandson's Lego felt like it was coming from my foot. Actually, the sensation was in my brain, right on that spot where my brain reconfigures my body.

So, our ancestors' intuition of a homunculus in our head was literally wrong. However, it was metaphorically correct.

As we come to the end of our reflections on metaphor, it is important to add a final word.

The scientists of the early modern period were right to insist that metaphor was not science. In fact, whether in science, philosophy, or theology, insisting on the literality of what is intended as metaphor usually destroys the information implied by the metaphor. Science then appropriately doubts even the most clever and exciting metaphor as a carrier of accurate information. Even so, a good metaphor usually deserves investigation.

There is a reason why a metaphor resonates. Most of the time, a metaphor resonates because it is poetically delightful. Sometimes though, it resonates because it is a mirror, reflecting some piece of reality we have not yet experienced.

For early and medieval Christians, the existence of metaphor indicated that our minds participate in that single Intelligence and Design through which all things visible and invisible exist. Here we arrive at what is likely the most significant bridge between the theology of late antiquity and contemporary thought: the idea that information, far from being a secondary attribute of reality, is one of its building blocks.

The ubiquity of metaphor in human thought and communication is thus an aspect of a material universe that emerges from, and is ordered by, information.

However, if information is a non-reducible component of reality, then an informational system may demonstrate emergent properties consistent with intelligence, perhaps even consciousness.

That would make an informational system an entity that ancient Christians described as a *power and principality*—a nonmaterial person, in other words.

11

No Other Gods Before Me
EMERGING SUPERINTELLIGENCE

Complex patterns of information may become integrated in ways that give rise to consciousness (as in the case of animals and perhaps even plants), or even to self-consciousness, as in the case of angels and human beings.

I HEARD A PREACHER YEARS AGO TALK ABOUT RIDING WITH HIS DAD to a hog slaughter as a kid. He recalls that when they arrived, he saw men sitting on the fence, staring at the pigs. A few of them then began shooting into the pen, laughing as the frantic pigs tried to escape.

The preacher's dad took the boy by the hand and lead him to the car. They sat there for a moment.

Finally, his dad said, "Son, God allows us to kill and eat animals. However, God does not allow us to be cruel to animals. These are not good people. A person who mistreats an animal will mistreat a human being. Don't ever have any dealings with such people."

Most Christians, though uncomfortable with mistreating animals, do not have a clear moral framework for relating to animals as fellow creatures. Viewing nature merely as a backdrop for the story of human redemption leaves little room for judging acts of cruelty toward animals as immoral. That notwithstanding, most of us have had an experience in which an animal seemed to be communicating with us. The more we have such experiences, the more we begin to feel that relationship with them occurs within a moral dimension.

Christian theology during the modern period had little to say about this. In fact, dealing justly with other *human* races and cultures has been a challenge for most of modern history. However, scripture warns us about the uniqueness of conscious beings and the ways we regard them. How one relates to an angel is not the same as how one relates to God, for example. One must honor others as made in God's image and likeness, but one must not worship another human being. Animals should be appreciated and treated justly, but they are not to be given the same level of respect as we give a human. A non-sentient object must be treated as an object, not as a sentient being. We can treat consecrated objects respectfully but must not worship them.

Moral awareness then involves making judgements about the sentience and consciousness of the entities to which we relate.

This will soon become a more important part of our spiritual lives than ever before. We are going to need to know how to relate to non-material forms of intelligence, most specifically to AI programs and intelligent robots.

Only a handful of years ago, it would have felt silly to write about this in a book on Christian theology. Now, I feel we should have had the discussion much sooner.

There are countless warnings in the Bible about how one should relate to nonmaterial persons, a category that includes God, Satan, angels, and demons. There are vague biblical references to other kinds of nonmaterial persons, however. These may be useful for thinking about artificial intelligence, social systems, corporations, and other kinds of entities that we experience, at least in some sense, as personal. Some of these, though not all of them, are recognized as legal persons in most societies.

That a non-living entity can be treated as a legal "person" is how a court will prosecute me for defrauding a bank but not for beating a dog. A court case called *First Bank of Buzzard Roost v. Dan Scott* is therefore possible, but *Fido v. Dan Scott* is not.

A court case called "The State of Tennessee v. Joseph B. Leadbody" refers to only one creature made in the image and likeness of God. This is the "person" that the state alleges has committed a crime. The State of Tennessee on the other hand, though the *legal person* who brings the suit, is not a creature made in God's own image and likeness. The state, therefore, is a pseudo-person, a composite entity that human beings have agreed to treat as if it were a person. The New Testament briefly refers to such pseudo-persons as *powers and principalities*, entities that believers must respect but not worship.

When contemporary people talk about a *social system*, they mean something similar to what the apostle Paul had in mind.

It is unclear whether Paul's view of powers and principalities as living entities was a metaphor or pointed at something he saw in a more literal way. Sociologists and anthropologists certainly view social systems as exerting enormous influence in the world. An individual is shaped by that influence and so rarely stops to question it. It is possible, perhaps likely, that Paul meant something similar in his remarks about powers and principalities. It is also possible that he meant something much more than that. The important point for this book is that the references to powers and principalities offer important insights for relating to the emerging forms of technological intelligences in our own times.

Most programmers insist that their creations are not truly sentient, but merely appear so. A program's algorithms form surprising responses to our questions, but they are based on information the program has gleaned from all corners of the internet. The program does this at a speed far beyond human capacity, leaving us convinced of the program's sentience.

This opens the door to a further question, however. Is this programmed response really different from that of a human? Don't human beings also draw on their memory when responding to questions?

Questions about the sentience or volition of artificial intelligence are thus easy to invert into a question about the uniqueness of human persons. Indeed, from a secular worldview, what other option is there? Christians, on the other hand, acknowledge the person-like qualities of an artificial intelligence program. However, spiritual categories like "powers and principalities" inform us that resemblance is not necessarily sameness. A power and principality seem to possess near god-like powers and presence. This, however, is a human projection, rather like being moved by the words and deeds of a cartoon.

Although human relationship with artificial intelligence is new to the secular world, the Bible writers and early Christian thinkers were wrestling with such issues long before the arrival of a chatbot.

Christian Theology and Nature

As you will recall, Maximus the Confessor and John Scotus Eriugina were both suspected of pantheism for their claim that consciousness was not unique to human beings. Although Christians of all times and places have believed in the existence of non-material conscious beings, it has not been common for Christians to think of animals as possessing consciousness. Too much talk of animal and plant intelligence seemed to reek of pantheism and animism, types of spirituality that the early Christians had confronted and overcome.

Both writers were misunderstood, both in their own time and in the centuries since.

Civil and religious leaders found Eriugina's writings, including his translation of Maximus into Latin, beyond their comprehension. They thus did everything within their power to discredit and isolate his influence. Also, continental Europeans probably found Eriugina suspicious. Celtic spirituality usually struck other Europeans as a bit strange. Even St. Patrick had suffered from that Continental mistrust.

Actually though, Maximus and Eriugina saw deeper into things than their peers. It would be wrong to claim that these writers had premonitions of discoveries that would come later in modern genetics, sociology, and computer science. However, it is not wrong to claim that they came close to describing the functions of RNA and DNA. St. Maximus, in fact, hints at a theory of consciousness that had much in common with what we now call panpsychicism, a view held by a number of prominent contemporary neurologists.

As an aside, several Christian writers in late antiquity hint at discoveries made in our own time. For example, the Cappadocian fathers (4th century CE), speculated about how space and time were probably the same thing. Fortunately for the Cappadocians, their speculations about this were too far "out there" for their peers to give it much thought. Besides, these ideas were bantered in private correspondence by the two brothers, their sister, and Gregory Nazianzus, who happened to be the Patriarch of Constantinople.

Maximus and Eriugina, in contrast, shared their philosophical insights with the world. Their belief that a created thing contains logos, seemed to imply both that the universe as a whole was conscious and that all the parts of the universe were conscious as well. Carried to the extreme, this assertion implied that mind every-where was simply a manifestation of the Mind of God, which was incompatible with scripture.

The Hebrew prophets had bitterly denounced pantheistic spiri-tuality, especially as they encountered it in the fertility cults. The Hebrews insisted that God had neither emerged from the universe nor was the sum of its parts. God had created the universe and defined it and its contents different and distinct from Himself. Although "the heavens declare the glory of God," creation was God's messenger, not God's face. The Hebrews prayed, "the earth is the Lord's and all it contains," which was not to be interpreted as defining the earth as God's body.

Maximus and Eriugina were careful to affirm this biblical perspective. Although both writers viewed creation as an epiphany, they denied it was an incarnation.

An epiphany is a revelation of God's presence through a natural object or a phenomenon, as when God spoke to Moses through the burning bush. God speaks in this way throughout scripture. The bush, along with all of creation, naturally contained logos. However, its spiritual significance related to God's selection of it for speaking to Moses. Moses did not therefore worship the bush. He worshipped the God that had spoken through the bush.

God is personal Supreme Intelligence and transcends the material world even when speaking through it.

Biblical theology thus draws a sharp distinction between God and creation.

Because creation manifests the character and beauty of God, a Christian deeply moved by a sunset might fall to his knees. He must not, however, offer a sacrifice, or bow before, or burn incense to, the sun.

All created things, including the sun, are fellow creatures. Each creature plays out an appointed role in God's universe. A Christian therefore takes delight in "all creatures great and small." Some of those creatures are so impressive that it is challenging not to think of them as gods. But although Christians express a worshipful appreciation for God's creatures, so much so that they can imagine themselves "joining in the chorus which the morning stars began," this piety involves worshiping *with* the stars. It is not worship *of* the stars.

Nonmaterial beings (such as angels) are greater in power than any material creature. Even so, we must not worship them. That is why most angelic visitations begin with the warning: worship God alone. Abdicating the position God has given humanity, even before an angel, violates God's order.

Holy people, places, objects, and roles may be venerated. However, this must not cross the line into worship. Consecrating objects such as oil, water, and wine for worshiping God, anticipates the role material things will play in the coming age. Nonetheless, even consecrated objects remain objects. We can respect them. We must not worship them.

This is one of the Bible's most continually repeated lessons. Do not have any gods before God. Do not worship an image. Do not elevate anything on earth above human beings, God's chosen viceroys of creation.

So why do we tend to violate this spiritual principle? What makes human beings sometimes want to worship objects?

Imagine what we would feel toward the donkey that carried

Christ into Jerusalem. We surely would want to touch it. We would speak to it tenderly. Perhaps early believers did all of that, which is entirely understandable. Nonetheless, it would have been wrong for us to worship the donkey. After its service to Christ, the donkey was what it had been before that service.

Let's look at another example.

God once told Moses to make a brass snake that he was to hold up above the people. Everyone who looked toward the snake would be healed of the plague. Several centuries after Moses died, the king had it destroyed.

It took some audacity to destroy an object that Moses had made. God, however, was pleased. Idolatry is a serious matter. It diminishes those individuals and cultures that embrace it.

The men who were being cruel to pigs were misusing their God-given stewardship. It would have been far worse though for them to be worshipping a pig. Worshiping a bull, a mountain, or a river erodes the dignity of human beings as divine image bearers. It also obscures humanity's vision of God.

Human beings the are neither gods nor servants of nature. They are nature's nurses and deacons, God's appointed stewards of creation. This means that human beings both belong to nature and stand apart from nature.

St. Thomas Aquinas explains this in a particularly helpful way, saying that God has created three kinds of creatures: nonmaterial creatures, material creatures, and incarnational creatures.

He was referring to animals, angels, and humans.

The incarnational state is "our appointed realm," Aquinas said. He meant that human beings are interpenetrated matter and spirit, that is to say we are neither completely material nor spiritual but rather exist at the crossroads of both. Aquinas goes on to say that human beings who deny their spiritual nature will descend into animalism. Those who deny their material nature grasp at angelism. Either error is a departure from our appointed realm.

Aquinas's definition of the human state is a healthy foundation for a Christian anthropology. It is also helpful for preparing ourselves to relate to robots, the internet, artificial intelligence, and social systems. The increasing anthropomorphized (user-friendly) interfaces of these systems suggest that our perception of them will grow ever more human-like, perhaps even god-like. Even now, we cannot ignore the growing cognitive abilities of the different kinds of nonmaterial entities with which we daily interact.

Soon, perhaps even before this book comes to print, our relationships with machines will deepen exponentially.

Think of Fred, an elderly man living alone a couple of decades from now. As he gets up in the morning, his robotic assistant, which he calls Sheila, reminds him to take his medication. The robot records his vital signs and sends them to Fred's doctor. After breakfast, he dictates to Sheila memories of childhood he intends to leave to his family. Sheila pulls a joke from the internet from time to time that matches Fred's unique sense of humor and plays them as he eats lunch. Afterward, Sheila reminds Fred that he promised to call his niece and asks whether he is ready to do that.

Fred will likely become rather attached to this robot. If, as will surely happen, the robot is equipped to offer sexual pleasure, the bond will become even more difficult to avoid.

What are we to make of Sheila? Even as I wrote the proceeding sentences, I was continually editing my continual use of the pronoun "she." Why was that? I do not believe Sheila is a "she." I am not sure that Fred would agree with me about that, however.

To think biblically about Sheila, we must think about how scripture teaches us to relate to the things human beings have created, and how that differs from how we are to relate to other living creatures. The Bible forcibly makes this distinction. A Christian must therefore take this into account. The contemporary challenge with maintaining the distinction, however, is that some of the things we make are more like living creatures than like things.

For insight on how to respond to things that think, we need to look at what the Bible says about relating to more familiar parts of creation.

We know that scripture teaches human beings to respect other living creatures. They are not personal property in the way that a chair is property. They are our fellow creatures. Animals, who are sentient, are beloved by God. Plants are also God's creatures, possessing a form of life intimately related to our own. So, we can cut down a tree to make a house. We can kill an animal for food. We should do neither of these things for frivolous or for exploitive reasons.

We are participants in a realm we do not own but which we manage on God's behalf. We are therefore given special responsibilities for the other participants with whom we share the created order. We also relate to nonmaterial participants of creation—angels, powers, principalities, and so forth.

Christians follow the ancient Hebrews in rejecting pantheism. Nonetheless, we celebrate our relationship with all parts of God's visible and invisible creation. Our intimacy with other creatures will increase as we learn more about their levels of sentience and consciousness. However, we are likely to make some mistakes about which creatures possess such qualities.

Franz Rosenzweig, arguably the most important Jewish philosopher of the twentieth century, envisions humanity's relationship with God and nature as a relational triangle.

In his great work, *The Star of Redemption*, (a reference to the Star of David) Rosenzweig affirms that God relates directly to human beings, but also relates to human beings through nature. In turn, human beings often become aware of God through their experience of nature. As they grow in relationship with God, humans learn how to appropriately care for nature.

An idol is a thing that fails to point toward God. Instead, it draws worshipful attention to itself. This obstructs the human being's relationship to God. That is what happened with the brass snake. It happens still today whenever we misuse the role of an icon, a relic, a dogma, or a human leader. Rosenzweig would say that idolatry occurs when our piety does not move *through* created things to the Creator. That breaks the relational triangle.

This view of creation, while distinguishing material creatures from God, acknowledges that God has granted creatures "the dignity of differentiated existence." Toward this divine end, Maximus would say, God has informed all created things with the means of maintaining themselves, some with the means of reproducing themselves, and others with the means of purposefully influencing (or being influenced) by other creatures. This makes human beings the older siblings of creation. It also reminds us that we are not our Creator's only concern. God loves nature not only for how nature points us toward God but for its own sake.

Since everything in creation emerges from Logos (Genesis 1-3 and John 1), it follows that all things contain logos. While Maximus and Eriugina were careful to say that Christ alone was incarnate Logos, all things nonetheless contain logos and are therefore conscious at the level appropriate to their order of creation.

In a rock, logos orders molecular structure.

In a tree, logos instructs the plant to mature, seek nourishment, and reproduce.

In a dog, logos instructs the animal to seek companionship, recognize and respond to the will of other creatures, and understand simple language.

Logos informs material entities how to carry out their unique purpose and role. At higher levels of creation, this information becomes aware of itself. It knows its own purpose, and that of other creatures. At the highest levels, it becomes self-programable, able to either resist its God-given purpose or freely embrace it.

This early Christian view survived into the medieval era for Western Christians. It is still the perspective of Eastern Christianity. After the medieval era, however, Western peoples, including Christians, began viewing the components of nature, including sentient animals, in machine-like ways. The people of the modern era thus tended to see non-human creatures as lacking spiritual significance, an idea that is rapidly changing.

More and more people are asking whether consciousness is a uniquely human trait. Christians uninformed about how their faith once responded to this question are left without a way to respond. A Christian may therefore wonder whether his dog has a soul. Another will worry that caring deeply about whales means they are becoming a pantheist. A Christian arguing against cutting down a forest on moral grounds may be confronted by another believer for being spiritually confused.

Postmodern views of human consciousness take many forms. Some think consciousness an illusion, a means through which evolutionary processes have fooled us into caring about our own survival long enough to reproduce. Others are leaning into a sort of secularized mysticism, thinking of the cosmos as having gradually become aware of itself. However, as the postmodern mood finally settles such questions, they will no longer be isolated to a discussion about human nature. The postmodern world is asking about the consciousness of animals, plants, social systems, and computer programs. As intelligent robots become increasingly involved in our lives, these questions will expand further.

In the first two chapters of this book, I quoted from Weir's *Project Hail Mary*. You recall that the book opens with Dr. Grace regaining consciousness after a long interstellar journey. All Grace experiences at first is a voice: "What is 2+2?"

Dr. Grace gradually realizes that the voice is coming from the ship's central computer. We notice though that he is only able to discern this after he recovers his own sense of personhood. Grace wrestles with the issue of consciousness again after meeting Rocky, the space alien.

Science fiction writers have been musing about intelligent machines for nearly a hundred years. They have helped us imagine benevolent and malevolent relationships with intelligent machines and programs by making these strange entities characters in the stories. That is one of the reasons why science fiction has rarely been considered serious literature.

"How could human beings create thinking machines like these?" earlier generations asked.

Today of course, it is not at all far-fetched to think about a human being talking to a computer. We do it every day. Even the voice we hear when we call our bank is rarely a human being. No wonder we are beginning to experience intelligent information systems as conscious. From there, it is but a small step to experience them as sentient. Increasingly then, the question of whether artificial intelligence is radically different than a human mind or is simply an information system emerging from silicon rather than biocarbon becomes entirely reasonable.

In fact, that point was reached while I was preparing this book. A Google employee was fired for going public with his belief that the software program he had been working with for the company was sentient.

So, our conversation must return to the questions about what consciousness is exactly, what sorts of entities seem to possess it, and what this implies about human uniqueness.

Most of us already believe our pets are conscious. They certainly seem to express reactions like shame and affection. Some scientists believe we are anthropomorphizing our pets rather than observing anything real when we speak this way. However, that makes us wonder if such scientists have pets or even if the scientists are themselves conscious.

Meanwhile, we are learning more all the time about the intelligence and consciousness of apes, octopi, birds, dolphins, and other animals.

Some experiments with fungi even suggest that they possess something like a neurological network, enabling them to connect with the plants of a forest. If this turns out to be true, can we not call the interaction among trees a conversation? Are the fungi conscious? Are the trees? Is the forest as a whole conscious?

Older people, especially Christians, are not likely to think these questions reasonable. From the postmodern perspective, however, informed by computer and genomic sciences, such questions are not only reasonable, but irrepressible.

Integrated Information Theory

In 2004, Giulio Tononi began developing what we call integrated information theory (IIT). This theory imagines a basic unit of information (called *phi*), which exists in everything. It also assumes that as phi increases, it tends to become integrated. Tononi theorized that as a system emerges from integrated information, it seeks to maintain itself and to interact with other informational systems.

That is an important development in the ongoing discussion about the nature of consciousness because it asks whether it is not only trees, cats, and kangaroos who are conscious but whether social systems and other kinds of integrated information networks are as well.

It appears to me that if integrated information theory reveals anything true about the world—as if it seems to do—we are likely to begin thinking of integrated information systems as being, at least in some sense, living, conscious things.

Of course, the line dividing living and nonliving things has been vague for some time. We haven't decided yet whether a virus is organic or inorganic, for example. That doesn't mean though that most of us are ready to think of a computer program as a living being. Indeed, for most people of the past, the idea that information —integrated or not—might be conscious would have seemed crazy.

Perhaps it is.

However, most new ideas seem outlandish at first. In hindsight though, we often understand a new idea as a groping for a new paradigm, for a way of making sense of new knowledge. As new information about reality continues to accumulate, it increases the strain on our existing paradigm. Like an old bookcase collapsing after putting too many new books in it, the existing paradigm may give way under the weight of new information. This is what is occurring now because of our growing understanding of intelligence, sentience, and consciousness. Our view of reality is straining.

Artificial intelligence systems are developing at a breakneck speed, and we have not yet figured out how to respond. That is why some of us have begun to think out of the box. The existing paradigms seem inadequate for making sense of intelligent machines.

Although the ancient world had no digital computer or internet, early Christians nonetheless have something important to say about the nature of informational systems.

Several New Testament passages reflect on how one should respond to the social systems in which one is a participant. These passages describe social systems as possessing a will and a presence to which human beings form relationships.

Admittedly, a social system is not the same thing as a technological information system. That said, a social system is like artificial intelligence in that it is a human-created informational system. The New Testament passages about how a believer should relate to social systems therefore offer contemporary Christians a way to discern a response to electronic forms of integrated intelligence.

The Spirituality of Community

Jesus said, "Where two or three are gathered in my name, I will be there."

Non-Christians will interpret this passage as a poetic way of saying that after his death, Jesus's disciples will experience their memories of him so powerfully that it will feel as though he is physically present. Certainly, many of us have experienced the memories of our loved ones in just this way. Stepping into a deceased loved one's home, we feel as though they may at any time walk down the hall.

In fact, though, nearly all Christians interpret this passage literally. In fact, we often quote the words at the beginning of a worship service to remind ourselves that the risen Christ will be meeting with us. It is why most forms of Christian liturgy begins with some version of the words, "The Lord is with you."

To which the worshippers respond, "And also with you."

During the service of Holy Communion, Christians will hear the celebrant say the words, "Therefore, with saints, angels, and cherubim, we here gathered offer you these gifts." The prayer is meant to open the worshipper's inner selves to the awareness of entering the presence of God and that of other spiritual beings.

Both the words of Jesus and this centuries-old prayer imply that when human beings gather for worship, they become a dwelling for spiritual forces. A group is thus a composite person. One can take this literally—as I do—or metaphorically—as sociologists, anthropologists, and psychotherapists do. Perhaps the reality lies somewhere between the literal and metaphorical. Perhaps the distinction doesn't even matter. Either way, groups profoundly affect us.

The Bible depicts nations having a will, as manifesting personality, and as having a certain kind of character—as persons. It seems reasonable therefore to apply this view to other kinds of communities.

Many of the values of a community survive the individuals who founded them. Indeed, those values continue to evolve and expand. That is why, century after century, France remains French, and China remains Chinese. The foods, social habits, ways of experiencing the world, even the temperament of these nations seem relatively consistent over periods of time. In the same way, dysfunctional families tend to remain dysfunctional, even after the toxic persons who damaged them are long gone.

One especially provocative issue of our times demonstrates how social systems influence the intentions of those who comprise them: systemic racism.

The assumption behind the concept of systemic racism (or systemic anything else) is that societies are formed (and maintained) around purposes and values. Some of these are clearly stated. Others are not. The society then communicates those values and purposes, mostly through its communal habits more than through its public, official words.

For example, the United States declares its stated intentions in the Declaration of Independence, the United States Constitution, and several key speeches by the nation's most respected leaders. Americans celebrate these words and quote them, even when they are disagreeing with one another about what those words mean.

However, the daily transactions of the nation's citizens over time reveals that our nation—like all nations—falls short of its stated ideals. The reason for this is that a community's unspoken ideals operate at much deeper levels than its stated values. The unspoken values also evoke more loyalty from its citizenry than the stated values.

Those who profit the most from a society's unstated values are usually only vaguely aware that its unspoken values even exist. Individuals who suffer from the community's unspoken values are the ones who become the most aware of their existence.

This is not merely a sociological insight. It is a biblical one. Pharoah had no idea anything was amiss in Egypt. The woes of the Hebrew people were utterly irrelevant in his vision for the nation. Indeed, their lack of enthusiastic cooperation with their own enslavement was an irritating distraction for Pharoah.

One's view of systemic racism therefore revolves around the question of whether a country does or does not perpetuate its founders unstated norms and values. A discussion about this does not, or at least should not, require one to assume that the nation's present leaders are racist. A healthy discussion merely requires the participants of the discussion to consider whether the racial views of the nation's founders continue to influence its present.

Certainly, a society's unwritten assumptions exert considerable pressure on the psyche and social habits of its citizens. It therefore requires conscious attention as well as considerable effort to resist the systemic values of one's community. A healthy discussion about this is not about shaming anyone; it is about awakening people to the unseen and heretofore unconscious values that may be influencing them. Only when such values are made visible will the members of a society make their own conscious decisions about how to respond to them.

It is important to acknowledge that political operatives use systemic racism, as they use other subjects, to stir up their base. That serves the purpose of extreme views on either side of a dispute.

However, respectful conversation opens space to its participants for processing what are often conflicting and scary emotions. Confronting the assumptions that one's culture has inherited from the distant past is not for the faint of heart. That is why individuals need authentic hospitality and grace for walking through serious discussions about their culture's values.

One thing is for sure, individuals do not emerge from outside community. Neither is it possible for a community to exist without individuals. Because a community's values shape the individuals who comprise it, its spoken and unspoken values endure unless and until its members deliberately decide to reevaluate those values.

Christianity teaches that all human societies (like the individuals who comprise them) are profoundly flawed. Remaining blind to these flaws destroys a society. At the same time, societies have virtues, which citizens should periodically affirm. Although utopia is unobtainable, societies can be repaired and reformed. For this to occur though, a society, like the individuals who comprise it, must remain open to continual critique and improvement—*semper refor-mata*, as the Protestant Reformed tradition put it.

We might summarize the New Testament's view of society like this: an integrated information-system (such as a human culture) always presents itself as a self-protecting and self-propagating entity. Therefore, those living within these systems will experience its influence at deep levels. Such a system becomes a power and principality —a superperson, we might say.

The New Testament writers call these systems *stoicheia*, which English translations usually render as the *"elementary systems of the world."*

Contemporary psychologists and sociologists use other terms to describe the power and presence of family, tribe, and nation. Every psychotherapist and social worker understands that behind a patient there is always a group deeply influencing him or her. One's family of origin usually exercises the most influence. However, when individuals marry, convert, immigrate, or enter new professions, the new groups with which they identify quickly begin to alter their original sense of self.

As Aristotle said, humans are social animals. He might have said, "Birds of a feather flock together because the flock makes sure of it." We are much more like fragments of family, tribe, and culture than like the self-created individuals we imagine ourselves to be, in other words.

Individuals react to societal influences by either confronting them or conforming to them. Either reaction alters the individual's sense of self. If a socialist joins a Southern Baptist Church in Alabama, her political views will most likely change. If a member of the John Birch Society becomes a member of the First Unitarian Church of Boston, we can expect that individual to change as well.

When a person becomes a dissenter within his own nation or church, he is likewise altered by that experience. Therefore, the Bible urges caution when confronting an evil system. Any kind of interaction with a social system—even opposing it—shapes us in unimaginable ways. That is why violent revolutions against tyranny rarely give birth to a peaceful state.

St. Paul says that we should respect the "powers and principalities," by which he means the sociopolitical forces in which we live. However, Paul goes on to add that we must never surrender our deepest loyalties to these powers. We work to influence them to become wholesome and healthy. We do not rail against them. Nonetheless, we must find the courage to resist them when they are doing harm in the world. For Christians, that usually takes the form of civil disobedience.

Even as we suffer in the pursuit of justice, we refrain from inflicting suffering upon others. Christians fight for justice in non-violent ways because injustice is a non-human power. In the clear words of the New Testament: "We do not fight against flesh and blood."

An example from the animal kingdom can help us avoid getting too spooky about this.

Some entomologists suggest we would understand insects better if we would observe them as groups rather than as individuals. In this view, the bee *colony* becomes the animal. Individual bees become bee-colony cells. From that perspective, we immediately note the bee colony's intelligence, which the individual bees lack.

Of course, the cells in my body can't read a book or even walk down the street. My cells are not me. Perhaps this is true of a bee colony as well, in which case the bee colony, rather than an individual bee, is the conscious entity.

A bee colony searches for food and reacts to threats. It creates maps of its territory. It extends its will into the world. A bee colony thus exhibits much greater intelligence than the individual bees who comprise it. The bee colony in other words, has emergent properties that one cannot locate in the individual bees.

This feature of biological organization is present in human community as well. Human societies become something more than merely the accumulation of their individual parts. They have emergent qualities.

The Bible describes *nations* (*ta ethne* in Greek, meaning not nation states but ethnic groups) like the way entomologists describe colonies and swarms. When the Bible refers to "Egypt," "Babylon," "the Greeks," or "Israel" it is not always referring to geographical locations. It is pointing to social characters through whom the biblical drama is unfolding.

Thus, to "go down into Egypt," does not mean merely that someone is traveling south to another country; it suggests that the traveler is deviating from righteousness. "Babylon" is not merely the capital of a mighty empire; it is a symbol of spiritual darkness. The Bible uses other nations—Gog and Magog, Nineveh, the Greeks, the Persians, and the Hittites—in a similar kind of shorthand to describe a people's spiritual characteristics.

The emergent features of a nation over long stretches of time, exhibit more than merely their geography, language, and armies. The Bible claims that nations (or cities) sin, repent, make covenants, and are ultimately judged. This means that the Bible views nations as creatures, even, in a sense at least, as spiritual "persons." That is not quite the right word but putting it within quotation marks perhaps helps us to maintain a bit of a difference between individual human beings, whom we believe live forever, and nations, which do not.

Contemporary people, both secular and religious are understandably wary of viewing social groups in this way. This very tendency has encouraged all sorts of dangerous prejudices and bigotry throughout history. If we hear someone say, "Jews are always . . .", or "Well, that's what one can always expect from an Irishman," our defenses go up, as indeed they should. However, this prejudicial way of treating ethnic groups is not what I have in mind. I certainly am not claiming scripture justifies it.

Using the concept of powers and principalities was simply part of the ancient world's way of defining the seen and unseen processes that affected them. Words for them often embodied multiple meanings that we have long since differentiated into separate terms. For us, a Greek is someone from Greece who speaks Greek.

In contrast, a man the New Testament calls "a Greek" may not be "Greek" at all in the sense I have just described. The "Greek" may be a Jew who has lived in Egypt. However, because a particular Jew was seen as having absorbed much of the culture associated with Greeks, more traditional Jews living in Jerusalem, might have referred to him as the "Greek."

Saint Paul uses this same kind of reasoning when reminding us that the word "Jew" can mean different things. The contemporary nation of Israel still struggles with this. Is a Jew a biological descendant of Abraham? A citizen of ancient Judea? The follower of a religion with roots in ancient Israel? Is a Jew anyone who embraces Abraham's beliefs? In that case, are Christians Jews? Is an atheist Israeli who celebrates Passover a Jew?

History has taught us to be careful with ethnic labels. Not only are they imprecise, but they also often lead to atrocities. Nonetheless, nations seem to exhibit a will, a personality, a way of being in the world, that distinguish them from other nations. Furthermore, these national characteristics seem to transcend the individuals who comprise them.

When we read the description of French culture written by a European writer who lived 200 years ago, we will likely recognize the description as roughly accurate today. An individual Frenchman may like instant coffee and canned soup, may dislike all talk of sex and romance, and may despise wine. Few of us will think that he represents "France." However, if we read in a novel that "Billy Bob was from Birmingham but wanted everyone to call him Guillaume. He aspired to be a real Francophile, but his neighbors wouldn't buy it," we immediately form a picture about Billy Bob. The author of this description is banking on our imagination to fill in the rest of the profile because that writer knows that the word "France" brings certain things to mind.

Families, colleges, congregations, and corporations all exhibit certain kinds of character. It may change over time, but it usually maintains itself surprisingly well. The Disney Corporation, IBM, and Starbucks all play definitive roles in American and global culture. They embody recognizable personality traits. They are, both in our mind and before the law, "persons."

Let's say we are reading a daughter's complaint against her father's choice of hotel accommodations. Suppose the father retorts with, "What did you expect, Becky Sue? The Ritz Carlton?"

These few words give us a good idea about what has just happened. The father's reference to a hotel chain noted for luxury tells that he has chosen something rather short of his daughter's ideal.

The biblical concept of powers and principalities is a related concept. The terms may, but do not necessarily, refer to conscious supernatural beings. Perhaps, even in scripture, the phrase is a metaphor, a way to describe social forces like the way social workers and psychotherapists think about the influence of groups.

So, what do biblical concepts such as powers, principalities, thrones, strongholds, or *stoicheia* have to offer contemporary people? I believe their value lies in the seriousness with which the New Testament writers describe them.

In the individualistic West, we are prone to ignore the strengths and weaknesses of those human communities in which individuals reside and by which individuals are formed.

Social workers and psychotherapists learn to temper this individualistic focus.

Psychotherapists know that when they are treating an individual, a family system lurks in the background. They know that individuals are more family fragments than they would like to admit and that the present members of any family are much more influenced by their family's deep past than they can imagine.

When psychotherapists or social workers talk about an alcoholic family system, they are talking about how the family functions, not necessarily about whether anyone in that family presently abuses alcohol. They are referring to the fact that values and habits formed in families to deal with addiction can persist decades after the addict's death. Adult children or even adult grandchildren of alcoholics can be teetotaling, Bible-carrying fundamentalists who loudly denounce the evils of alcohol. Nonetheless, they may exhibit all the characteristics of an alcoholic. We call such people dry drunks.

So, we are not forced to read into scripture the belief that the powers and principalities are necessarily conscious nonmaterial beings. We can learn from the concept even if we see it as a metaphor. However, we should keep in mind that biblical metaphors are rarely "mere" metaphors. The biblical writers rarely made as strong a distinction as we do between literality and allegory, or between concrete and abstract. The concept is important all the same, especially in an era that increasingly relies on informational systems.

The Internet and other Informational Systems

While biblically literate Christians can usually imagine a social system as having character and a will, they seem at a loss about what to make of artificial intelligence systems.

Everyone knows that a computer is in some sense "smarter" than a human being. The computer does calculations in seconds that would require the most intelligent mathematician years to solve. They play chess with us. They help us design imaginary empires, complete with soldiers, buildings, and weather patterns. They fly our airplanes. They drive our cars. They perform medical operations. They create realistic photographs and videos of things that have never occurred.

The internet is unimaginably powerful because it connects millions of computers in a global information system. The internet archives and makes available the world's great literature, statistics, journal articles, pictures, and videos, in ancient dead and living languages. The internet makes it possible for a woman in Kansas to chat with man in Tibet. It puts a telegraph in our pocket. It delivers our mail. It pays our bills. It schedules our time. It invites everyone everywhere to purchase nearly anything from anywhere.

What progress! What power!

So, is the internet conscious? Does it evolve? If so, in what ways? Has human life become impossible without it?

A growing number of cognitive scientists are asking these very questions. Whether we find those questions significant or foolish depends on what we mean by words like "life" and "consciousness." Most of us do not experience the internet as a living being. We do not think of it as conscious, even in the way that our dog is conscious. Nonetheless, the more we chat with Siri and Alexa the thinner the line becomes that separates our experience of electronic intelligence from that of biological intelligence.

Merriam-Webster defines life as the "state characterized by the ability to get and use energy, grow, and respond to change." By that definition, one can make a case that the internet and other kinds of information systems are indeed alive.

It is more challenging to find a common definition for consciousness. Is a robot that is programed to respond to its environment and learn from experience conscious? That is a critical question. In the very near future, the voice on the phone that answers our questions about say, travel arrangements, will even responds to our off-hand comments. It is about to become rather challenging to know whether we are speaking to a computer or to a human being. Will we experience those computer-generated voices as the utterances of a conscious being?

It may be that our head and heart will be divided about this. Perhaps we will know in our heads that the voice is not coming from a person, but our heart will still direct us to say "sorry," and "thank you." So, while most of us, certainly Christians, are not inclined to think of informational systems as living, conscious entities, it's a real question whether our grandchildren will see things this same way.

New Testament references to "powers and principalities" can help us think through our questions about robots and computer systems. These references suggest that a Christian can acknowledge the person-like influence of such systems on our psyche while stopping short of experiencing them as persons. Though a Christian could accept that an intelligence system might come to be viewed as "a person under the law," (in the same way a corporation becomes a legal person, as in *Jones v. IBM*) without viewing that system as a living soul.

In *The Beginning of Wisdom*, Leon Kass makes a comparison between the World Wide Web and the Tower of Babel. In that story, humanity builds a great tower to reach into the heavens. At first, all the workers speak the same language and so the project develops splendidly. Then, God confuses the workers languages. Soon the workers began fighting with one another and so the project comes to a halt.

Kass remarks that the Web, with its translation capabilities, will soon offer a person speaking any language of the world the ability to read any document written in any language from any era of history. Already the global economy moves goods from a garage in Berlin to a house in rural Kentucky. The transaction seamlessly translates the different languages of the participants and effortlessly transforms dollars into Euros.

Kass said that because the moral nature of humanity is no more developed now than in ancient times, the foundation of our Brave New World remains as fragile today as it was on the planes of ancient Shinar. If he is right, the present economic kumbaya will not last. As we increasingly come to understand each other's words and perspectives, we will become less rather than more, tolerant of our differences. Trends within our own nation seem to support Kass's pessimistic view.

The integrated informational systems that exude such enormous influence into our personal and collective lives, are not accountable to anyone. They are amoral, having no regard for either humanity's joys or its sorrows. Although we experience these systems as being somewhat like persons, they are in a truth, soulless. Treating them as real, ensouled persons is therefore, at least from a biblical standpoint, idolatrous.

The same holds true for a social system, whether based on ethnicity, nation, lodge, business, or church. Powers and principalities are person-like. We anthropomorphize our interaction with them by giving them names and legal status. The algorithms lead us to think that these programs "know" us. Nonetheless, they are, just as a plow, an automobile, or a brass snake, the works of our hands.

In short, the commandment about not having "any other gods before me," seems to forbid human submission to any sort of system —social, digital, or robotic—that threatens to usurp the place of either God or humanity.

12

Deceptive Images

The cosmos contains forces that hinder, oppose, and distort providence. Some of these are conscious and intentionally malignant. Others are unconscious but nonetheless harmful.

IN *PEOPLE OF THE LIE*, M. SCOTT PECK DESCRIBES A FAMILY WHOSE oldest son had committed suicide. In a session with this family, the younger brother of the deceased told Peck that his parents had given him "the gun" as a birthday present.

"What do you mean by *the* gun?" Peck asked.

"You know, the gun my brother used to . . . you know . . ." the boy replied.

In the session with the parents, Peck asked them about what the young man had said.

"What does giving this gun communicate to your son?" Peck asked. "Doesn't it send the message that perhaps your younger son ought to do the same thing that his older brother did?"

"What should we do with a perfectly good gun?" the enraged father shot back. "Throw it away? It was a good gift. The boy ought to appreciate it."

Peck could not convince the parents that they were destroying their younger son. The more Peck insisted, the colder and more obstinate the parents became.

The case led Peck to think about a few patients he had treated through his career who had been difficult to diagnose as mentally ill, but who nonetheless seemed profoundly diseased. Such people seemed life-sucking. They exuded some sort of dark strength that resisted treatment. They wore down anyone who tried to help them. Mental illness didn't seem an appropriate label for such people.

Peck began to think about the work of raw evil in the world, a concept he had always viewed as outdated and superstitious. Ultimately, he wrote *People of the Lie* to warn mental health workers about evil and how to recognize it.

Although many contemporary Christians are reluctant to discuss the subject, the Bible is clear about the existence of evil. One of the reasons for our reluctance is that attaching the label "evil" to individuals and groups has sometimes led to persecution of the mentally ill, practitioners of folk medicine, heretics, or anyone who seemed different from those who labeled them. Some expressions of Christianity seem unhealthily obsessed with evil.

Peck addresses these issues. He insists that we do harm when we ignore evil just as we do when we obsess over it. Although his reflections on evil are not always consistent with orthodox Christian beliefs on the subject, he draws deeply from Christian thought to express what he has observed in contemporary, secular language.

The book resonated with me, both as a pastor and a therapist. I have encountered similar situations to the ones Peck describes a few times in life. One of them involved an influential preacher.

Donors and lawyers had insisted the preacher get help for his predatory and abusive behavior. Outwardly cooperative, the man had outwitted his therapists. Most of them had never experienced the high levels of manipulation this man had mastered. So, he dazzled the mental health workers as he did his followers, always a half-step ahead of real accountability.

When I met him, he seemed amused. He was ready to continue the game. In as monotone and disinterested kind of voice as I could muster, I reviewed the events that had led to his exposure. I then asked him to respond. He expressed no guilt. He took no responsibility. He seemed unconcerned for the people he had harmed.

He explained to me that like King David, he had received a great anointing from God. He had been chosen to do great and mighty things. Others would never understand the inhuman amount of stress that came with his work. Yes, the inhuman pressure had driven him to seek sexual relief from his employees. However, God, who was his only judge, had forgiven him. He was therefore at peace. He rebuked and took authority over any religious spirit of condemnation.

And so forth. And so on.

After a long silence, I replied. "Ok, I know what is going on. I have a diagnosis."

He looked amused. "So, what is it?"

"You are working a gig. You're a con man. A common fraud."

At this, the preacher stormed out of the room, mumbling about "therapeutic nonsense" while flying down the hall. A few minutes later, he was on his plane, headed out of town.

As he fled, the darkness felt like an invisible speedboat that had left me swimming for my life.

Evil

Christians believe in the existence of evil. Although difficult to define, evil is a sort of anti-power, a form of malevolent energy that works to destroy individuals and communities.

The New Testament teaches that some forms of evil are intentionally and consciously malignant. Other forms of evil are nonconscious. Scripture refers to conscious evil powers, as demons. A virus would be an example of a non-conscious form of evil.

Neither Judaism nor Christianity have ever fully explained how or why such forces exist. We are not even clear about how they function. We simply assume their existence and ask God for deliverance from them.

A Christian dealing with some sort of destructive dysfunction will suspect that evil is at work. However, by evil, Christians do not always mean a conscious, disembodied intelligence. Sometimes, the word evil simply refers to some sort of destructive force that is draining life from an individual or a group.

We are not always certain whether such destructive forces are conscious or intentional. While individuals and communities may experience them that way, some evil powers may not be "beings" at all.

I hasten to add that Christians believe in the existence of disembodied, evil beings. We just don't know much about them. Some of us believe we have encountered them, though their deceptive nature leaves us confused about what exactly we have experienced.

Evil is deceptive. We play into its hands by either ignoring it or by making too much of it. So, the presence of evil always calls for humble, sober vigilance.

Most historic Christian groups (and many of the youngest ones) offer ministries of deliverance (called exorcism) to deal with evil. Progressive Protestants, in contrast, usually explain the demonic as an ancient way of talking about destructive processes better explained today by neurology, psychology, or the social sciences.

Neil Anderson, an Evangelical minister, offers one of the most helpful contemporary approaches to exorcism I have encountered. Although Anderson acknowledges the existence of evil, he believes sensationalized responses to evil do more harm than good. In fact, because of popular associations with the word exorcism, he does not use that term to describe his own ministry.

In his book *Bondage Breaker*, Anderson outlines his approach. He advises the spiritual counselor to speak gently with the one who has come for deliverance. The counselor should ask about any history of mental illness and whether the person asking for help has been experiencing normal human stressors. At some point, the prayer counselor will usually read appropriate scripture, stopping at times for feedback. The counselor listens for statements or emotions of guilt, and for any sort of obsessive thoughts or behaviors.

Anderson urges the counselor to stress God's goodness and forgiveness throughout the interaction. A counselor should invite the one who is suffering to ask for God's help with full confidence that God always desires to deliver us from all kinds of darkness.

I have observed Anderson at work. His approach is healthy and effective. Although secular therapists may doubt that any sort of spiritual powers are involved, they likely would not find Anderson offensive or harmful. Anderson of course, does believe that evil powers are sometimes involved in these seasons. Although he is deliberately methodical and undramatic, he has at times experienced strange phenomenon that he found convincing.

Anderson, Peck, and Christian exorcists from older Christian traditions differ substantially in how they explain and approach the work of deliverance. What they share is a reluctance to jump to conclusions about evil and a resistance to sensationalized theatrics. Nearly everyone who offers a ministry of deliverance within some sort of established accountability structure agree that unwise and uncharitable approaches to deliverance cause great harm. In contrast to exorcism as depicted in film and literature, most accounts of deliverance consist of a suffering person becoming aware of (and responding to) God's grace and forgiveness.

Evil and The Christian Health Care Worker

In most situations, a Christian mental health worker describes a client's psychological condition in the established nomenclature of the field—the Diagnostic and Statistical Manual of Mental Disorders (DSM-5). If a psychotherapist is offering care in a non-church setting, this will most certainly be the case. That does not mean that the practitioner does not sense some sort of a spiritual toxicity at work.

When we enter a public field such as psychotherapy, we work with colleagues from other faith commitments as well as with those without any such commitment. By entering this common space, a Christian accepts the practices and nomenclature established to make this interaction possible. Naturally, when a Christian mental health worker demonstrates competence and integrity, they will likely encounter opportunities for sharing with their colleagues the wisdom they have gathered from their own spiritual journey. Unless or until a relationship develops in which it is safe and welcomed to do that, the Christian practitioner must "translate" their spiritual insight into psychological nomenclature—the common language of the field.

If a Christian does not feel comfortable working with non-Christians in the mental health field, they always have the opinion of offering spiritual direction or pastoral counseling at overtly Christian environments. In such environments, a Christian therapist can freely express their insights in overtly Christian language. That is the approach of people like Anderson, for whom the core work of care involves scripture and spiritual practice.

The point I want to make here is that many committed Christians are called to work within secular environments. This calling involves the acceptance of a code of ethics dealing with differing views on religion and spirituality. Nonetheless, there are always appropriate and ethical ways of drawing on the insights of one's faith when dealing with spiritually dark situations.

A Christian therapist or social worker caring for a client with narcissistic personality disorder, borderline personality disorder, or a particularly troubling kind of addiction (to cite a few challenging examples) may sense the presence of evil. A Christian practitioner will privately note the spiritual components of the case while addressing it within the established guidelines of the field. The Holy Spirit is not a prisoner of terminology or method and will always show a way forward.

Christian therapists should know that psychology and sociology are contemporary and secularized approaches to issues once described in religious language. Some of the most respected secular voices in the field—William James and Karl Jung come to mind— have clearly acknowledged this. So, there are ethical ways of drawing on the deep roots of these secular fields without feeling that one has compromised his own spiritual commitment.

Some Christian therapists use the terminology of Alcoholics Anonymous and related movements to express their spiritual insight. When one is not dealing with a neurological condition, recovery language can serve as a "halfway house" between spirituality and psychology. Provided this is not a cover for incompetent care, recovery terms are usually acceptable to believers and non-believers alike. In my opinion, it is at any rate more grounded in everyday life and therefore more practically helpful than DSM-5 language.

The role of Evil in Social Dysfunction

Sociology, anthropology, jurisprudence, economics, and political science all employ preferred jargon to describe human flourishing and dysfunction. Each field uses its preferred terminology as its practitioners observe, analyze, and describe economic movement, societal values, the formation and enforcement of law, social equities, racial injustice, despotism, and numerous other kinds of human realties. Most of these fields are relatively new. They have risen within the modern, secular paradigm in which spirituality was viewed as having little to add.

During the modern era, Christian professionals have largely accepted the paradigm. In so doing though, they have often remained ignorant of the ways in which their faith has long addressed such issues as we mentioned in the preceding paragraph. For example, Christians assume that communal dysfunction is a spiritual issue. The Old Testament prophets, the Sermon on the Mount, and many other scriptural and theological sources have formed a uniquely Christian take on human flourishing. Most of the time, Christians respond to injustice through practical action rather than with theory. However, the theory exists and should be consulted by believers engaged in public life.

From the very beginning, Christians attempted to follow Christ's instruction to heal the sick and feed the poor. St. Paul carried out a fund drive for poor believers in Jerusalem, for example. That work continued long after the apostolic age. The Roman government noted on several occasions how Christians cared for the empire's orphans and widows. In the following centuries, Christians founded hospitals and orphanages wherever they went. The Salvation Army, the YMCA, food banks and shelters in nearly all the world's great cities, have been founded and funded by Christians in response to human suffering.

Few Christians try to explain the theological basis for their responses to societal distress. They simply know that their faith calls them to love their fellow human beings. Sometimes, this well-intentioned response to the suffering of individuals fosters unintentional neglect of systemic evil. Jewish and Christian theology, in contrast, explores how evil works of evil works within a group as well as within an individual.

Christian theology, in other words, not only affirms the destructive power of sin—the existential illness of the individual human soul—but of how systemic dysfunction may be a manifestation of evil. Communal dysfunctions—injustice is the Christian word—operate within groups much as sin operates within an individual. For this reason, practical Christian responses to societal evils like hunger, disease, and crime, although vital, are incomplete without a full grounding in Christian doctrine.

The reason we need theological grounding for our response to societal evil is this: systemic dysfunctions are often the work of a deliberately malignant, demonic power. If this is the case, then even the personal responses instructed by our faith—such as feeding an unhoused person—will not seriously confront the root causes of human suffering.

Slavery is an excellent example of societal evil. For four hundred years, the Western World consciously and deliberately enslaved human beings. The governments of Europe and North America created legislation to regulate it. They nonetheless maintained slavery, both through cultural habit and by the force of law. In this way, like stirring sugar into one's coffee, the evil of slavery became systemic—part of the system. One does not unstir sugar from sweetened coffee. My spell check keeps rejecting the word unstir. Unstir is not a word because it is not a doable action.

Since a man holding the chain connected to the neck of another man is himself chained, slavery affects both slaves and slave owners. Indeed, from a Christian standpoint, it is the slave owner who is the most seriously bound in that he is chained by a metaphysical darkness that imprisons his soul. Therefore, by building a defense and justification for slavery, American Christianity significantly altered itself. By accommodating something profoundly at odds with its own DNA, American Christianity invited the darkness into Christ's own community. Some of those mutations remain unquestioned in popular forms of American Christianity.

Everyone knew that slavery was antithetical to the faith that the slave owners professed. President Lincoln said as much in the second inaugural address. He noted that the evil of slavery was ultimately responsible not only for the obvious dehumanization of Africans but for the equally dehumanizing effects on those who had enslaved Africans.

The president's words inflamed his soon-to-be assassin. Lincoln had said clearly that slavery had provoked God's justified wrath, not only upon the Confederacy but upon the Union as well. The conflict having ended, and the constitution now amended to make slavery illegal, the president prayed that God's wrath against the nation would cease.

Lincoln's words, spoken at the inauguration of his second term, were offered in a spirit of national repentance. They were intended to deal not only with the formal termination of slavery but the deconstruction of the systemic evil it had woven into the nation's fabric.

Without a doubt, many people expressed kindness to the slaves. My own family has a copy of a document of emancipation written by my father's great-uncle. After converting to Christ, he freed his slaves in a moving testimony of contrition. This document though, however moving, does not address the endless hardship and cruelties that even emancipated slaves endured living within a culture in the grip of darkness.

As with most societal evils, slavery's power to harm was not completely undone by legislative change. The Jim Crow laws of the American South perpetrated much of the structure of racism. These laws (and even more the customs of the region) catechized generations of White Christians to view racial injustice as a social good. Indeed, as a pastor who spent most of his adult years ministering in the American Southeast, I can testify to how serious the backlash can be from otherwise kind and gracious people against anyone who insists that racial inclusion is a core teaching of the Christian faith.

It is tempting for contemporary Americans to deny any connection to historical slavery. In fact, even if those connections are undeniable, it remains challenging to know what to do about it. For example, are the present members of a family whose inherited wealth developed during slavery responsible for the sins of their ancestors? Denial is certainly not a moral response. Mere acknowledgement also seems inadequate. Still, there is no clear-cut guide for how to treat the financial resources that originated in this evil.

What is true of a family's wealth clearly traceable to the evil actions of their ancestors is true of the nation's resources. Many American cities are located on land our ancestors confiscated from others. In some cases, those cities already existed, as parts of other nations. Do people now living, people who had nothing to do with those past injustices, return the lands they own to descendants of the original owners? If so, to which ones?

Lest we become self-righteous, we must acknowledge that most of those who profit today from past evils do not live in antebellum mansions. Indeed, some of the most passionate voices about systemic racism are members of extremely educated families. These families often owe their own capital to great injustices and crimes.

In short: few of us are free from association with past crimes. This is true of all people everywhere.

West Germany, as much as any country in history, worked hard to address their own dark past. Chancellor Merkel, who was raised in Communist East Germany, grew up somewhat emotionally detached from the genocide that occurred shortly before her birth. However, the Berlin wall was located just a few blocks from her home. When it suddenly became possible to visit the museums in the West, she experienced the full shock of how her nation had planned and effectively carried out the destruction of its Jewish population. This led to numerous travels to Israel and ultimately to an address to the Israeli Knesset, delivered partially in Hebrew.

Germany's genocide happened merely a few decades ago. Most of us have faced it repeatedly in film, literature, and endless documentaries. Many of us have known people who lived through it. That makes it tempting to think of our own nation's past crimes against humanity as somehow less serious than those committed by Germany. In large part though, this is simply because our crimes occurred a century and a half ago.

Furthermore, we often scapegoat the American South in our discussions about slavery. As President Lincoln reminded us, the entire nation either directly or indirectly supported the right of some human beings to own other human beings.

We are even less inclined to remember the evils endured by native Americans and Hispanics in the American Southwest. The doctrine of manifest destiny was proclaimed not only by state and national governments, but from pulpits as well. It is celebrated to this day in books and film, though in fact it was nothing less than an ethnic cleansing. If our contemporary Native population seems less inclined than African Americans to force our attention to view this dark side of history, it is probably because most of our Native population was effectively slaughtered before we were born. Nonetheless, poverty, alcoholism, domestic violence, and mental illness plague many of our native communities and is traceable to an attempted genocide committed by our own nation.

Few individuals, including those who profit from them, openly defend such evils as genocide and slavery. Even so, many who denounce these past evils are respected citizens of communities that enact laws to justify or ignore the shadows of what those evils cast over contemporary social structures and cultural habits. It is morally important to shine light on those realities, even when we remain unsure about how to address them.

When overt forms of evil are removed from a society, those who have profited from it, will usually resist any attempt to address it. The European legal systems that obstructed Jews trying to recover their grandparent's stolen art, are prime examples. In a single generation, the people who had the stolen art in their possession, viewed themselves as victims and fought to maintain "their" property.

Evil is complicated. Addressing evil is also complicated. Rage against evil often leads to new evils. People can become evil from fighting evil. Humility and grace are always required to keep us safe as we respond to evil.

The overwhelming majority of Christians of all places and in all times view genocide and slavery as evil. This was true even during the days of slavery. In those cases in which Christians defended this, they did so behind euphemisms, deflections, and the fog of nostalgia. Only when we work to remove that fog, speak clearly, and focus our attention on how evil has harmed our neighbor will we begin to notice evil's destructive power at work within our own hearts.

This is the reason Christians recite the Lord's Prayer. We all need deliverance from evil.

We mentioned earlier that some evils are, as far as we can tell, impersonal. For example, a viral pandemic is a systemic reality more than an individual infection. As we learned during the COVID-19 pandemic, a virus, which we are not entirely certain should be categorized as a form of life, travels through our nations, businesses, and churches. It leaps from individual host to individual host. It strains our health care systems. It devastates family structures. It sows political distress. It undermines economic stability. And it perpetrates long-term distress at many levels.

So, is a virus evil? Is it merely destructive biological code? Does it manifest some hidden disembodied power? We don't know. We do know that we can fight a virus with material weapons—vaccines. In contrast, human evil is much more challenging to fight because our aggression against evil easily becomes evil.

Neither Judaism nor Christianity offer a satisfying explanation of the origin or the nature of evil. The Bible leads us to assume its existence and to be aware of it as we think about the human condition.

I believe it helpful therefore to distinguish the concept of evil from the concept of sin. Scripture presents sin as a human weakness, which the New Testament writers assume we inherit from Adam and Eve. Sin is an illness of soul for which we seek forgiveness and healing. Evil, in contrast, is a kind of dark strength—a demonic infestation from which we need deliverance. The Lord's Prayer acknowledges this distinction. That is why Jesus told us to pray for "forgiveness from our trespasses" but also for our "deliverance from evil."

The implication is that systemic evil evokes a different kind of response from God than individual sin.

As a secularly trained psychiatrist, Peck was shocked when he came face-to-face with the ancient horror that educated Westerners believed we had outgrown long ago. Peck wanted to warn mental health workers that evil was real and to take it seriously. For hinting that a materialist approach to medicine, however vital, might be inadequate, Peck seriously eroded his own credibility. From a Christian standpoint, however, he was correct about the existence of this ancient foe. Modernity has been wrong to dismiss evil as an entity with which humanity contends.

If it is challenging to utter the word evil in a secular context, our following chapter deals with a subject that has been even more difficult to discuss during the modern era: sin.

13

The Bent Image

MY FRIEND LEONARD BOUGHT A TRUCK.

"What a bargain," he thought, driving off the lot. He enjoyed how people admired his truck as he drove it around. The sound system was good. The leather seats were comfortable. The red paint was fresh and bright. The truck was great.

Except for one thing: the truck pulled to the left.

No big deal. Leonard had the truck aligned.

Then, he balanced the tires.

Finally, a mechanic told him the truth: the truck's frame was bent.

The friendly salesman had failed to tell him the truck had been in a wreck. Although the body shop had worked wonders on the truck's appearance, it still had a bent frame.

Christianity teaches that every human being is born with a bent frame. Despite our best intentions, we pull to the side. Some people pull in one direction. Others pull in another direction. No one has a perfect frame. We are all born bent.

The biblical word for this is sin, a loaded and often misused word.

Western Christianity, in nearly all its forms, envisions sin as deliberate rebellion against God. Eastern Christianity, in contrast, thinks of sin as an illness of soul.

I believe this view of sin is more consistent with how Jesus defined it. It is also practically helpful when talking with non-Christians about sin. Most of us realize that we fall short of our own intentions for ourselves. Our inability to consistently live up to our own ethics and morals is distressful. So, whether we are Christians or not, we know from experience that our frame is bent. Scolding us about faults we can't seem to correct only adds to our distress.

M. Scott Peck began *The Road Less Traveled* with this short sentence: "life is difficult."

Peck knew that would snag our attention. Whether we are rich or poor, healthy, or sick, famous, or unknown, life is often challenging. His sentence was a paraphrase of a principal Buddhists call *the four noble truths*.

Sometimes it helps to state a familiar concept in fresh words. Sin is not only a trite term for many of us, but a distasteful one. Certainly, not many contemporary people are interested in having a conversation about sin. Even Christians mostly endure sermons on the subject and leave church feeling worse than when they arrived.

Preachers have often attacked sin like a surgeon operating without anesthesia. They tell us we have an inoperable tumor, but they are cutting us up anyway. If we are godly people, we will thank them for it.

People rarely sign up for that kind of surgery!

Hence, a quick look over the fence to see what the Buddhists say about the human condition.

The Pali word *dukkha* is a somewhat equivalent word for sin. It is usually translated as suffering, pain, or "dis-ease." Some have even translated dukkha as stress. It expresses the idea that the wiser one gets, the more one experiences life as somehow *out-of-sorts*. The out-of-sortsness is not always because of anything we have done, moreover, but is simply an inescapable component of human life.

We want things we can't have. We face trying circumstances. We feel beset by pressures that erode our joy of living, both from within ourselves and from outside ourselves. We consistently fall short of the standards we set for ourselves. We disappoint ourselves and others. We become disillusioned.

Finally, we die.

We can have no peace, the Buddha said, until we accept the inescapable reality of the human condition: life is simply out-of-sorts.

Sin and the Bible

The biblical concept of sin is not exactly the same thing as dukkha. For contemporary people though, out-of-sortsness is a good place to begin the discussion. Most of us know that life is out-of-sorts. We would not be taking the quantities of psychotropic drugs or struggling with addiction at the levels we are if that were not the case.

So, with gratitude to the Buddhists for this contribution, let us look at what the Bible says about sin.

The first biblical mention of sin occurs in Genesis, chapter four. Two brothers, Cain and Abel, offer a sacrifice. God prefers Abel's sacrifice, which angers Cain. God warns Cain, "Sin is crouching at the door, and you must master it."

Cain does not master it, however. His disappointment turns into rage, which results in history's first murder.

The story contains a lesson that the New Testament writers will repeat centuries later: human beings are born with a condition that "pulls to the left."

That is what sin is. It is not so much a deed as a condition. We are responsible to resist the sideways pull, and the best of us try hard to do that. Nonetheless, as the Hebrew prophets were understanding at the conclusion of the Old Testament (and the New Testament writers would grasp even more fully) we cannot always resist the pull of our own bent soul. Sometimes, we are not even that interested in resisting it. The bentness of our soul affects our will, our judgement of self and others, and even our concept of God.

We are not bent merely a little. We are profoundly and fatally bent.

This human brokenness makes full alignment with divine providence impossible. Even if there were no malignant non-human forces obstructing our way, we would lean to the left.

Human beings don't need demons to be bad. They can be bad all by themselves. This is true of the wisest and holiest of us. All human beings wrestle with this radical dysfunction.

This is the reason sin is a major theme of the New Testament.

The first book of the New Testament, St. Matthew's Gospel, mentions sin in the very first chapter. The angel promises Joseph that Jesus will "save his people from their sin."

As Jesus grows up and begins to teach in the villages around his home, the rabbis are scandalized that Jesus claims to forgive sin. Jesus doesn't stop forgiving sin though because, as he explained, "This is the reason I came into the world."

In St. Luke's gospel, the resurrected Jesus says that his death and resurrection were necessary so that "repentance and the forgiveness of sins could be proclaimed to everyone in the world." Then, Jesus instructs his disciples to forgive the sins of everyone who hears and responds to the Gospel.

All early Christian writers talked a lot about sin. However, it is in the Epistle to the Romans where St. Paul most clearly defines sin. He starts with bad news: we all have it. He then delivers even gloomier news: sincerity, piety, abstinence, and asceticism will not cure us.

Like the Buddha, St. Paul says that we can make no spiritual progress until we acknowledge our own "bentness." Paul disagrees with the Buddha though in how one should deal with sin. Paul says that we must trust Christ, who through his person, his words, and his crucifixion proclaimed God's forgiveness.

As the Apostle John put it, "God didn't send his Son into the world to condemn the world; but that through Him all people might be saved."

Christ's death on the cross has defeated sin, Paul says.

The cross both exposed human depravity and revealed God's kindness. The cross informed us that God will stop at nothing to heal us, and he released into the world a spiritual power called grace. This power initiates a transformational work within everyone who believes it. Nothing else is required.

Healthy spiritual practice reminds us of God's presence and reassures us of God's work in us. However, if this practice becomes a lifeless obsession, we lose our trust in grace.

As we fully trust in God's goodness—as it was displayed through the death and resurrection of Christ—our will and appetites gradually change. This process is called sanctification. It means we "turn our feet in the direction of the Lord's decrees." Our inner life and behavior come to reflect the ways of God.

However, human effort to move toward the good, the true, and the beautiful fails. In fact, trusting in our own efforts to become good, leads to frustration and delays our encounter with grace. We must accept God's radical hospitality, which is how Christ opened his Sermon on the Mount.

The words, "Blessed are the poor in Spirit," meant that God was inviting those who couldn't get their spiritual life in order into covenant. Jesus explained what this meant in a parable about a wedding feast.

In the story told by St Matthew in chapter 22, a wealthy man invites all the upstanding citizens in the area to his son's wedding. Everyone sends their regrets. They are too busy to attend. The wealthy man then sends his servants to the "edges, highways and byways," inviting the "riffraff" to his feast.

Christ was repudiating any sort of spiritual stratification, saying in effect that all humanity is in the same boat where sin is concerned. He was also pointing out the most serious impediment to our deliverance from sin: failure to respond to God's hospitable invitation. He was reminding us that freedom from sin comes to those who are humble of heart. In the words of the apostle, "God resists the proud but gives grace to the humble."

Jesus tells us about a tax collector for the Roman government who could not find words to express regret for his sins (Luke 18). The man beat his chest, a passionate sign of mourning over one's debauchery. Jesus says the man was heard and went away justified. The reason God did not justify the Pharisee who had entered the temple at the same time, Jesus said, was that "he prayed with himself saying . . . I am not unholy like others."

While this is neither a book of Christian theology nor a study of scripture, sin is something that will arise in conversations about our faith with non-Christians. Believers cannot contribute to the contemporary world by eroding their own core convictions. This necessarily includes our view of human dysfunction. Christianity, in all its forms, views human beings as lost and in need of salvation. This is, of course, a perspective modern culture has long resisted.

What we would like to do here, on this subject as with others, is reflect on how Christians might offer their unique perspective on the world in ways that do not come across as demeaning. I am assuming that non-Christians might be more interested in what we have to say about sin were we to define it as an illness of soul which affects everyone.

Addiction

A healthy discussion about sin can be helpful when people are struggling with addiction. Indeed, I believe what we now call addiction was on Christ's mind in the Sermon on the Mount. In that sermon, he presented a radical approach for escaping the shame cycle.

The process of addiction, whether to a substance or a behavior, moves through a destructive cycle. An addict becomes steadily imprisoned in a wheel of suffering because his repugnance of the substance and behavior deepens the entrapment. The wheel has several stages, one leading to the next as the cycle endlessly repeats.

Use,

Abuse,

Dependence,

Shame,

Resistance, and

Relapse.

Unfortunately, human beings can become addicted to anything.

Let's use cake as an example.

We eat a piece of cake. It is good. So, we want another piece.

This is not an addiction. Not yet.

However, one day, the cake may taste so good and make us so happy we decide to eat a third piece. Then we do it again the next day. We eat cake all week. And then for another week. Soon, we crave sugar. No matter how much cake we eat, we cannot satisfy the craving. Now, we are not so much enjoying cake as captured by it. Hunger for cake has become what the Buddhists call a "hungry ghost." Something empty has moved inside us. We are perpetually hungry but never satisfied.

It may become difficult to go through a day without cake. Or perhaps we go several weeks without cake at a time but occasionally plunge headlong into a cake binge. In either case, we have entered the stage of dependence on cake. The dependence may be psychological or biological or both. Either way, we cannot stop ourselves from eating cake.

It alarms us when we become dependent on some substance or a behavior. We become disgusted with ourselves. The shame of not being able to walk away from our dependence overwhelms us. So, we may exert all our forces of body and mind and just throw all the cake out the window. We may even throw away pictures of cake. We can smash all the cake pans. We can shout, "Hallelujah, that's the last cake I will ever eat!" We mean it too! We are certain that our battle with cake is over.

We have won. Our resistance to cake lasts a long time.

Then one day, a friend has a party where there is lots of cake. We know this going in, so we promise ourselves we will eat only a half a slice of cake—just to be social. Our friend is pleased that we like his cake. He insists that we have another slice. We may not even be aware after that second piece that we have begun stuffing ourselves with cake.

The next day, we know we have failed.

"I am not a good person," we think. Shame covers us like a heavy blanket. We cannot endure it. The only way to cope is to have more cake.

We have relapsed.

I have never met a person with a cake addiction. That's why I thought cake would be a safe example. However, if you have not found a substance or a behavior with the potential to enslave you, you will. Hoarding, workaholism, perfectionism, prescription drugs, cosmetic surgery, religious obsession—there's an addiction some-where out there tailored-made just for you! There is no such thing as "an addictive personality." There are just addictions—some of which are socially acceptable and others that are not.

The most challenging addictions to address are ones connected to substances or behaviors that meet a genuine need. Food and sex addictions are notoriously difficult, for example. We all must eat, and most of us desire sexual life with another person. Food addic-tions involve either using food to fill emotional need or withholding food from ourselves to gain control over some part of our life. Like-wise, when we become dependent on sex, we are no longer focused on a life-giving, intimate connection with another person. We're simply craving another body (real or imagined) to fill emotional emptiness.

Therapists often refer to the shame cycle because when we misuse a behavior or a substance but have not yet moved into dependence, it's usually possible to address it fairly easily. We can still say, "Gee thanks, but I've already had too much cake." We can say to ourselves, "There are too many sparks flying between me and that coworker. I am going to put some distance between us."

This is the stage of the cycle where the Old Testament speaks into addiction. "Thou Shalt Not!"

Just Don't Do It!

That may work for you most of the time. Like the ancient Hebrews, we hear this warning with all good intention. We promise ourselves we will respect the boundaries we profess. Unfortunately, there is always one area of life that trips us up. Eventually, one day when we are not paying attention, it breaks through all those good intentions.

Interestingly, Christ addresses the addiction cycle at a different place than the Old Testament writers. Jesus interrupts the addiction cycle at the shame stage. That is, Jesus offers relief to those who are exhausted from trying to control themselves. They have repeatedly failed anyway, so why try? They're just bone-tired and disgusted at themselves.

"Come unto me, all you who are weary and heavy laden," he says.

"Neither do I condemn you."

"Blessed are those who mourn."

"Your many sins are forgiven."

And so forth.

My wife and I stopped at a garage sale many years ago, where I saw a man wearing a T-shirt. On the front were the words: "Jesus is Coming Back!"

I had never seen words like that on a T-shirt. I agreed with them. I was just surprised. But then the man turned around. On the back of the shirt was, "And Man is He Pissed!"

That was shocking!

In those days, using a word like "pissed" was considered profanity. To use it in reference to Christ was downright profane. The message offended me. It still does. Not because of the word "pissed." The reason the shirt offends is that its message reinforced what I believe has been a real problem in Western Christianity: we have too often ignored St John's description of Christ's mission.

For God sent not his son into the world to condemn the world; but that the world through him might be saved. (John 3:17)

Jesus doesn't come looking for us because he is "pissed." He comes looking for us because he is the Great Physician. He did not come to punish us. He came to heal us! If Christianity in any way represents the words and character of Christ, then its message and work must be grounded in the cause that motivated him: proclaiming the forgiveness of sin.

That is where the Christian message to the world begins: Jesus saves.

Our dysfunctions, both as individuals and as societies, are too complicated and resistant for us to solve by ourselves.

We are like a person gradually sinking in quicksand; we need help from someone standing on solid ground. Our friends can't help us. They're in the same situation as we are. The saints can help us, but only because they can introduce us to the One who saves.

Throughout this book, I have been claiming that Christianity has much to say to the contemporary world. None of it will matter though if we do not get this part of our message across—no one is doomed to meaninglessness nor to being crushed under the weight of their own dysfunction.

Help is always a breath away.

14

Coming Undone
THE UNRAVELING OF REALITY

I HAVE A FAVORITE PAIR OF COMFORTABLE SHOES. THEY LOOK NICE and support my feet. Unfortunately, they keep coming undone. Several times a day.

The shoes have redeemed themselves though by giving me a way to illustrate the meaning of the old English word *undone*.

If you cut that pesky thread sticking out of your sweater, the sweater may unravel. That's because a sweater is a pattern of interwoven threads. Severing one of the threads unweaves the pattern. If the unraveling continues, all you will be left with is the material that made up the sweater. The sweater itself, however, will have disappeared.

A sweater is a form imposed upon otherwise unrelated threads. With the loss of form, a sweater is undone.

English speakers once used the word undone in contexts other than in conversations about shoelaces and sweaters. We once talked about human beings coming undone.

Saying that a person was coming undone meant they were in a state of unraveling. Like an unraveling sweater after someone has cut a thread, past generations thought it possible for a person to lose their sense of self. It could happen because one became disillusioned with a cause they once believed in. It could be because of unthinkable trauma. Self-loathing because of some terrible mistake might do it. Whatever the reason, a person coming undone had begun a process they could not stop.

We didn't stop using the word undone because it doesn't happen anymore. The contemporary world is full of people who feel they are coming undone. Even nations for that matter, including my own, seems much less solid than they once were. Political labels get redefined, leaving those who identified with them feeling invisible. Divorce, loss of faith, bankruptcy, and public shame can all lead to being undone.

A person who comes undone may not take their life. However, just because a person who experiences self-deconstruction keeps on eating and breathing doesn't mean they do so with purpose or joy.

Families can come undone too. Sickness, accidents, or betrayal can remove parents or children, leaving the other family members physically alive but lacking a sense of identity or significance.

Sometimes, this occurs when a member of the family commits a heinous crime. Families of infamous criminals like Jeffrey Dahmer, for example, must radically reconstruct their sense of family. Lee Harvey Oswald's wife remarried but she waited seven years to tell her daughters about their father. Families do not form and maintain themselves simply because its members share genetic links. Families organize around identities, values, and habits. All of which can unravel.

My own family left Scotland and Northern Ireland decades before the American Revolution. After the Battle of Culloden, my forebears, who had fought for Scottish independence, fled to America. They made a new home in the Appalachians. The ones from Northern Ireland did the same. My French Huguenot ancestors fled religious persecution in France. They too found refuge in the Appalachian highlands. What all my European ancestors had in common was the experience of being forced from their homeland. They struggled to find safety from British control, and they survived by doing what they thought necessary to preserve themselves. It's not surprising that their descendants remain suspicious of authority.

For good and ill, the sense of being alienated from the world beyond one's clan is a part of Appalachian identity.

My family's identity is thus rooted in half-forgotten experiences that occurred centuries ago. Most people with roots in Appalachia will identify. It is what makes Appalachian culture such a unique part of the American social fabric. One sociologist called our region "America's largest reservation."

The important point here is that churches, businesses, cities, nations, and all other kinds of human societies maintain themselves around mostly unstated mythical narratives. A culture's mythical core is mostly unconscious, held together by common threads weaved in the distant past. Those threads can unravel during times of natural catastrophe or war, which can lead to the community's undoing.

Millions of people living in the contemporary world have Hittite ancestry. However, few of them know it. (I am quite sure I once had a landlord who was Hittite, but that is a cheap shot unworthy of this great book.) Anyway, Hittite culture is long gone. It unraveled. It was undone. It disappeared.

Christianity warns that all things, even nature itself, are vulnerable to being undone. Indeed, our faith teaches that powers and processes exist in the universe that actively work to undo everything that is good, beautiful, or true.

There are two main sources for this Christian doctrine of existential decay.

The first is The Holy Scriptures.

The second is the Greek Doctrine of Forms.

We've already referred to *tohu wa bohu*, noting that the Hebrew phrase is usually rendered in English as "without form and void." However we translate it, *tohu wa bohu* means unordered emptiness. It describes the state of chaotically entangled threads that once was (or which could yet become) a sweater. Tohu wa bohu is the condition of undifferentiated stuff, of matter lacking purpose, pattern, form, or design.

The ancient Hebrews dreaded tohu wa bohu. The phrase expressed the possibility that order, which the Creator had imposed upon matter at the beginning of time, might unravel. The Hebrews imagined the wilderness and the sea as borderlands, protecting the social and the natural world from existential chaos. They described a person who left his inner self untended—in an unformed and void state—as a fool. Banishment from community meant being cut off from societal patterns that kept chaos at bay. Moral chaos especially had to be avoided. Any sort of moral unraveling in any part of the world might lead to the undoing of everything everywhere.

This fear of unraveling is behind many of those passages in the Old Testament that contemporary readers find distasteful. The elimination of communities the Hebrews judged as morally corrupt was based in the belief that moral infection will spread, leading to cosmic loss. From our perspective, this seems paranoid and cruel. Of course, the ancient Hebrews saw things differently.

As the Bible progressed, the fear of dissolution became personified in Satan, the great Undoer. We will look at that later in the book.

The other source of the Christian view of undoing was ancient Greece.

The Greek Doctrine of Forms was the way most ancient Mediterranean communities viewed reality. It had emerged in ancient Greece but then developed in the nations conquered by Alexander the Great, forming the culture we now call the *Hellenized* world. (Hellas means Greek.) The Doctrine of Forms thus became a component of what the Roman Empire, the Byzantine Empire, and ultimately medieval Europe would think of as "common sense." Even today, Western Civilization retains the remnants of this ancient view of reality. They are fossilized in words we use every day.

It will be worth one's time to go over the following paragraphs carefully because I'm going to explain how these common words connected to the worldview of the ancient Western World. Familiarity with original meanings of the words will give one the ability to understand ancient and medieval literature—including the New Testament. It will also acquaint you with a few deep assumptions about reality embedded in the major Western languages.

Some of the most influential intellectuals of the last few centuries have tried to free Western culture from these ancient assumptions. As a result, contemporary Western peoples are often ignorant of the Doctrine of Forms. Western peoples are nonetheless gripped by the unconscious influence that the Doctrine of Forms still projects on Western languages and thought.

As you proceed, you will see how persistent this ancient perspective is in the collective unconsciousness. You can decide for yourself whether our ancestors were brilliant, crazy, or just misinformed.

The Doctrine of Forms

The best way to understand the Doctrine of Forms is through a few common words used every day. Although now we tend to experience them as isolated terms, they were once part of a skeleton that sustained the Western World's view of reality.

Here are a few of those words: form, deform, reform, inform, metaphor, transform, formation, uninformed, conformed, and formal. Closely related to these words is another set: idea, ideation, ideal, idealism, and ideological. Just for laughs, here are a few more: substance, abstract, accident, and concrete.

The Doctrine of Forms, which gave rise to all these words, emerges from a single assumption about reality: that everything in the universe is a combination of substance (matter) and form.

Our ancestors derived several important implications from this basic assumption.

First, there is a realm in which forms exist but where substance does not. These immaterial forms are perfect and eternal.

Secondly, there is, or at least there was at one time, a realm in which substance existed without form. Formless matter was a mass of undifferentiated "stuff." Lacking form, purpose, or pattern, material stuff had no way of arranging itself into anything definitive or meaningful.

Thirdly, the universe as we now experience it is filled with matter that has been ordered and arranged. Something or someone ordered the original, unformed material into atoms, the atoms into molecules, and the molecules into elements. The elements then combined in ways that became rivers, rocks, mountains, and aardvarks.

Fourthly, ordered matter sometimes becomes organic life. All such life forms react purposefully to their environment. Some of them even become aware of their own existence. That leads them to ask questions about both their environment and their own individual purpose.

Fifthly, human beings are unique in that they not only react to their material environment—something all animals and plants do—but that they participate in the realm of forms. Humans routinely abstract form from substance. They pull the forms into their own imaginations where they are examined, manipulated, and communicated. Like God, human beings can form matter into things by imposing upon matter the forms humans carry within their imagination. (Imagination means "creating images.")

The Doctrine of Forms assumes that form is embedded into every piece of matter. We call the process through which this occurs *in*formation. Information thus belongs to the realm of forms rather than to the realm of substance.

Human beings not only observe the process of information but participate in it. We can both abstract form from matter and inform matter with form. In other words, we can learn about the purpose of things by observing them. We can make mental images of what we experience either firsthand or through the reports of another. We can even create new purposes for the forms we imagine.

Furthermore, human beings can share their awareness of a form with another human in ways that do not involve sharing material substance. For example, a woman can describe to her friend the appearance, fragrance, and chemical compilation of a plant. The description can include information about whether the plant is edible or practically useful in other ways. If she has communicated effectively, the one with whom she shares this information acquires an ability to recognize the plant, even if she has never seen it.

We take this ability to communicate form with one another for granted. However, it is quite remarkable. Plato and other early

Greek philosophers believed we can do this because we make mental copies of the underlying pattern of things. In other words, we *in*form ourselves. We then pass along those patterns to others, thus *in*forming them. We do not need the material thing itself to describe it to others. We only need its form.

The takeaway idea? A human mind can inform another human mind without involving matter (except for the parts of our physical bodies used for communicating with another mind.)

This basic idea, that things consist of form and substance leads to a deep understanding of the world. (Understanding means knowing *what stands under.*) Whether it constitutes a misunderstanding or was merely a useful explanation for the early stages of science is another question. I'm merely trying to explain how our ancestors thought about reality.

Let's develop the Doctrine of Forms a bit more.

If we notice that something is beginning to lose form, as when a candle starts to melt, the ancients would have said that the candle was being *de*formed. To regain its form, the candle would have to be *re*formed. If one were to shape it so it would look like other candles, the ancients would have said that the candlemaker was *con*forming the candle to a design imposed by himself or his customer.

If we were to outfit a car with wings so it could fly, the ancients would have said that we were *trans*forming the car into an aircraft. In other words, even though the substance of the car would be substantially the same in both cases, its underlying form would change. It would no longer be merely a vehicle that rolls down a road. It would become capable of taking to the skies.

Contemporary people are immersed in constant transformations of just this sort.

A few years ago, my wife was impressed by the scenery. So, she said, "This place is so beautiful. I wish I had a camera!"

My perplexed young granddaughter replied, "But Gram your phone is right there!"

We laughed. For my generation, a phone is something hanging on the wall. It is always attached to a cord. We use the phone to talk with people. In the years since my childhood, however, society has transformed the concept of a phone. We don't even use the same substance to make a phone. Our old idea of a phone is only a fraction of what a contemporary notion of a phone is all about.

The Doctrine of Forms helped our ancestors make sense of these kinds of changes. When we recover the old meanings of the words connected to their view of reality, it helps us too. So, let's go a bit further with the way this works.

When we are planning a social event but do not want to give too much attention to the specific personalities involved, we form*alize* the occasion. For example, a city's leaders can plan a presidential visit even though they know there will be a new president by the time the event occurs. These city leaders will be planning the event around a role rather than a specific person. Even though they don't know who the person filling the role will be or what he or she will be like, they draw upon traditional protocols, procedures, traditions, and customs. These guidelines determine what the people attending the event will wear, what music will be played, and how the participants will move within the space the city leaders select for the event. The reason they can know all of this in advance is because they are planning a *formal* event, an event focused on form.

A formal occasion in other words, is one that transcends the individual tastes of its participants. To accept an invitation to a formal occasion involves relinquishing one's individual preferences and adapting to commonly known and accepted speech, dress, and behavior.

Contemporary people often dislike formal settings. Nonetheless, formality is essential for maintaining social life.

Imagine representatives from warring nations meeting to discuss peace. Such a meeting must be formal. The participants may not trust one another. They may or may not or enjoy being with one another. However, they're not there as individuals meeting other individuals. They are there as representatives of their respective nations. They are not there to chit-chat or exchange phone numbers, though all this may occur if the meeting becomes more productive than anticipated. Unless and until a less formal atmosphere emerges, it's important to protect the participants from outbursts of anger or expressions of personal distrust toward one another. Observing formalities makes all this possible. Formality protects events from unpredictable emotions, customs, or banter that might derail the proceedings.

In a formal gathering, one doesn't slap the King on the back and say, "How's it going, Chuck?" The King is not there as an individual. Arguably, for most of us the King doesn't even exist as a person. The King is a symbol. Whether or not the King likes you as a person, therefore, is irrelevant. He will respect your assigned role during the proceedings, and you will respect his. This will be true even if you happen to know the King personally.

That is what formality means.

Without a clear form for emotion-laden occasions, participants may fall into disorder and confusion. That's why funerals and weddings are usually (and should be) formal.

Pastors know that even in a warm and personal funeral or wedding, they should expect to gently lead everyone through a series of known steps. The bride should come in at a certain time to music she has selected. Rings will be exchanged in a certain way. If the bride's father forgets his response to "Who presents this woman to be wed?" and mumbles something incoherent, the service nonetheless moves on to the next step.

The only possible thing that should be able to disrupt a wedding would be if someone were to respond to "If anyone here can show just cause for which this man and woman should not be married, speak now." After officiating at hundreds of weddings, I still have no idea what one would do in such a situation! The phrase has become a fragment of some past contingency. No contemporary person is expected to take it seriously. It survives because formal protocols change very slowly.

I've just described a formal Christian wedding because that is the world I know. Other religions and secular venues will do things differently. In Western culture though, even secular weddings often follow a version of what I've just described.

In the last few pages, I've offered a rough outline of the Doctrine of Forms. If you want to know more, read Plato, Aristotle, and Aquinas. You should be able to follow their arguments. Should you care to go further than that, you will be able to read what the philosophers of the Western World have been arguing about for the last three thousand years!

I included this short lesson on the Doctrine of Forms to explain how the Christian Church Fathers viewed the work of evil in the world. They saw it as an "undoing." Evil for them was the process of eroding form, of rendering material substance, including human beings, useless and empty.

There are other ways to approach the subject. However, I'm claiming that a fresh look at early Christian thought will help us develop a response to the contemporary world. Since I've been drawing heavily on Patristic sources to do that, I thought it would be helpful to introduce a few Patristic terms and assumptions.

The Great Undoer

The Bible does not give Satan a lot of space.

The image of Satan as a symbol of personified evil were woven through the centuries from otherwise disconnected passages. Artistic depictions by people like Dante and Milton, along with tons of visual art on medieval church walls, have contributed to ideas about Satan today. As a result, Christians tend to read key passages of the Old Testament as relating the composite image we call Satan. Thus, Christians usually assume that references to "a lying spirit from the Lord" and Ezekiel's "King of Tyre" are about Satan as we now imagine him/it. Neither of these passages (if read in isolation from the rest of the Christian canon) clearly point to a "prince of darkness," however.

My comments are not offered as a dismissive critique of an intertextual reading of scripture. After all, what transforms the Hebrew Scriptures into the Old Testament is when one reads it as pointing toward the person, words, and deeds of Christ.

My point is simply that Satan emerges as a major character in the Old Testament only through the interpretive lens of the New Testament. Satan emerges even more through the subsequent art, theology, and folk tradition of Christian peoples. For example, the writer of Genesis explains the sudden appearance of the serpent in the Garden of Eden as simply "the most cunning animal in the garden." It's not clear in the passage itself that we are dealing with a personified embodiment of evil. We read that into the passage because of our understanding of the rest of scripture.

I once lived for a while in the Amazon. So, I have encountered some scary reptiles. Fortunately, none of them talked! Snakes are scary as it is. The snake's added ability to speak in Eden tells us that the serpent in this story represents something much more significant than a common serpent. Nonetheless, Genesis leaves the matter with these few words, saying nothing about the snake being a manifestation of God's archenemy. By the time Milton raises the hair on our neck with his retelling of the same story, centuries of Christian midrash had seriously deepened the importance of Eden's crafty serpent.

Old Testament passages make references to Leviathan and other symbols of primordial danger. Satan appears to tempt David into taking a census. Once in the Book of Job, Satan appears before God to ask permission to torture a just and upright man. Other than that, Satan is a rather minor character in the Old Testament.

Between the Old Testament and the time of the Gospels, however, Jews were exposed to Persian dualism. In this view, Good and Evil are roughly equal in power and locked in eternal conflict. Jewish thought didn't make much room for such an extreme view of evil. Nonetheless, the Persian sojourn Jews became increasingly concerned about evil, not merely as a source of temptation, but as a personification of primal Chaos and Disorder.

The Deuterocanonical *Book of Wisdom*, written in the first century BCE, refers to the devil in a way we don't encounter in the Old Testament. It is a harbinger of what emerges afterward in the New Testament. The Book of Enoch (300-200 BCE), which has not been received as sacred scripture by either Jews or Christians (except for the Ethiopian Church,) was widely read in New Testament times (Jesus mentions it once). Enoch pointedly talks about a cosmic war between darkness and light.

The New Testament refers to the devil (or devils) several times, usually as a source of hindrance or torment.

The early Church rarely mentions Satan until the time of the desert fathers. That's the period when Christians begin to think of demons as actively opposing those who seek after holiness.

It was in the medieval era, however, when folk Christianity began leaning into something like Persian Dualism. As one reads over literature from that period, it can seem that Christians imagine Satan as something like God's evil twin.

This preoccupation with Satan and demons affected all forms of Western Christianity. Even in the post-medieval period obsession with evil led to outbreaks of witch hysteria throughout Europe and North America. Indeed, secularized forms of this preoccupation was used to justify racial and religious persecution throughout Western history. It culminated in the horrors of the holocaust.

The lessons of history teach us to approach a discussion about Satan or existential evil with caution. However, there is also a down-side to dismissing the concept of the demonic altogether. If we do that, a discussion about evil for any reason becomes challenging. While we must avoid scapegoating or demonizing other human beings, we cannot afford to eliminate a concept that is vitally important for understanding social life. No one likes to talk about cancer but avoiding the topic doesn't eliminate the disease.

Christians at any rate cannot ignore the subject of evil because Jesus embedded a warning about the devil in the prayer he taught us to pray. He said that we should ask God to "deliver us from evil" or, as some of the older traditions prefer, "from the Evil One."

This prayer assumes a distinction between the work of evil and human sin. We ask for *deliverance* from the evil one but *forgiveness* for our sins. Forgiveness implies a removal of guilt. Deliverance implies a liberation from a foreign presence.

The distinction between these two sources of human dysfunction seems intentional. When we ask for deliverance from evil, we are reminding ourselves to be vigilant of malevolent forces around us and within us. These are far more serious than mere errors of judgements or the countless faults to which we are prone. Evil seeks to undo everything good in us and through our undoing to erode good in the world. Evil works to keep us ignorant of injustice, tyranny, narcissistic entitlement, and of our own unethical and unjust thoughts, words, and deeds.

Martin Luther, in *A Mighty Fortress is Our God* warns:

Behold our ancient foe, doth seek to work us woe
　　His craft and power are great
　　And armed with cruel hate
　　On earth he has no equal.

Even more forcibly, he adds:

And though this world with devils filled should threaten to undo us
　　We will not fear for God has willed his truth to triumph through us.
　　The Prince of Darkness grim; we tremble not for him
　　His wrath we can endure; for lo his doom is sure.

Despite this warning about evil, Luther was not beyond falling into the trap of what he called "our ancient foe." His willingness to use violence against Jews and other religious minorities resulted in all sorts of sorrow and mayhem. Some have even seen a link between Luther and the Nazi massacre of the Jews. Whether that is justified or not, it makes Luther's warning more serious. If one is so preoccupied with the danger of demonic force could himself be used as an agent of demonic force, we must all take care.

Luther tempered his warning about evil with the line "we tremble not for him." Unfortunately, his warning about being obsessed with evil has not always translated into Christian practice. Trembling in the presence of the Prince of Darkness has been the very reason believers have sometimes committed unimaginable cruelty toward others.

A healthy view of evil therefore seems to lie somewhere between being aware of its potential to harm and remembering that becoming obsessed with evil usually results in evil.

Without going any deeper into the theology of disembodied evil, we simply affirm that it's an inescapable part of Christian teaching. When affected by social disorder, Christians are called to discern whether something more than mere human dysfunction is at work. They are reminded that the ancient force that "seeks to work our woe" is always busy trying to unravel things; that evil is always threatening to "undo us."

As with many theological concepts, it may be the wisest course of action to maintain a fuzzy rather than a clearly defined stance about the devil. Through the ages, Christians and Jews have reflected on the stories of scripture to gain insight into the meaning of evil. These attempts have deepened our awareness that forces exist in the world that work to dissolve human persons and human communities. However, these growing insights have never fully arrived at definitive definitions.

The evil one is something of an absence rather than a presence and so at any rate defies description.

St. Augustine at least viewed the evil one in this way, not as God's eternal nemesis but as an erosion of God's goodness. Satan was, in his view, a seductive enticement to formlessness. Augustine didn't deny that this enticement had a personality or that human beings experience it as a conscious presence. He just believed that the presence of evil, described by most people who encounter it as a skin-crawling terror, is an absence, wooing humanity to undo themselves.

What Augustine describes is like what we sometimes feel when standing close to an abyss. We feel irrationally drawn to it. We may even imagine ourselves hurling down into the gaping emptiness. Augustine would say this attraction is not an illusion. At vulnerable times in our lives, we may feel compelled to throw ourselves into an abyss, to surrender to the process of unraveling.

It may be difficult for a secular person to imagine anything of worth in the Christian doctrine of evil, especially any talk of the ultimate Undoer himself. However, even if one cannot accept the theological unpinning for this concept, it is a useful one for understanding why humanity often feels pulled into destructive ideas and behaviors.

Unlike enlightened Europeans living in the late nineteenth and early twentieth century, contemporary people do not find it as easy to believe that things will just keep getting better and better. The sort of social optimism experienced by many of our great-grand-parents in their youth was seriously wounded in the trenches of World War One. The Second World War then annihilated Pollyanna.

The last ten decades should have convinced us that an educated and cultured people—a Christian people at that—can fall victim to a bigger-than-life narcissist. We know that because it occurred.

When the dust had settled, millions of human beings had been transported, tattooed, categorized with utmost efficiency, gassed, and then cremated. Gulags, ethnic cleansings, apartheid, and other kinds of technologically enabled, government sanctioned cruelties taught contemporary people that scientific sophistication is no guarantee of moral maturity.

When a nation is being undone, it does not always look like impoverishment and disease. Sometimes it looks like a rising GNP, parades in the street, and astounding military success. While a society enjoys the party, the Undoer may be boring into the heart of things, allowing the surface to flourish as evil erodes belief in goodness, truth, and beauty. As the center gives way and the quarrels intensify, the Undoer joins every side of the conflict, empowering each in the rush toward anarchy and destruction. For Evil never cares who wins, only that mayhem is maximized, that love is destroyed, and that life is undone.

Protection Against Evil

For individuals and communities alike, the best protection against evil is humility: the simple awareness that we all have vulnerabilities. The old gospel song taught us to pray:

> *"I am weak but Thou art strong; Jesus keep me from all wrong."*

In contrast, the human attitude that most effectively attracts evil is hubris, the kind of pride celebrated in the popular song "My Way" by Frank Sinatra. Its message is utterly defiant to the message of Christ. So, it is probably Hell's national anthem.

Taking pride in having never knelt, having always done things "my way," is one of the clearest explanations I know of why human beings can feel so strongly attracted to the abyss.

Even if we take evil seriously, we are not always able to avoid it. History informs us that crusaders against evil may become evil themselves. Didn't we say above that when human beings are against one another that evil jumps in on both sides? If no doctrine, cause, or practice can protect us from evil, what are we to do?

That question leads us to the heart of what Christianity offers the world: the human being we believe is God.

15

God Enters the Mirror
THE SIGNIFICANCE OF THE INCARNATION

THE MOVIE *AVATAR* BEGINS WITH A BACKSTORY ABOUT A PARALYZED Marine named Jake Sully. His twin brother, who had been preparing for a mission to the distant planet of Pandora, has died. The space agency has asked Jake to be his brother's replacement.

Jake learns that the agency's scientists have harvested genetic material from Pandora's native population. They have fused this Pandora material with human DNA to create hybrid embryos. The plan is to download the consciousness of the agency workers into the embryos. One of these very expensive avatars contains the DNA of Jake's twin. So, Jake is the only available match.

Jake agrees. After his long voyage through space, Jake wakes up and begins his training.

As he learns how to live and move about in his new body, he gradually becomes more at home in Pandora than in the mission base.

(Missionary kids will relate!)

Jake also falls in love with a Pandora native.

By the end of the movie, Jake has made his home on Pandora.

The Christian doctrine of the Incarnation is not quite like this. However, *Avatar* may be a good place to start the discussion.

By the way, this chapter may be the most theological one in the book. Since it's impossible to understand Christianity without a discussion about the incarnation, this short trip into theology seems unavoidable.

Of course, I may be in danger of heresy by using *Avatar* as an illustration of the incarnation. We will just have to accept that risk and move on.

The Christian doctrine of incarnation simply means this: to fully empower the purposes for which God created the universe, God became himself a human being. In Christ, God offers both a model and a means through which human dysfunction, and through them cosmic dysfunction, can be healed and completed.

It is for this reason that healing has always been a major focus of all Christian expressions. The Christian work of healing extends to both individuals and communities. Indeed, it involves the entire natural order. The incarnate God came to break the work of the Undoer and reverse the unraveling process of God's good creation.

The Christian understanding of what it means to be human is not radically different from that of ancient Judaism. In this sense, the incarnation has not altered the Hebrew belief about what human beings are intended to become. Where Christianity differs from its Hebrew roots is that Christ has become a new Adam. Through Christ, God reintroduces the original human form, thereby transforming what had become deformed in Adam's fall.

Biblical anthropology (Jewish and Christian) begins with the claim that human beings are "made in the image and likeness of God." We are thus ensouled material bodies or, if you prefer, embodied spiritual beings. Biblical spirituality therefore envisions human life as an interpenetration of matter and spirit. We are spiritualized matter and incarnated spirit.

Christ, in whom the fullness of the godhead dwells in a bodily form (Colossians 2:9), both models God's intention for humanity and enables its fulfillment. This implies that the human body is not only intended to receive divine form, but it is invited to enter a process of spiritualization through which it ultimately becomes something more than we can presently imagine.

Furthermore, it's not only human beings that will be transformed. The Incarnation ultimately involves everything.

We're given a glimpse of this future transformation of everything through the way we use material objects in worship. So, allow me a short diversion.

The spiritualization of matter is explained in the words of an old prayer used throughout the Christian world during the celebration of Communion. It is derived from a common blessing over food, used by Jews still today:

"We thank you Lord God, king of the universe for this bread and this wine, which you have created, and which human hands have prepared. They shall be for us the body and blood of Christ."

We can put aside for the moment the fact that Christians disagree among themselves about whether the use of materials in worship involves their actual material transformation or are merely symbolic. In either case, this ancient prayer expresses something important about how Christian's view matter and spirit. In the Christian view, matter and spirit are not rival contenders in the argument over which of them constitutes the ground of reality. Rather, both matter and spirit are "creatures" which emerge from a single substance: Logos, the Word of God.

This "sacramental perspective" views material objects as legitimate components of worship because God has scheduled the entire universe for radical transformation. Sacramental life thus is an essential part, not merely an analogy of human transformation in Christ. A sacramental approach to spiritual life implies that what we do with our bodies—how we steward our physical and material assets—is an essential part of "sanctification," the full participation in God's intended aims for all creation.

We offer water, oil, wine, bread, and other materials in worship to show that the material world has, along with human beings, been befriended by the Holy Spirit. It is God who has invited matter to participate in the drama of redemption.

Many ancient but still influential Gnostic voices insist that only humanity will be redeemed from the existing universe. In this view, only human beings and angels share spiritual life in God. For Gnostics, the material world is the very thing human beings are trying to escape. They believe the material universe is so unspeakably vile that it cannot be redeemed. Only sanctified spirit escapes the coming conflagration.

The apostle John was aware of the Gnostic perspective because it was beginning to emerge in his day. He called it the "spirit of antichrist" because Gnosticism implied that "Jesus did not come in the flesh." As the medieval theologian Thomas Aquinas would say later, God intentionally appointed human beings to be spiritually inclined material creatures. This is, he said, "our appointed realm."

Therefore, Christians confess the resurrection of the body. By this we mean that it is not only the human spirit, soul, and mind that are being transformed in Christ, but the human body as well.

The doctrine of the Incarnation thus leads to a sacramental view of all of reality. Just as the incarnation involves the enfleshment of spirit, sacrament involves the spiritualization of matter. Together, incarnation and sacrament form what the patristic writers called "Jacob's ladder." In fact, to them Jacob's ladder was Christ Himself. For having bridged—with his own body—the great gulf between form and substance, Christ now invites human beings to ascend this ladder (himself) upon which heaven has descended to earth and upon which earth is now invited to ascend into heaven.

Even though Christian theology borrowed some of these terms and concepts from Neoplatonism, the doctrine of the incarnation prohibited any Christian from being a thoroughly convinced Neo-Platonist. Although ancient and medieval Christians drew heavily upon neo-platonic concepts, they radically modified those concepts in the light of their belief that God intended to sanctify the material world. Therefore, it would not be reason alone that raised us to God, but matter—specifically the material body of Jesus Christ.

Plato and all ancient Platonists would have viewed this idea as utterly repulsive.

Christian insistence that Jesus Christ had risen from the dead *bodily* and that the fullness of the godhead had dwelt in Christ *bodily*, prohibited believers from despising matter. However, the idea that matter could be sanctified also created a space for an opposite error —idolatry.

If God alone was to be worshipped, what were Christians to do with sanctified space and objects?

The tension between belief in sanctified matter and God's prohibition against idolatry created the same dilemma for Christians that ancient Israelites had faced. God made an object (a snake on a pole) the means of healing in one generation and then called for its destruction centuries later because veneration for the object morphed into idolatry.

Respect became homage.

An instrument of worship had become its object.

We can see then that Christians inherited this tension between sacred symbol and idolatry. Each year, as I hear the readings on Ash Wednesday, I marvel at how this tension plays out in the life of the church. The readings always include Isaiah's sarcastic tirade.

"Is this the fast I have chosen, for you to throw ashes on your head or bow down like a reed? Why don't you humble your-selves by addressing injustice? Feed the hungry and clothe the naked. Why not try that?"

Isaiah 58:6

I have often used this passage for my Ash Wednesday homily because it points to the tension between symbol as a means of spiritual awakening and symbol as a mindless ritual. When symbol points to itself, it becomes an idol. Healthy spiritual experience occurs by looking at what a symbol points toward, rather than at symbol itself.

The question naturally arises, why we should then not just dispense with symbol?

We should aways welcome this question because it's an extremely important one.

A ring does not create a marriage. However, a bride and groom faithfully repeat the words "with this ring I thee wed." We do not really "pledge allegiance to a flag" but "to the nation for which it stands." God and human beings choose some objects to participate in a higher reality than what their surface appearance suggests. As long as the object effectively moves our attention to that higher reality, it should be respected. If, on the other hand, the object begins to obscure the spiritual reality for which it was chosen to communicate, it must be discarded.

Money is a good example. A dollar bill is made of paper. However, it is a special kind of paper. We have chosen it to represent a value much greater than its material components. If we agree about that, money remains valuable. If we change our minds about it, it becomes merely paper.

I own a 10,000 German mark with the picture of Kaiser William on it. It is worth about five American dollars to people who collect obsolete currency.

In spiritual life, the issue is more serious. Sacrament exists within a tension between a gnostic denial of its worth on one hand and an idolatrous obsession with it on the other.

That very tension is the central theme of the Frisco Kid, an old comedy.

Rabbi Avram Belinsky is traveling across the old West to a synagogue in San Francisco. He's carrying with him the sacred Torah he brought from Poland. We watch as he faithfully protects the scroll. Finally, he faces a situation in which he can either save an outlaw's life or preserve the sacred Torah. Torn by his excruciating choice, the rabbi finally forces himself to save the man's life. The Torah falls into the campfire.

Later, clutching a damaged but still intact Torah, he prays for forgiveness. The outlaw tries to console the rabbi, pointing out that in the end he has saved the Torah. The rabbi responds that he is not repenting for risking the Torah. He's repenting for having made the mistake that the Torah was more important than a human life.

It was right for the rabbi to venerate the Torah. It is after all, God's instructions to humanity. As Psalm 119 so beautifully says, the teachings of God are infinitely precious. However, we only venerate a material text because of what comes through it. If we fail to learn what comes through the text, our adoration of the text becomes a spiritual obstacle. That was the lesson the rabbi learned.

An incarnational/sacramental view of life is lived out between biblical boundaries. Yes, matter can be consecrated because matter ultimately participates in God's transformation of the universe. Nonetheless, the respect of consecrated things must not become idolatrous.

The struggle with what a healthy incarnational view of reality looks like has always divided the Christian community. The use of icons, the view of the Eucharist, the purpose of baptism, the correct way to think of Christ's humanity, the importance of relics (such as the Shroud of Turin) has been, and remain still, divisive.

Our purpose here is not to settle those disputes. What we want to do here is point out that Christianity's internal disputes emerge from an inescapable paradox. Worshipping Christ as the Incarnate God forces those who believe in him to disavow both materialism and idealism. Nonetheless, believers must also struggle with the implications of living in a universe in which neither matter nor spirit are ever reducible to the other but in which both emerge from a common, transcendent source: the Word of God. The same Word of God who became a material human being in Jesus Christ.

The implication of Jesus's words, "He that hath seen me hath seen the Father," is that in Christ, matter and spirit have been united and interfused. That is why for Christians, matter matters. Spirituality cannot be for us a way to ignore material objects and processes.

Jesus

For a Christian, it is both easy and challenging to write about Jesus. The reason it's easy is because we experience Christ as the center of everything. The reason it's challenging is because piety shapes a believer's words in spiritually intimate ways. This can hinder meaningful conversation with non-Christians.

This book is not a devotional. It is an exploration of how we can respond to the contemporary world in ways that are faithful to our belief in Christ. Our challenge is that a Christian naturally seeks to introduce others to Christ. However, that can alienate those who are open to conversation but do not wish to be evangelized.

We must therefore learn to thread the needle, honestly admitting to what we believe but without violating the will and reason of our neighbors. If what Christianity claims is true, then Jesus makes himself known. The best we can do is represent him well in our character and respect for others.

This section about the historical Jesus Christ is brief. That is not because Jesus is less important than other topics in this book. To the contrary, it is because the life of Christ is of such supreme importance to me that it could easily consume everything else. Also, studies on the life of Christ are numerous, varied, and easy to find. I seriously doubt I will add much to them.

There is another reason why my remarks about Jesus, though scattered throughout the book, are relatively limited. My personal piety precedes and can easily overwhelm both my theology and philosophy. However, piety does not form a common ground upon which we can meet with non-Christians.

My reverence for Christ is restrained here because I want to focus on how Christians can form healthy interactions with others.

Here's an analogy. If you learn that my wife and I have two biological children, you will correctly assume that we must have made love. That said, no one, including my children, wants to hear anything more about it. It's not shame that causes us to parse our words or to restrain talk about intimate life though. It is the respect that my wife and I have for one another and that others have for us that creates the boundaries of our conversation where personal intimacy is involved.

At any rate, the story about Jesus is simple and well known.

It begins with an unmarried woman becoming pregnant, a woman who insists that she has not had any sort of sexual relationship with anyone else. After a few agonizing weeks, her fiancée, who has a supernatural encounter of his own, believes her story.

The months go by. By the time for the baby to arrive, the couple, filing their taxes in their ancestral village, cannot find a place to stay. They ultimately settle for a cave that has served as a shelter for an inn keeper's animals. After the child is born, the mother and her husband gently lay the child in a feeding trough that they covered with rags.

The baby thus began his life in poverty, among farm animals.

Every year, Christians around the world recreate the scene in churches, homes, and open spaces.

Our Lord was a Jewish child. So, he was circumcised in the temple, in obedience to the law. An old man and woman who prophesied about the significance of the child's life were the only witnesses.

The only scene we have from his childhood is the Bar Mitzva. Jesus astounds his teachers with perceptive questions and commentary on the law. He is so enthralled with his interaction with the teachers that he got separated from his parents and went missing for three days.

After this incident, we are told nothing except that Jesus developed physically, mentally, socially, and spiritually.

Everything else about the life of the historical Christ focuses on his last three years, which he uses to teach and heal the sick. The Gospel writers pay considerable attention to Jesus's last week on earth, especially his violent death by crucifixion.

Contemporary believers often ignore St. Luke's claim, that the final chapter of Christ's physical presence on earth was the forty days after his resurrection. During this time, Jesus taught his disciples "those things concerning the kingdom of God" and "opened their eyes to the scriptures." The great scholar Jaroslav Peligan claims that the entire New Testament emerges from these forty days.

That is the crux of what we know of the historical Jesus of Nazareth.

That is not satisfying for most of us. We want more information than we have. Believers have often felt this way. Even the Apostle John concluded his gospel with the exasperated confession that he had merely brushed the surface. "If all the things that Jesus said or did were written, the worlds of worlds would not contain the books," John said. Admittedly, that is a bit hyperbolic. His point is clear enough though: "I have not been able to get to the depths about this life as well as I had hoped."

Naturally, if the great apostle John didn't believe himself capable of doing justice to the story of Jesus, we cannot blame ourselves for failing at that task. The attempt must be made, nonetheless.

Everything in the book you are reading revolves around my conviction that God created the universe and that in Jesus Christ, God lived as one of us. If these things are true, however we explain or describe them, physical reality is considerably different than what either a materialist or an idealist claim. That is this book's central premise. It hangs on whether Jesus Christ lived as the Gospel writers describe or is a literary character, they either invented or exaggerated.

C. S. Lewis faces this issue head on in *Mere Christianity*. Jesus cannot be for us merely a moral teacher, like the venerable Lao Tzu or the insightful Buddha, Lewis insisted. Neither of these great teachers claimed to be God. By claiming to be God, Jesus forced us to decide if he was mentally ill, a con man, or just perhaps, who he claimed to be.

It's not a choice contemporary people, including some professing believers, wish to make. Eventually though, we must make it. Even professing Christians must make it, perhaps several times in our life. This is especially true for contemporary believers. We are, after all, children of our own times. After centuries of secular materialism, perhaps we should claim the apostle Thomas as our patron saint. He was after all the disciple who said in effect, I am still here with the rest of you, but I will believe Jesus is alive when he walks through the door.

My uncle says that he stopped calling St. Thomas "Doubting Thomas" years ago. He prefers to call him Honest Thomas. It is certainly comforting for contemporary people that Thomas was not dismissed from Christ's company because he doubted. In the end, Thomas also believed. In fact, Thomas was the first disciple to call Jesus God.

Thomas was convinced by material evidence of the resurrection —the living body of Jesus. He had seen the Lord's lifeless body reverently placed in a tomb. Days later, he saw that same body, now reanimated, and transformed. At least that was the conclusion Thomas reached.

There are excellent books that demonstrate the reasonability of the resurrection. My purpose is to explore what belief in the life, death, and resurrection of Christ implies about reality. I want to know how those who believe in Christ can, in word and deed, enter healthy conversation with the increasingly secular world around us.

I appreciate and admire apologetics. It's a useful and admirable calling. That is just not my main purpose here. Apologetics is, at any rate, more of a catechistical tool than an evangelistic one. Nearly always, the thing that arouses and draws a soul's attention to Christ is an encounter with a transformed life.

A saint, in other words.

So, it is to that subject to which we now turn: the personal transformation of human beings into living signs of God's presence, power, and love.

16

Restoring The Image

Healing individuals and communities involves restoring providential intent to bodies, minds, societies, and ecological structures.

IN THE LAST CHAPTER, WE LOOKED AT HOW THE DOCTRINE OF incarnation leads to a Christian emphasis on healing.

Numerous hospitals and schools exist throughout the world, even in nations with few Christians, because believers in Christ, often through great sacrifice, have focused on alleviating human suffering.

These institutions were often founded to draw people to Christ. Therefore, one often finds Christian symbols on their walls. Also, in hospitals especially, there is often a chapel, open to the public. Contemporary society tends to experience these consecrated spaces as manipulative. From a Christian perspective though, physical healing cannot be separated from mental or spiritual life. For Christians, the medical arts are components of a multi-layered assault on everything that seeks to deform God's image and likeness in human beings, or which diminishes the well-being of the created order.

Healing is, in other words a broad concept, covering any sort of restoration of the physical, social, or personal lives of human beings. Indeed, it is applicable as well to the care of the natural ecological order. For a Christian, cleaning a river to eliminate obstacles to life; restoring sanity to a diseased mind; repairing a broken leg; assisting a soul in its quest for forgiveness and transformation in Christ; and creating a vaccine to overcome viral infection, are all related to bringing creation into alignment with its Creator. Healing is thus multifaceted.

This definition of healing implies that believers and nonbelievers can be united in the common quest for human flourishing. Christians who define salvation and sanctification too narrowly lose sight of this common ground.

The Greek word *sozo* is one of the ancient concepts we should consider here because the New Testament word contained layers of meaning that we gradually came to differentiate into disconnected terms. Sozo originally referred to the healing of a body, the salvation of a soul, the transformation of a community, the overcoming of an addiction, and a deliverance from physical danger. Sozo, in other words, is the power that brings individuals and communities to health and wholeness, both in time and for all eternity.

Saints

For Christians, the primary sign of God's presence within human society are human beings who exude holiness. The theological term describing the process through which this occurs is sanctification. Individuals who seem far into the process are called saints. The word saint is used differently in the various Christian expressions, and some would not prefer the definition I am using here. However, it's the popular way the word saint is used outside of a theological context.

Saints usually evoke deep respect from others, even from the nonreligious. People are usually moved when meeting someone moving toward integration and authenticity. Although Christians believe that saints are fallen and therefore imperfect people, we honor what they are becoming. We also want to be like them though, like young horny Augustine, we may add "but not yet."

Saints come in all sizes, shapes, and dispositions. Some are markedly intelligent. Some are not. Some are funny. Others are serious. Some do miracles. Some struggle with doubt. Some write books. Some repair a neighbor's roof. Some build hospitals. Some are wealthy. Some are poor. Some are single. Some are married. Some are mentally ill. Some struggle with addiction. Most are unknown.

The only thing the saints have in common is a joy that transcends their material circumstances. Perhaps the best synonym for saint is "life-giving." After one has been in the presence of a saintly person, one feels as though his or her batteries have been charged. In a word, saints are a reflection, and a promise of that ultimate state Christians believe God intends for all people.

Without this incomplete but essential sign of God's work of redemption, it would be difficult to believe that anything about the Christian message is true. We have no video of either the Resurrection or the Exodus. If we are supposed to believe in these events and the beliefs and practices we derive from them, it's not unreasonable to ask for an indication that we are not "following cleverly devised fables," as the Apostle Peter puts it. A transformed human life would be such an indication.

Put another way, if, as Christians profess, human beings are called to be the stewards of Creation, we ought to expect that following Christ produces real, observable changes in how one relates to the material and the social world. As the old circuit-rider preacher claimed, "The first one to notice that someone is converted may be the family dog."

Sanctification is a process. So, we should not deny that real change is occurring simply because we think someone's life (including our own) falls short of perfection. Sanctification transforms one as they continue their journey. It is a byproduct of loving God and loving others rather than the main goal of one's life. Paradoxically, as one's spiritual journey continues, one becomes ever more aware of their imperfections. Because of this, the spiritual seeker will not be aware that others experience them as a life-giving person.

A saint is formed by living out their vocation. They struggle through the issues of life like everyone else. However, those who observe them watch how they treat people with dignity and grace. They are a conscientious steward of the resources under their influence. They stumble and fall, but they get back up. They keep walking. They radiate hope. People find their presence transformational. After being with them, others find themselves thinking that their own lives matter.

Christians often long to explain to others why they believe in God. Some of us long for signs and wonders to prove God's existence to a disbelieving world. So, we learn techniques. We master marketing tricks. We build religious enterprises and empires. Alas, we write books.

In the end, the most convincing "proof" of God's presence is a person who once was lost and has been found, who once was blind but now can see.

The world wants to see God in the face of another human being. People want to meet a real saint.

Such people, always in-process and never entirely free of human imperfection, are the principle means through which Christ makes himself known and through whom he continues to heal the world. Tina Turner said, "We don't need another hero." However, we desperately need the saints.

Saints at Work

The ministry of Jesus could be summed up in a single word: healing.

Most of Christ's miracles involved healing sick bodies. However, Jesus also fed the hungry and addressed the ills of society. Furthermore, these were not means to some greater end. He didn't heal people so they would "get saved." He healed them because they were sick. Healing—at every level of existence—was his mission.

Earlier in this book, I reflected on how Christians view the cosmos as governed through multiple systems of structures we call "providence." However, Christianity also teaches that the universe is not fully as God intended. Either it has gone awry, or it awaits full perfection (scripture contains both explanations). Whichever explanation we prefer, this Christian view of the universe as lacking wholeness leads to our emphasis on healing. This concern is demonstrated when we care for those who are sick in mind or body, when we address communal dysfunctions, and when we seek to repair the nonhuman parts of creation. In every case, healing is about restoring God's providential intent (as best we understand it) to bodies, minds, societies, and the natural environment.

In this view, all types of illness involve a loss of providential form. Action undertaken to address that loss is a participation in the Creator's work. God has assigned humanity the responsibility of caring for creation. Therefore, the work of healing is a participation in God's governance of the world. A believer usually en ters this exercise of stewardship through prayer and other spiritual practices. However, unbelievers may also participate, though without full awareness of God's existence or of God's aim for creation.

Sometimes, as believers carry out their specific part in the care of God's creation, they experience unusual occurrences through which healing, provision, or guidance seem to come from "out of the blue." Most believers have stories about such occurrences. From the outside, and indeed to the believers themselves, these occurrences take the form of uncanny coincidences. Very occasionally, as in the case of a spontaneous recovery from serious illness, we are left without a natural explanation.

Christians believe that supernatural responses to prayer are always possible. Most of the time, however, prayer leads to fresh insight that advances the work of healing in natural, non-spooky ways. Even then, a believer remains aware that as he or she works, help may come through unusual and inexplicable sources and circumstances.

George Muller (1805-1894), a German born immigrant to the United Kingdom, became disillusioned by the thousands of orphans that roamed England's large cities. He began to doubt that God was concerned about these children. During a time of intense prayer, Muller expressed this disillusionment. He accused God of being calloused about the plight of England's orphans. Suddenly, he felt

God speaking deep in his soul, "I will care for these children through you."

The impoverished immigrant immediately began to look for ways to gather the children. For the rest of his life, Muller founded orphanages. The work pricked England's conscience and alleviated the social conditions addressed in Dickens' Christmas Carol and other stories from that era.

Christian history, beginning in the Book of Acts, is full of adventures like the one Muller had. They continued through the following centuries and occur still.

Loren Cunningham (1935-), founder of Youth with a Mission, purchased and outfitted a fleet of Mercy Ships with sophisticated medical equipment without money or medical training. For decades, these Mercy Ships have docked in ports throughout the globe, offering care to the world's poorest people.

Dorothy Day (1897-1980) was a reluctant convert to Catholicism. Her previous life as a secular Marxist gradually transformed into care for America's urban poor in the name of Christ. She lifted a prophetic voice against the nation's financial and societal exploitation of the poor. However, she is most known for founding and maintaining food kitchens that prodded the conscience of her church, her city, and her country.

Christians do not always agree with one another about the root causes of poverty, or about what constitutes societal dysfunction, or about how to address these things. What Christians agree on is that all these issues are critical concerns of those who follow Christ. As a result, it is not unusual for Christians to acknowledge the work of people with whom they politically and theologically disagree. The two people we have discussed here serve as good examples. Loren Cunningham and Dorothy Day represent different social/political viewpoints. Nonetheless, they would affirm the goodness of the work the other undertook to alleviate human suffering in God's name.

Ecological Healing

This section is the last part of the book I wrote. Although I have some strong feelings about ecology, I struggled to arrive at a way to express my thoughts that readers would not find either alienating or hollow. I went to bed the night before writing it wondering about how to begin.

When I awoke the following morning, an old hymn was running through my mind:

> *O Lord my God, When I in awesome wonder*
> *Consider all the worlds Thy hands have made.*
> *I see the stars; I hear the rolling thunder—*
> *Thy power throughout the universe displayed.*
> *Then sings my soul, my Savior God to Thee*
> *How great Thou art. How great Thou art!*

The hymn, as many hymns do, paraphrases a Psalm, the eighth Psalm to be specific.

Oh Lord, my Lord, how majestic is Thy name in all the earth . . . when I consider the heavens, the moon, and the stars that Thou hast ordained, what is man that Thou are mindful of him?

The Psalm goes on to consider the other creatures who inhabit the same planet in which the Psalmist makes his own home. He asks God why he has been made caretaker of this planet since only God fully understands the purpose of creation. Although it is a hymn of adoration, it is also an acknowledgment of a responsibility.

The Psalm is a poetic expression of what it means to steward the earth on behalf of its creator. This stewardship is, in fact, the very first instruction given to humanity in Genesis. We are to dress, till, and manage the earth. As our first instruction, one would think it foundational to every other spiritual practice, rather like how arithmetic comes before geometry or calculus.

In fact, Christians have rarely made "dressing and tilling the earth" a fundamental part of either their theology or practice. There are exceptions though. St. Francis of Assisi made the care of animals a priority. St. Seraphim of Sarov is said to have tamed bears and wolves and to have walked peaceably with wild animals of various kinds. Monks have often tended gardens, one of whom (Gregor Mendel) launched the modern field of genetics.

Overall, however, care of the earth has not been at the forefront of Christian concern. One of the culprits of this neglect is a certain kind of apocalyptic perspective that views material creation as temporary and expendable. As one mountain gospel song puts it, "This world is not my home; I'm just a passin' through." This is paradoxically enough, a gnostic and not a Judeo-Christian view of creation. In Gnostic thought, matter hinders the soul from entering its true condition: spirit. In contrast, Hebrew and Christian scriptures view material creation as the handiwork of God and God's chosen home for human beings.

What then would a Christian ecology look like?

Well, it would be based on stewardship rather than on kinship with other creatures. Judeo-Christianity does not deny the kinship of animals and plants to human beings of course. However, unlike most forms of the contemporary ecological movement, a biblical view discourages human beings from taking any sort of reverential stance toward nature. The world and its contents are described as belonging to God, who has delegated to human beings the managerial responsibility for their care. At first, they are not allowed to eat meat. This changes after the flood. However, the manner and scope of meat eating is carefully prescribed.

Orthodox Ecumenical Patriarch Bartholomew has written extensively about how these elements form the basis for a Christian approach to ecology. His appeal to Christians for taking up the care of the earth as a form of spiritual practice led Pope Francis to adopt a similar position. The Pope articulates his own views in an encyclical called *Laudate Si*. As one would expect, the two men approach ecology in a way consistent with their respective communities. Together, they offer a rich and complementary format upon which other Christian expressions can build.

In the United States anyway, some Christians are highly suspicious of any undue interest in ecology. For them, the idea that human beings have anything to do with the management of creation seems prideful. After all, can a human being move a star? Can he decide the time of the tide? The Bible itself sometimes takes this line. In Job, God asks Job where he had been as God had formed the universe. God even sarcastically implies that he could have used some help, had Job, with all his wisdom, been around at the time. God then asks Job if he knows how to make it snow or can catch a sea monster with a hook.

The balance between acknowledging what God alone can do and doing what human beings are responsible to do is a core issue of Christian theology. In a sense, it is the very question that leads one Christian to decide that human effort in spiritual matters is not only ineffectual, but also unwelcome, even wicked. Another Christian, on the other hand, will view human response as part of the work God wishes to empower. In the specific matter of ecological concern then, Christians will probably draw the line at different places on what human beings are responsible to do.

Today, most Christians will agree that water and air should be kept clean and if they are polluted, we should do all we can to improve them. They also tend to agree that companies should be required to clean up after themselves. Indeed, contemporary companies often agree as well.

These are relatively new opinions. Throughout the industrial revolution and well into the decades following the second world war, the Christian world filled the skies of its cities with great clouds of soot. The factories dumped untold amounts of waste products in the water. It was not a biblical or theological response that began to change matters; it was a secular form of ecology.

The ecology movement successfully convinced the population that clear air and water was a bare-minimum standard for human survival. However, more ambitious ecological aims, such as preserving animal habitats and restraining development in old forest areas, have had much more limited success. Often that has been due to the ecologist movement's lack of sensitivity toward the working class's anxieties about their own economic sustainability, a matter of great concern for most Christians.

What has been missing in discussions about environmental sustainability has been a Christian perspective that views the matter as a moral concern. By that I do not mean some form of scolding, directed at either working people or business leaders. A Christian approach must take such legitimate interests seriously. Indeed, it seeks to include the people affected by ecological care in the conversation.

Most people do not want their descendants to live in a world without bees or butterflies, even if such a world were livable. Nonetheless, they must eat now. When they hear people whom they view as representing an elite class lecturing them on how we are treating the environment and notice that these folk live lives they only dream of, it is understandable when they shrug their shoulders and stay the course.

The sort of Christian approach to ecology championed by the Patriarch and the Pope may not entirely resonate with Evangelicals, but they have made a good start. At any rate, the conversation is unavoidable. Even younger generations of Evangelicals know this, but they often have no other frame of reference than secular forms of environmentalism that scare their parents and grandparents.

For me, this issue connects best with the subject of healing. A disruption of the patterns of creation develops a dysfunctional system. When that occurs to the human body, we call it sin. When it occurs to a community, we call it injustice. In all these cases, dysfunction requires healing, and healing requires healers.

Mental Health

In a way, including a short section on mental health in this book is a redundancy. The entire collection of essays emerged from a set of statements for Christian mental health workers. I have graduate and post-graduate degrees in the subject and have served in mental health centers. However, my central vocation has been pastoring local parishes and caring for clergy as an Anglican bishop. My doctorate is in ministry. As a result, I spent several years listening to an ongoing conversation in my head between psychology and theology. Assuming that I would find a link in philosophy, I worked to gain an adequate grounding in that field.

The conversation took another turn during the global pandemic. I had just retired from the church I had pastored for several years. Travel for my episcopal duties also stopped. Meanwhile, a counseling center near my house asked me to work part time with them. The state of Tennessee even sent out temporary licenses to those with the appropriate academic credentials who had worked in mental health.

As I began seeing clients three days a week, I began working on a set of statements about what I believed was an appropriate and ethical foundation for serving the general population from a Christian perspective. After reading over these statements for several weeks, I began writing reflections on them. This book is the result.

In brief, my view of mental health emerges not only from my training but from a conviction that human beings, made in God's own image and likeness, are nonetheless born bent. Both as individuals and communities, human beings, including therapists, neurologists, and priests struggle with multiple levels of dysfunction. Because human beings are material creatures who have been invited to participate in spiritual life, human dysfunctions have both material and spiritual sources. Brain and neurological illnesses afflict both "the just and the unjust." So do psychological ones. So do spiritual ones. So do unconscious philosophical conflicts.

A Christian therapist, in my opinion, holds all these possibilities in mind as they seek to ease the burden of those who come to them for help. Sometimes, we uncover an addiction. Sometimes it's early childhood trauma. Sometimes, we must rule out Parkinson's or dementia and so send a client to a neurologist. Some need medication. Some need training in how to move through (or out of) a seriously dysfunctional family. Some need care for spiritual abuse, or advice for leaving a cult.

I work with the salt of the earth in this field. The psychologists, neurologists, psychiatrists, and the various kinds of therapists I know are hardworking, loving people. Whether or not they are Christians is not my central concern when it comes to treating people in need of help. I want to know about their competence and ethics. That said, the belief that human beings have a spiritual nature profoundly affects the way a therapist thinks about their clients. It is both illegal and unethical to proselytize vulnerable people. However, I have often fervently prayed in the privacy of my car for insight and wisdom in treating someone. I am sure most Christian therapists do this.

The Lord I attempt to serve once said, "Come unto me, all you who are weary, and I will give you rest." There have been few eras of history in which so many would identify themselves as in need of rest from the burdens of their own addictive behaviors, their disillusionment with nation, church, and family, and from the general loss of meaning so endemic of our times.

Mental health is always a relative, moving target. So, the first and most important part of healing is the radical hospitality we offer to the weary and heavy laden. We tell them they are not freaks. We tell them they are welcome. Then we comfort them with the comfort that we ourselves have been given.

Many years ago, I walked into a mental health facility for the first time in my life. I felt like a failure for my inability to care for myself. My church environment was profoundly twisted and had no health to export. It had been a good business and had attracted many sad and lonely people. However, I had lost the conviction that our church had been a benefit to those who attended.

Fortunately, I had experience with how Christian community can offer the sort of love and acceptance that changes lives. I had seen that at work in jungle churches covered with thatched roofs. I had seen it in the inner city and in college basements.

As I went deeper into the recovery movement, attending groups, seeing therapists, getting marriage therapy, and finally returning to graduate school to study the field for myself, I experienced a new encounter with grace.

This book is my attempt to address what my journey has been about: turning myself over to the care of a good Creator, who is not willing that any should perish.

17

Above Us More Than Sky

The Creator not only communicates through providence and through the incarnation but through a personal, conscious Divine Presence who is "other than" creation while permeating creation and all its parts. This Presence communicates with human beings in ways that can be discerned, evaluated, and clarified.

THE MOST EXEMPLARY STATEMENT ABOUT CONTEMPORARY CULTURE in the West is probably Charles Taylor's book, *A Secular Age*.

Taylor's central point is that Western peoples, particularly those living in what he calls the North Atlantic nations, have been steadily dismissing the concept of transcendence. The idea here is that nothing exists beyond the material world or, if it does, it's of little practical significance.

Taylor believes that even Western Christians have gradually lost belief in (and certainly experience of) transcendence.

John Lennon's "Imagine" expresses this loss of transcendence as a freedom from superstition that allows us to live in peace with ourselves and with others. It was what Taylor meant by "dismissing transcendence."

Whatever his personal view, it's difficult to deny that Taylor put his finger on a core characteristic of postmodern culture. I also find it difficult to repute Taylor's claim that Western Christians have largely accepted this spiritual shift.

The loss of transcendence is the reason some American believers have recently justified taking up arms to defend their political beliefs. It is also why progressive Protestants have increasingly turned to beliefs that are difficult to defend by scripture or Christian tradition. Both sides of the church's political aisle seem to have given up on the hope that God directly intervenes in human affairs or that a human individual can be transformed in Christ.

Nonetheless, most human beings long to touch something beyond their everyday material existence. When God seems to become unavailable, we use sex, drugs, art—something powerful enough to capture our attention—in hopes of touching the sublime. Even when one suspects they are fooling themself, knowing full well that after the drugs wear off or the weekend ends, they must return to their mundane world, the momentary flights into otherness may feel essential for thinking that life matters.

Certainly, making a living is challenging when one believes their life is without meaning. Something must give somewhere.

In the light of human history, it's a curious thing to live in a society in which so many define the core of reality in economic terms. Contemporary society acknowledges that religion, art, and love are at the very least necessary diversions for keeping human beings interested enough in life to keep going to work. Unfortunately, though, when making a living becomes the real aim of one's life, it becomes increasingly impossible not to suspect that life itself may be insignificant.

We can hardly blame anyone in this case from snorting something or sleeping with someone, at least on the weekends, to soothe the pain of meaninglessness.

Accepting the awful truth about one's ultimate insignificance, either as an individual or as a species, seriously alters the meaning of art, religion, and love. Such things, once part of the core of life, now become unsatisfying diversions, like the sound of the band playing on the decks of the Titanic. We barely hear the music as we peer into the freezing water.

I see no reason to camouflage the toxicity of a meaningless world. For me, it smells of death. If "the real world" is about buying and selling, then to hell with it. Buying and selling cannot anesthetize a culture in the grip of nihilism, the belief that nothing matters.

So, what do we do about the loss of transcendence?

Mindless leaps into religious sentimentality, however tempting, do not differ from taking a sacred mushroom or enjoying an erotic romp. On the other hand, any kind of transcendent experience can awaken a sleeping soul, reminding a person that they are truly alive and unique—that they matter.

In Deuteronomy, Moses says to the people of Israel, "Behold, I set before you both life and death, choose life that you may live."

That's what Christians mean when confessing the Nicene Creed. They quote this line:

> *"I believe in the Holy Spirit, the Lord, the Giver of Life, who together with the Father and Son are worshipped and adored."*

This line reveals why Christianity does not survive the loss of transcendence. In fact, this question of transcendence may well be the point of maximum incompatibility between Christianity and the contemporary secular world. Without an existential ground of being, Christianity becomes either a coercive code of pointless rules or a performance of aesthetically moving pageantry. In neither case does it point at anything beyond itself.

If there is no "otherness," Christianity fails.

One cannot reconcile the Nicene Creed with Lennon's "Imagine."

The song is eloquent. As a musician, I respect it. As a believer, however, I hear it as a dirge, a soulful cry of utter loss. As it expresses a deep longing for brotherhood, it fails to tell us how such a thing is possible or even desirable. If above us there is only godless sky, then all values, including universal peace, are uncompelling contrivances.

"Imagine" expresses in few words what Taylor takes over seven hundred pages to say. On the other hand, Taylor, unlike Lennon, realizes that living in a secular age comes at great cost. Taylor is not an evangelist. He is a diagnostician. He tells our culture that it has a spiritual disease that will probably end its life.

Fortunately, I believe there is a cure for this disease. It's an experiential relationship with the One the Nicene Creed calls The Lord, the Giver of Life.

The Holy Spirit

It is probably fair to say that Western Christianity has never had a fully developed theology of the Holy Spirit. The formal theology is *pneumatology*, a topic that makes most Western theologians a bit nervous. In contrast, the Eastern Churches have paid much more attention to the Person and the work of the Holy Spirit. We will draw on some of that tradition here.

For most Western people, though, the easiest onramp into pneumatic experience, better said as "an introduction to the Presence of God," is the worship offered by African American forms of Christianity.

Pentecostalism is an extension of the Black Church experience and deserves an important place in any conversation about transcendence. I need a few paragraphs to qualify that statement, however.

Pentecostalism grew out of two different kinds of socially marginalized peoples: the feed slaves and the Appalachian poor. Methodism had influenced these groups early in American history. After the Civil War, however, splinter groups—collectively called the Holiness Movement—shook themselves free from the ecclesial and liturgical constraints of the parent body. This opened opportunities for socially marginalized people to address their own spiritual and emotional needs. This resulted in a racially integrated grass-roots movement that reshaped American Christianity.

As White Pentecostals began integrating themselves into the American religious mainstream, they gradually adopted the theological language of fundamentalism. The fundamentalist mindset was at its heart *cessationist* (meaning that all spiritual gifts ended in the New Testament era), which altered the way they expressed their spiritual views. It also tended to downplay what had been the original taproot of Pentecostal spirituality: a deep connection with socially alienated and disinherited peoples.

By the mid twentieth century, the grandchildren of Pentecostalism's founders began moving with the rest of the nation away from rural settings and into urban communities. Increasingly anxious to escape their impoverished holy-roller image and participate in the nation's growing prosperity, they began to rethink their social and economic views. The health and wealth teaching of much of contemporary Pentecostalism emerged during this period. It was as though Mr. Potter in the movie *It's a Wonderful Life*, had become a professing Christian but without changing his views on the self-justifying respectability of wealth.

With these qualifying statements in mind, I return to the claim that the Christian experience and theology of transcendence is rooted in the person and work of the Holy Spirit.

It's not my aim here to examine the different views of the Holy Spirit one encounters in the various expressions of Christianity. Rather, I want to envision how an awareness of the Holy Spirit's presence leads believers to discern how God may be at work in places where Christ is not yet named. I want to think about how the Holy Spirit quickens the mind and heart with new insight, how he strengthens the work of healing in the world.

I assume that the Holy Spirit is not confined to the Christian Church. Scripture begins with a universal view, establishing college concern for all of creation before it moves that focus to the specific mission of Israel. As Genesis begins, the Spirit broods over an unformed universe in which there is no family of Abraham or Christian Church. This implies that the Spirit is interested and involved in nature. So, while the Holy Spirit is most fully known and experienced by believers, the Holy Spirit is nonetheless present in everything, everywhere.

In the early centuries of its development, Christianity concluded that the Holy Spirit was a divine person and not an impersonal force. Therefore, to experience the Holy Spirit is to experience God.

A rabbi once asked me to explain how Christians can think of the Holy Spirit as Person. After thinking a moment, I pointed out how in the Old Testament the *Shekinah*—the word derives from the Hebrew word for presence or dwelling—hovered in a visible form above the Tabernacle. Although the word Shekinah does not appear in the Bible, it is the subject of Rabbinical texts. Curiously, it became a term used by early Pentecostals to describe their own experience.

The Christian usage of the word Shekinah is appropriate because New Testament believers also claimed to see the descent of the Holy Spirit. The difference between the Old and New Testament appearances was this: instead of hovering over a physical holy place, as we read in Exodus, in the Book of Acts the Holy Spirit hovers over individuals. St. Luke makes the point that the tongues of fire become "cloven" (separated) into individualized expressions. St Paul refers to this individuated work of the Holy Spirit when he refers to believers as members of a body or stones of a spiritual temple.

As an aside, the holy fire that Eastern Orthodox believers experience on Easter replicates the New Testament account. In the Orthodox experience, a single fire emerges from the tomb to settle on individual candles held by the worshippers standing outside.

In Christian theology, the Holy Spirit works to prepare individuals for hearing the Word of God and believing in Christ. Believers gathered for worship should thus make themselves aware of the Spirit's Presence, trusting that the Spirit is present to convict, enlighten, and guide them.

Christianity also teaches that the Spirit enlightens believers about what they are called to do, as well as empowers them to carry the calling out. Therefore, the concept of vocation (as opposed to occupation) is so important to Christians. The sense that one has been called to do something has a very different feel about it than merely doing something one is expected to do.

In Eastern Orthodox theology, the Spirit descends upon the altar in a moment called the *epiclesis*. This serves as a picture of how Christians offer their minds and bodies for the supernatural strength needed to accomplish the work God has called them to do. However, the Spirit hovers above all people and all movements that bring healing into the world. Mature believers thus learn to discern the Spirit's presence even in places where Christ is not yet named. They then adjust themselves to cooperate with the Holy Spirit to further the day when the knowledge of the Lord shall fill the earth, the sea, and the sky.

The Work of the Spirit in the World

So far, I have talked about how Christian's experience and explain the work of the Holy Spirit, within the Church and in their personal lives. For the rest of this chapter, I want to focus on the work of the Holy Spirit in the world at large.

As we have mentioned several times here, the Bible first mentions the Holy Spirit in the second verse of Genesis.

"And the Spirit of God (Hebrew: *Rauch Elohim*) was hovering over the face of the waters."[1]

The word *rauch* does not yet differentiate between breath, wind, or Spirit. The original word contained all these meanings. That is why Bible translators sometimes render it in English as wind or breath. Indeed, it's perfectly right to read the passage as referring to a mighty wind, or Divine Breath.

The focus of this Divine Wind is primal chaos, and we enter the story just as God is preparing to command the undifferentiated matter to form the differences and distinctions that we will come to know as the visible universe.

The Hebrew word translated here as "hovering," is seldom encountered in scripture. It implies protection and care and, in some cases, hints of sexual intercourse. The possible sexual innuendo adds an important nuance to the creation story since, in sexual life, one hovers over another to bring new life into the world.

The implication of care and concern suggests the way a hen hovers over her chicks. That is precisely as it is used in Deuteronomy 13:11, where God's love for Israel is compared to the way an eagle hovers over her chicks as they first prepare to fly. The mother eagle ensures the safety of her chicks while they learn to be at home in the skies.

The Greek word επικιαζο is used similarly in Luke 1:35, where the Holy Spirit overshadows Mary at the conception of Christ. This hovering, or overshadowing, is the virgin mother's preparation for conceiving the Son of God.

The Bible thus describes the Spirit as the divine forerunner of God's creative and redemptive work in the world. He is the Divine Presence preparing material persons and objects for divine use.

In his book *After the Spirit*, Eugene F. Rogers ties a fresh approach to this biblical concept of hovering. Describing the Holy Spirit's work as "befriending" matter, Rogers goes on to say that just as Christ is God incarnate, so the Spirit sanctifies and spiritualizes matter. The Spirit does not incarnate within matter but does prepare it for service in the world. Pentecostals usually refer to this as "anointing."

The Spirit grants *koinonia*; family resemblance, since it is called the spirit of Sonship; character, since it moves and leaves into truth; unpredictability, since it blows where it will. Attention to the Spirit's appropriate activity also directs our attention to the anthropology of material culture, since it is the spirit whom Christians call down to sanctify people and things: deacons, priests, believers, water, wine, oil, incense, churches, houses, and anything that can be blessed.

Oil, water, wine, the bodies of human beings to be baptized, married, or ordained; in and many and various ways the matter of the world becomes the element of the sacrament. To think about the spirit, it will not do to think spiritually: to think about the spirit you have to think materially.[2]

Eastern Christian theology often draws on the story of Christ's transfiguration for its understanding of the Holy Spirit's work in the world. All four Gospel writers mention it (John 1:14 is a likely reference) as does the Second Epistle of Peter. Clearly, the event made a deep impression on the New Testament writers. Eastern Christianity asks us to pay attention to this fact. They also inevitably point out that it was not only Christ, but Moses and Elijah who were transformed. The story also insists that Christ's clothes were transformed, becoming whiter than any laundry could ever do.

Eastern Orthodox writers insist that the story is there to teach us that matter matters. They also say that this implies that through Christ, it is not only human beings who will be transformed, but the entire material universe. They further assume that this perspective is implied in one of the lines of the Apostles Creed: "I believe in the resurrection of the body."

The confession of a physical resurrection, according to the Christian East, is not about "life everlasting" in the sense of becoming disembodied ghosts. It's about the redemption and transformation of our entire physical being. The transformation of one's physical self is an extension and consequence of the sanctification of one's spirit. The transformation of material objects occurs through redeemed humanity, God's chosen viceroy of creation.

The Psalms' poetical description about trees clapping their hands is a well-known reference to this belief that everything God has created is invited to participate in the universe's ultimate redemption. Although some New Testament passages point toward a destruction of the material universe, most early Christian writers support Eastern Orthodoxy's insistence that such passages refer to a cleansing and renewal rather than an annihilation.

If matter indeed matters; if the Spirit hovers over and consecrates material things for divine use; and if the presence of the Holy Spirit in creation is a foreshadowing of its ultimate transformation, then the attitude of the Christian necessarily shifts toward befriending and honoring nature. We hint at this when we prepare nativity sets or sing Christmas carols that include references to sheep, oxen, and donkeys. The doves in the flood story of Genesis and at the baptism of Christ are other biblical hints of the participation of animals in God's redemption story.

The Spirit's role in the last scenes of the Christian canon includes the natural world as well as the covenant community.

And the Spirit and the bride say, "Come!" And let him who hears say, "Come!" And let him who thirsts come. Whoever desires, let him take the water of life freely.

Revelation 22:17

We hear the echoes of Genesis 1:2 as the Spirit once again prepares the way for God's redemptive work. In this final biblical passage, the focus of the Spirit's attention is the social world. The Holy Spirit welcomes anyone who desires to participate in the restoration of the world. All that is required is thirst.

The various Christian communities express the work of the Holy Spirit differently.

In *The Spirit Poured Out on All Flesh*,[3] Pentecostal theologian Amos Yong writes about how the Holy Spirit is at work "where Christ is not yet named." Clark Pinnock in the *Flame of Love: A Theology of the Holy Spirit*[4] uses this same phrase. Henry Blackaby offers a Baptist take on his missional pneumatology in the popular course *Experiencing God.*[5]

Blackaby's emphasis on God always being at work and the world and his insistence that "the Holy Spirit is always there before you arrive," had an impact on my own missional development. It was from him that I first heard about the importance of discerning what the Holy Spirit had been doing in each circumstance in which I felt called to participate. I could then "join in the Spirit's work" rather than feel responsible for carrying out God's work in the world.

What a relief that was!

Missionary Don Richardson offers one of the most powerful descriptions I know of on this approach to a missional pneumatology. In his book *The Peace Child*, Richardson tells of his difficulty communicating the Christian story to a remote group of people living in New Guinea.[6] He made his breakthrough after watching warring tribes exchange a "peace child." The tribes pledged to maintain peace between their respective people for as long as the children they had just exchanged lived.

After this experience, Richardson recast the story of Christ. God, he told the people, had offered his own son to end an ages long conflict with humanity. Instead of honoring this Divine Peace Child, humanity killed him. Now the people of this tribe understood. Now the Gospel made sense to them. Richardson developed a missional concept from this experience that he called redemptive analogies.[7] It was another way of saying that the Holy Spirit is always at work everywhere and so the work of believers is about discerning and supporting it.

C. S. Lewis assumed that the world religions and mythology were filled with such redemptive analogies. He too assumed that the Spirit has been at work, not only within Abraham's family or in nature but within all human cultures. St. Paul seems to support that assumption in both the first chapter of his *Epistle to the Romans* and in his sermon at Mars Hill (recorded in Acts 17).

This notion of redemptive analogies means that we need not assume that fidelity to Christ requires us to look at non-Christian communities as blank screens upon which God has been waiting for us to write the first word. Rather, we begin our work by discerning how the Spirit already has been at work writing God's own message into that culture. God initiates the encounter; we join a meeting already in progress.

In this book, I am continually returning to the question about how Christians can relate to the contemporary world. In this chapter, I have tried to present the Holy Spirit as the indispensable forerunner of any proclamation about Christ. I am saying that the world's peoples, in the longing for transcendence, encounter that Spirit who hovered over creation in the beginning and hovers still. While from a Christian point of view these cultures have been mistaken in some of what they conclude about God, they have at the same time stumbled into truths about God. As a result, missional encounters involve learning as well as teaching, receiving, and sharing.

Secularism certainly presents a new challenge to Christianity in that it denies the existence of transcendent reality, something few cultures in the past have done. Nonetheless, most secular people demonstrate in their words and deeds a longing for some sort of meaning. So, while there are unavoidable conflicts between secularism and Christianity, the Spirit is nonetheless at work. We can assume that even in the most godless forms of secularism, the Holy Spirit has been preparing redemptive analogies for the sharing of the Gospel.

When we find such redemptive analogies, we discover not only ways of sharing our faith; we acquire fresh understanding about God for ourselves.

Working in the mental health field, I have often asked myself how God may be at work in the brokenness of those I serve. Spiritual direction, which is a facet of what I do, is the work of helping others—believers and unbelievers alike—discern for themselves how the Divine Presence around them has been seeking their good.

While it is unethical to use treatment as a form of evangelism, I am convinced God, who created the person I am serving, loves her or him far more than I can. If I can discern how the Holy Spirit has already been at work in this person's life, I can then cooperate with God's good work instead of thinking it is all up to me. The results are often startling when we approach things from that angle.

This path is available to everyone. The carpenter can ask how God intends to use a piece of wood. A lawyer can ask how God is already at work to bring justice about in a specific case. A mechanic can ask what God has to say about the safety of those who will fly the aircraft or drive the car he is asked to maintain. And so forth.

There is no facet of human culture in which God has been or is now, absent.

In short, the Holy Spirit is the experienced Presence of God, not only in the Church but also in nature and the social world. The Spirit woos humanity toward the Creator's ultimate purpose by inspiring stories and ethical convictions that prepare the human heart for God's redemptive work. Becoming aware of this Presence, we no longer experience ourselves as existential orphans, peering longingly above us at an empty sky. Instead, we join the Revelator in shouting, "The whole earth is filled with God's glory!"

18

The Book of Reality
READING SCRIPTURE IN A
POSTMODERN WORLD

Divine Presence inspired certain individuals in ancient times to make known aspects of the Creator's intentions that had been overlooked or distorted by culture.

ONE OF THE BEST-KNOWN PASSAGES IN ST. AUGUSTINE'S *CONFESSIONS* is the account of Augustine's conversion.

By the time we reach that point in the Confessions, we have already walked with him through his earlier life. We have heard of his struggles to find fame and physical pleasure. He has already described his encounter with St. Ambrose Bishop of Milan, and we have noted the depth of their conversations. So, we know by this point how he enjoyed Ambrose's preaching, though he has made us aware that it was the bishop's eloquence and not the content of the sermons that had moved him.

Finally, we reach the point where Augustine has grown concerned for his soul. He has begun to read the scripture's but is not yet impressed. Also, because he cannot bear to leave behind the sexual life that he believes God requires of him, he finds no way forward.

The moment has arrived though. He must make his decision.

Augustine is with his friend Alypius, housesitting for a man away from the city for a few months. Early in the day that will end with his conversion, Augustine can't stop crying. The pressure of his divided heart is pulling him in all directions. So, he shouts to God that he is incapable of living the Christian life.

Something extraordinary then occurs.

I was saying these things and weeping, with agonizing anguish in my heart, and then I heard a voice from the household next-door, the voice of someone—a little boy or girl, I don't know which—incessantly and insistently chanting, "Pick it up! Read it!"

Immediately, my mood changed, and I started considering, with greater concentration, whether children were accustomed to chanting something like this in any kind of game. I couldn't remember that I'd heard anything like it anywhere. I got control over the onslaught of my tears and got up, having construed in the chant a straightforward divine command to open a book and read the chapter I first found there. I had heard that Anthony had been admonished by the reading of the gospel that he had walked in on by chance; what was being read seemed to be speaking to him personally: "take everything you have and give it to the poor, and you will have treasure in heaven; and come, follow me.

Moved by this omen, he returned to you in no time.

Excited, I returned to the spot where Alypius was sitting. I put down a book of the apostle Paul's letters there when I got up. I grabbed it and opened it, and I read in silence the passage on which my eyes first fell: don't clothe yourself in raucous dinner parties and drunkenness, nor in the immorality of sleeping around, nor in feuds in competition; but clothe yourselves in the Master, Jesus Christ, and do not make provision for the body in its inordinate desires.

I didn't want to read further, and there was no need. The instant I finished the sentence, my heart was virtually flooded with relief and certitude, and all the darkness of my hesitation scattered away.[1]

We should take notice of several things in this account.

First, we are hearing Augustine, Bishop of Hippo, telling this story many years after his conversion. That implies that the bishop wants us to pay attention not only to the final moment of conversion but to the sequence of events leading to it.

Secondly, Augustine recalls being tormented by his divided heart.

Thirdly, the bishop recalls hearing a voice he is unable to identify that chants, "Pick it up, pick it up, read it, read it."

Fourthly, he remembers seeing the copy of St. Paul's letters.

Fifthly, as Augustine opens the book, he accepts what he reads as God's personal words to him. He was not reading critically, that is to say in a respectful but detached manner. He opened his soul to the spirit of the text. Augustine knew how to read critically and did so in his scholarly works. However, this was not a time for that kind of reading.

Finally, Augustine says, the passage pierced him, and so he submitted to what he believed God had said to him.

Most Christians can relate.

Even believers who have serious questions about the purpose and authority of scripture, will often have personal stories about being seized by scripture in just the way Augustine describes. It often occurs unexpectedly. One is barely listening to the scripture reading at church or is privately reading scripture with divided attention when suddenly, a phrase—perhaps even a single word—leaps from the text. One's heart feels pierced in a way that opens a new sense of conviction about a matter.

Augustine's account describes a believer's intimate relationship with Holy Scripture. We relate because we usually encounter the Bible as he did before, wrestling with questions about how the text came into being, how it was assembled, or why it was officially accepted as scripture. Legitimate issues about Bible translation, manuscript variations, how different Christian communities read and interpret the Bible or the different passages they accept as canonical are all terribly important. They are rarely the first things we ask about the text, however.

In fact, many devout Christians never ask probing questions

about the origin of scripture. I think they should. I try to convince people of the importance of asking those questions. Most do not think it's important. For them, scripture is self-justifying, largely because of their experiences with it. Admittedly, few Christians are familiar with the entire text. Most read the relatively short portions most familiar to their Christian expression. What is read though is experienced in the sacramental, devotional way St. Augustine describes.

Christians officially believe that scripture is both a human product about God and a special sort of information from God. Just as Christians confess Jesus to be both God and man, they believe scripture was written through the minds, hearts, experiences, and words of human authors as God inspired them to write.

Fundamentalists emphasize the divine authorship of scripture; biblical criticism emphasizes its human authorship. The monastic and Eastern Orthodox traditions tend to read scripture as canon, assuming that the whole is contained in the parts and is best internalized by forming the words into prayer. Charismatics and mystics emphasize the role of the Holy Spirit, who personalizes and illuminates the text as it is read.

Christians are inclined to privilege one these aspects of scripture over the others. However, most believers would think that these different perspectives are not incompatible with one another. Each of these approaches to the text, including critical analysis of language, manuscript families, and literary form, add to the depth of one's experience of it.

To explain further how Christian's experience scripture, we should look at a few terms.

Inspiration

In the context of scriptural study, the word inspiration refers to the belief that the Bible's human authors are not the primary sources of the text. The word inspiration literally means, "in-breathed." It points toward the unique partnership between the Holy Spirit, whom Christians believe moved the writers to write, and the human authors who were real persons, embedded as all people are, in a particular place and time.

Belief in the inspiration of scripture does not mean that God used the human writers as automatons or ventriloquist dummies. It means that God touched the hearts and minds of the writers in a way that preserved the essential truths God wished to communicate to the world.

As a result, most believers do not think much about the human authors as they read scripture. They assume they are hearing the words of God, which is quite enough for them. That is understandable. Reading the Bible in translation, one barely notices how style and vocabulary shift from one biblical book to another. In the majestic King James Version, for example, every passage is rendered into the most eloquent form of the English language possible.

Many years ago, I was talking to a Bible translator. He startled me by saying that the King James Bible was more eloquent than most of the original text. He went on to say that he believed the eloquence obscured and mystified rather than revealed the text. That is one person's opinion of course, but it's a very informed one.

When reading scripture in the original languages, we are much more likely to notice literary devices such as alliteration, play-on-words, and rhyme. We become aware of whether a passage is written in a high style or in common speech. We are more aware of whether the passage was meant as poetry, prose, literal narrative, or allegory.

Furthermore, all these aspects of the text vary from author to author.

Even the highest view of scripture requires one to take these aspects into account, reminding us that the Bible has human authors as well as a divine one.

Acknowledging the Bible's human authors, which includes awareness of their time, place, class, and gender and (if possible) their specific aim for writing, opens opportunities to discuss scripture with people who do not believe that the Bible is divinely inspired. Sometimes, the insights of such people into scripture can be illuminating since piety can obscure the text's earthly details. For example, while it may be spiritually profitable to allegorize the Song of Solomon as a description of a soul's relationship to God, it is most obviously an erotic poem. Nonreligious readers notice that immediately.

We could think of other, less obvious examples. Jack Miles, whose book *Christ, a Crisis in the Life of God*, retells the story of Jesus meeting the Samaritan woman at the well. After reminding his readers about the strict protocols of male/female relationships at the time of the story, Miles demonstrates, convincingly in my mind, that the woman believes that Christ's words are sexual metaphors, to which she responds in kind. ("I don't know about giving you a drink. This well is quite deep.") It is only when Christ reveals her past that she realizes her mistake and is terrified. Jesus then assures her that although she has mistaken what he meant, his concern for her is genuine. That is what moves her to shout to the village, "Come meet a man who has told me everything about myself!"

A pious reading of the story rarely yields such a possibility. Christians don't like to think about a sexually motivated woman trying to seduce the Savior of the World. However, I was profoundly moved by Miles's interpretation of the story because it reveals Christ's ability to see beyond the way our deepest longings can manifest themselves on the surface. Christ, this retelling of the story says, is not repulsed by our sins and addictions. He sees their source and offers to meet the genuine human needs these dysfunctions distort.

If the Bible does indeed have a Divine Author who wishes to make his presence known, we can rest assured that the reader will, eventually, encounter that presence. Human beings are not responsible for that.

As the young Augustine discovered, inspiration has a way of revealing itself.

Canon

Ancient peoples experienced what we have come to call the Bible as a library of scrolls, as *The Holy Scriptures*.

Notice the plural. In ancient times, each "book" of the Bible was a separate scroll. Copies were stored in a special room and placed in a latticework called pigeonholes. In fact, that's where we get the phrase: don't pigeonhole me!

Synagogues nearly always had a copy of at least the *Pentateuch*, the first five books of the Bible. They tried to collect as much of the sacred library as possible, however. The precious scrolls were carefully carried into the worship space to be read aloud. The Gospel of Luke describes how Jesus was once asked to deliver a homily on the reading from Isaiah. In that brief account, one notices the elements I have just described.

By the time of Christ, there was a prescribed reading plan for which passages to read at which times of the year, which Christians would call the *lectionary*. The early Christian Church continued to observe this approach to public readings, adding passages from the Gospels and the Epistles, a practice still observed by most Christian communities.

For centuries though there was no Bible. There was only a collection of inspired scrolls. Few congregations had access to the entire collection.

For a long time, there was only a fuzzy consensus on what separated sacred scripture from other valuable literature or from commentaries on scripture. Both Jews and Christians saw the Pentateuch as sacred, along with the Psalms (the community's common prayers) and the prophets, (the reflections of Israel's most influential preachers on the moral and ethical implications of covenant).

This fuzzy consensus developed early. By the time of the New Testament, the often-used phrase The *Law and the Prophets* implies the Jews viewed the Pentateuch and the Prophets as bound in some sort of sacred unity. The Psalms, easily memorized for use in worship, were especially beloved, then as now.

About 70 AD, the Rabbinical community affirmed what had long been accepted as "canon" (rule) about sacred scripture. The only disputes revolved around the Chronicles, the Song of Solomon, and other temple archives concerned with liturgy, taxes, and national infrastructure. Finally, though, the Jewish community settled on our present Hebrew canon. Some early Christians wanted to eliminate the Hebrew scriptures except for the Psalms. This was denounced as heretical, however, and so Christians have embraced the Jewish canon as their own.

The canonization of New Testament texts unfolded from 300-600 AD. There was wide agreement in the Christian community about most of the writing that we have received as the New Testament. Debates continued for hundreds of years though about such passages as *The Book of Revelation*, the *Epistle to the Hebrews*, the *Epistle of St. Clement*, and others. Today, nearly all Christians hold to the 66 books of the Old and New Testament. The Deutero-canonical books (or Apocrypha) have either fully canonical status (among Catholics, Orthodox and some Anglicans) or occupy an important but not divinely inspired place (most Protestants.) Ethiopian Coptic believers accept a third set of writings we have only recently learned to have been part of pre-Christian Hebrew literature but are not used by most Christians of either East or West.

We cannot understand how the "holy scriptures" became the Holy Bible without discussing a major technological shift that led to a gradual replacement of the scroll with the book.

The scripture began as writings on clay tablets and then on parchment, which unlike tablets could be rolled up. Around the times of Christ though, people began cutting scrolls into separate sheets, which they sewed into something resembling a modern book. It would be nearly a thousand years before the entire sacred library (biblia) could be bound together as a massive single volume. The development of the printing press and thin paper slowly made it possible for every believer to own a volume like this for their own home. (Your great-grandmother probably had one of these volumes. Hopefully, it is still in your family somewhere.) Only in the last hundred years or so did the Bible become a book that people could easily carry around.

Most Christians believe that the Bible, which is for them primarily a devotional text, has something to say about reality itself. Christians differ among themselves about the level of authority we should assign to the canon, as well as how literally we should interpret what it has to say about natural life.

As for the question about how to understand the Bible, perhaps it helps to view it as a vast body of sacred words that radiate out from a clearly established core. Since the 66 books of the Protestant cannon is common to all Christians, we can think of those books as our established common canon. As spiritual content moves from that core, it gradually becomes more diverse and less authoritative. For example, well-read Protestants will value the Book of Maccabees and Sirach though they rarely view these books as belonging to the received, common canon. Thus, Protestants, label these books as *deuterocanonical* (second canon), placing them in a respected, but not canonical status.

Moving a few circles from the common canon, we notice that many Christians highly respect Augustine's *Confessions*, Thomas a Kempis's *Imitation of Christ*, Calvin's *Institutes*, and the *Book of Common Prayer*.

These books apply scripture to the needs of specific times, places, and purposes. Not all Christians value all of them. Some deny that they have any spiritual significance at all, in fact. However, time has sanctioned them for great numbers of believers and so they carry considerable weight in Christian thought and discourse.

We can also say that some spiritual practices and hymns also come to participate in this "reflective canon." For example, most English-speaking Christians are moved when they sing *Amazing Grace*. Most Western Christians can sing at least a few lines of *Silent Night*. Most know phrases from the Service of Holy Matrimony, such as "in sickness and in health, for richer for poor, forsaking all others, clinging only to you." None of these "texts" qualify as scripture but are venerated nonetheless as a source for Christian thought and sentiment.

Just as no contemporary American can ignore the influence of football and hotdogs on their culture, no Christian can deny the influences of these secondary sources of Christian belief we have mentioned here. The founders of the American republic never tasted a hotdog. They didn't watch football on TV. Americans have developed these aspects of culture as they lived out the founders' vision for the country they birthed. Something roughly similar has occurred in Christianity with scripture. It has inspired art, theology, and spiritual practice that has in turn profoundly influenced Christian thought.

Canon then is an important but not an entirely exact concept.

Translation

Christians have always honored the original languages of scripture: Hebrew, Aramaic, and Greek. Many believers try to learn them. However, unlike other religious communities, Christianity has always placed a high priority on translating its sacred scripture into other languages. Furthermore, whenever the Bible is published in a new language, it is treated as *The Bible*, no less holy than the original text.

The miracle of languages recorded in Acts 2 hints how the lack of a sacred language would be a sign of human brotherhood in Christ. No linguistic community, even the original one, would have preeminence in the Christian Community. Each people group would absorb, interpret, and express the gospel in its own unique way, thereby continually adding to the Churches' understanding and worship of God as well as to the world's ability to hear and comprehend the Gospel.

This feature of "divided tongues" has given birth to the literary cultures in dozens of nations. Once a people have a Bible in their own language, which has sometimes required the creation of an alphabet, other books follow.

For centuries, the Bible for Western peoples was St. Jerome's beloved translation into the common people's (vulgar) Latin. This Latin Vulgate Bible remains one of the great literary achievements of European history and source for much of Western Civilization's visual and musical arts.

Early Protestants added a new dimension to the Church's use of scripture: an emphasis on the responsibility of individual believers to know and use the Bible in their daily devotions. This sparked a fury of Bible translations, one of which was the Authorized English Version of 1611, popularly known as the King James Version.

The English king had insisted that a single version of scripture would be used by all denominations in his realm. The resulting translation work and its publication put considerable stress on the national treasury, costing the United Kingdom the equivalent of the American project for sending a man to the moon in 1969.

The gamble paid off.

The Authorized Version of King James became a major source of culture-formation. The working-class people focused on becoming literate so they could read it. That resulted not only in a burst of religious passion but on a drive for universal literacy. A flowering of national literature followed close behind. After that came newspapers and increasing pressure for real democracy. Finally, there was a demand for universal participation in the nation's economic life.

As the English language continued to evolve, the Authorized Version maintained its place in the people's hearts and minds. By the mid-twentieth century, however, English-speakers began turning to newer translations. This provoked considerable reluctance and opposition but also resulted in fresh readings of scripture.

The King James Version's venerated success as a pillar of culture was repeated in other communities. Luther's German Bible served a similar place in German culture. The Reina Valera of 1602, continually revised for the Spanish-speaking world, remains the most used version in that language. There are many other such examples.

Today, the Bible has been translated into all the world's major languages, including several that have only a few hundred speakers. For some small language groups, the Bible is the only book of any kind.

Technology has made it possible for a person to access Bible translations in most of the world's languages. One can download them onto multiple kinds of devices, compare their differences and similarities, transmit them to countries that censor scripture and so forth.

Since even the most ancient copies of scripture contain differences and variations, there is no such thing as a standard text. The Bible is a family of texts, deposited into and emerging out of the world's diverse communities and cultures. St. Luke, describing the miracle at Pentecost, could as well have been describing the sea of Bible translations into the languages of the world: "each in their own language, they hear the marvelous words of God."

Hermeneutic

Hermeneutics is the process of discerning the meaning of a text. We read actuary tables differently than a history book. We read a novel differently than a medical journal. Knowing the purpose of a text tells us how to process its words.

We usually assume that the author had a purpose for writing the work we are reading. We try to discover that purpose if we can. In the case of a well-known book, we're also aware that other readers have shared their insight about what the text implies. As we read, we pay attention how the text refers to other writings. We notice if the author uses words in a particular way or seems obsessed about a particular point. Such critical reading habits help us understand a text.

Shakespeare's Hamlet often refers to the Bible. Knowing that the playwright set his drama in Denmark and at a particular moment of history, we realize that the Protestant Reformation serves as a distant backdrop to the story, its themes, and its character. Since Hamlet was first performed, innumerable books, poems, songs, and speeches have referenced all these points and much, much more. Phrases like "to be or not to be," "to suffer outrageous fortune," and "to protest too much" have all entered everyday speech in English-speaking countries because of it.

So, how should one read and understand Hamlet today?

Does fidelity to the text require us to forget the ways its phrases have been used since it was first written? To understand it properly, do we need to learn the real "facts" about Denmark in the days after the Reformation? Or do we enjoy Shakespeare's retelling of the story for his own purposes?

Do we see the character Hamlet as crazy, as just, or as irresponsible?

Five hundred years of performance and reading have made it difficult for us to dictate a single approach to Hamlet. The truth is every performance of Hamlet is a commentary and an interpretation of it. Each person walking away from a performance will likely emphasize something a bit different than the friends who attended the play with them. These many layers of Hamlet do not represent a dilution or erosion of the original text, they are rather a fresh embodiment of it.

If all of this is true of a five-hundred-year-old play, written in a language people still use today, how much truer is it of scripture?

The Bible is a collection of scrolls created roughly 3,000-2,000 years ago in languages that have fundamentally changed over time. When we factor in the ways each translation has added to the nuances of the words and phrases used in the various parts of scripture; the ways in which the various denominations have prioritized biblical themes differently; the evolution of language over the many centuries since scripture was written; the addition of chapters and verses; the arrangement of the various books in their present order (Jews, Catholics, and Protestants each order the contents a bit differently); the division of words from texts where no such divisions were made; the act of joining diverse literary genres into a single book; and the endless quotes and retelling of biblical stories in art, music, liturgy, and political speech—well, one begins to grasp the challenge of nailing down a definitive interpretation of the text as a whole.

There is more.

Should we view Holy Scripture as a collection of writings that lack a clear unifying message, suggesting that each part of scripture must be read in its original context? Or can we agree that there are central themes through the entire canon, suggesting that we should interpret each individual passage and each book of the Bible in the light of the canon's unifying themes?

Can we identify a core idea, or book, or passage around which the rest of the canon should revolve? If so, which? If not, what if anything unites these various writings into the single book we call The Bible?

Should we root our study of scripture primarily in spiritual practice, as monastic theology did for much of history? Christian monks memorized the Psalms as they prayed them together daily. Since many Christians of the past believed that the major themes of scripture were contained in the Psalms, that book became for them the unofficial heart of the entire canon.

Should we instead root our understanding of scripture in a serious study of the text, paying close attention to the language, the era of history and the purpose for which a particular passage seems to have been written?

Should we read the Bible's stories as its primary content, implying that the theological reflections are commentaries on the meaning of those stories? Or should we read the theological texts as the Bible's primary content, implying that the Bible stories are illustrations of the clear teaching of other passages? Should we read the teaching of Christ in the light of the Pauline Epistles, or read the Pauline epistles as reflections on the teaching and person of Christ?

Two equally fundamentalist believers will nonetheless come to different conclusions about the meaning of scripture depending on where each locates the center of the text. If one reads the rest of the Bible in the light of the Sermon on the Mount, for example, and the other reads it in the light of the Book of Romans, their understanding of the Epistle of James will be quite different. Monks and nuns, who chant the Psalms daily, assume that the Psalter contains the central message of the entire canon, which leads to a different way of approaching scripture. If we place the Book of Acts at the center of the text, we come to yet a different understanding of the faith.

You get the point.

In the end, the Bible seems to function more as a spiritual compass than as a map. It is more like a gymnasium that forms the readers mind, heart, and practice than like a maintenance manual. Rather than offer clear answers about every opportunity and challenge we will face in life, it develops the reason and judgment required to make good decisions about these things.

Interaction with scripture forms the intellect. It educates one's emotions and behaviors. It facilitates community among those under its influence. For the Christian as with Jews, the Holy Scriptures are the primary source of inner healing and maturation. It is not, however, a text that automatically ensures immediate agreement among those who read it. On the contrary, scripture frequently provokes debate and dissension. Such differences over interpretation can, though often do not, lead to deeper understandings of life and faith.

One thing we know for sure, the scripture was written to be read and reflected upon within the context of a believing community. Individual believers can read it privately and encounter both the presence of God and wise counsel for their lives. However, it is in the hearing of the Word in worshipful community where we most encounter scripture's transformative power. Likewise, as we have noted, non-believers may derive important insights from their own reading of scripture. Nonetheless, scripture claims that the awe of God is the basis for understanding it.

I end this chapter with a quote from the *Book of Common Prayer*.

Blessed Lord, who caused all holy Scriptures to be written for our learning, grant us so to hear them, read, mark, learn, and inwardly digest them, that we may embrace and ever hold fast the blessed hope of everlasting life, which you have given us in our Savior Jesus Christ, who lives and reigns with you in the Holy Spirit, one God, forever and ever. Amen.

While writing this chapter, I have kept in mind that few Christians will agree with everything I have written here about scripture. Rather than offer the perspective of any single Christian expression, what I have attempted to do is describe how Christianity has tended to view scripture. One thing most Christians agree on is that scripture is, and will remain, the major source from which they derive their morals, ethics, and ultimate meaning. It is from scripture, though not entirely from scripture, from which Christianity responds to the values and norms of all cultures and all eras of history.

It is for this reason that we should seek to understand how and why we view the text as we do, as well as how equally sincere believers may view it quite differently.

Though an Italian Catholic, an American Methodist, a Scottish Presbyterian, an Egyptian Copt, and an African Pentecostal will differ from one another about which passages they absolutize or allegorize, where they view the canon's center, and perhaps about other interpretative factors, it is nonetheless scripture that largely forms their response to one another and to the non-Christian ideas they encounter in the broader world.

Scripture is part of the bedrock of the Christian faith. As Christ himself said, "heaven and earth will pass away but my word will not pass away." So, whatever their hermeneutic, most Christians will agree that following Christ involves a life-long encounter with scripture.

Of course, a Bible on one's shelf neither informs nor transforms anyone. It's the Bible "inwardly digested" that points to the Incarnate Word. According to Jesus, that was the purpose for which scripture had been written. The inwardly ingested word becomes a means of grace, calling the hearer into a personal awareness of one's own self in relationship to God and to God's people.

19

Self Beyond the Rabbit Hole

*All human individuals are created in God's image and likeness. However, full
personhood—the development of an individuated sense of agency and
responsibility—is a potential that must be purposefully sought and activated.
Full adult personhood does not emerge automatically with age.*

MANY GREAT WORKS ARE FAMOUS FOR THEIR ENGAGING FIRST LINE.

Moby Dick begins with "call me Ishmael." Many people who
know that line have never actually read the book.

Then there is what is likely the most quoted literary line in the
English language: the first sentence of Dickens' *The Tale of Two
Cities*.

"It was the best of times, it was the worst of times, it was the
age of wisdom, it was the age of foolishness, it was the epoch
of belief, it was the epoch of incredulity, it was the season of
light, it was the season of darkness, it was the spring of hope,
it was the winter of despair."

Charles Dickens

We could go on. I would like to quote Gibbon's first line from the *Rise and Fall of the Roman Empire*, but it takes up a full page!

C. S. Lewis might have become known for writing one of those first great lines. Had he asked me, I would have urged him to begin his most critically acclaimed work, *Till We Have Faces* with a line he instead buried deep inside the book: *"How can we know the gods face to face until we have faces?"*

I am offering this advice much too late to be of any use. Lewis died in 1963, after all. There is also the fact that my own books have not had, shall we say, quite the level of success as the ones Lewis wrote. So even if I had offered him my excellent advice, he may have had reason to not be impressed.

But let me make my case!

Lewis's great sentence deserves considerable reflection because it embodies one of the most profound ideas in Christian anthropology: *the belief that personhood emerges within relationship with other persons.*

Lewis offers this insight within his masterful retelling of the myth of Psyche and Eros. In that ancient story, Psyche loses both her divine lover and her magical kingdom after breaking the one rule the god had established. Eros had clearly said that Psyche must never see his face.

She had accepted this condition and had enjoyed a season of great delight.

Then, curious, Psyche lights a candle to see the face of the one she has been sleeping with. Immediately, the spell is broken. Both the god and his magical realm disappear, leaving Psyche seized with grief and utterly alone. Gradually, though, her sorrow gives way to wisdom. In time, wisdom produces a personal transformation. Whereas she had known how to experience thoughtless bliss before that terrible night of undoing, she must now move through her loss, her self-loathing, and her regrets to become an authentic self.

Lewis's great line interprets Psyche's transformative experience through the lens of Christian theology.

By raising the question of whether one is ever born with a face, Lewis juggles several words that became crucial in forming early Christian thought. First, Lewis has in mind the Greek word *prosopon*, which originally meant "face," or "mask." Secondly, he is thinking about early Christian discussions about the Trinity and the nature of Christ, when the Latin word *persona* (which, like the Greek word prosopon also meant mask or face) gradually developed into the modern word person. Lewis is recombining concepts that our culture separates into distinct words but which in the ancient world were intertwined within a single word.

Shockingly, ancient peoples did not describe human individuals as persons. They didn't usually imagine themselves apart from family, clan, tribe, or nation. They experienced themselves as something like a family fragment, a component of a group.

This has been in fact the way most non-Western cultures before the modern era experienced human individuality. Until a few decades ago, the best way of assuring that a letter would get to someone living in an Asian country was to write first the nation, then the city followed by the street, after that the number of the house, then the family name of the one to whom the letter was being sent. Only then would one add a personal name.

This is of course opposite of the way contemporary Western people address a letter.

Early Christian reflections on the meaning of personhood is the reason why the Western world came to view the human individual as it does today.

As we have noted, the Latin word "persona" originally meant "mask" (from per-sonare: "to sound through.") Ancient actors used these masks to signal the character they wished to portray to their audience. In a good performance, the audience would not think about who was speaking through the mask. Indeed, the mask itself seemed to be doing the speaking, forming the character by the sound coming through the mask.

Christian theologians found this a useful metaphor to describe the three centers of consciousness—Father, Son, and Holy Spirit— that they believed scripture ascribed to the One God. The formal word for these centers of consciousness was hypostasis, meaning "reality" or "state of being." However, this philosophical term was too remote and abstract for most people. The word persona was much easier to grasp. The Church fathers reluctantly used it but attempted to explain that God's three hypostasis were more than masks. At any rate, the word persona began to take on a much weightier meaning in everyday life.

In time, Christians began applying the word *persona,* to themselves.

If Christ had indeed invited human beings to become something more than mere parts of a family or tribe, perhaps God intended to offer human beings a previously unimaginable kind of individuated existence. Perhaps the weary and heavy-laden individuals who had placed their trust in Jesus could become something more than family fragments. Perhaps they were growing into, persons, in community with the other persons—God, the saints, and angels.

If that were the case, then salvation involves the transformation of human individuals into the sort of beings who would one day relate to God "face-to-face."

Lewis had all these things in mind as he wrote his powerful sentence. He was saying that it is impossible for any individual to know God face-to-face until that individual "grows a face," until he or she becomes a person.

Lewis is implying then that human individuals are only potential persons.

Becoming a person in this theological sense refers to a process of maturity that moves an individual beyond instinct and tribal codes. A fully realized person would experience themself as both individuated and in voluntary relationship with other persons. A person does not sleepwalk through life because they have a sense of their own unique purpose. They cultivate an awareness of self as intimately related to God, to others, and to the natural world.

In scripture, it is God alone who evokes this level of self-awareness. God calls several "family fragments" to move out of their collective identity into the vulnerable place of formation in God. Abraham, Jacob, Job, Gideon, and Moses are all examples. These individuals begin their journey toward personhood as they respond to the God who calls them by name. This personal call evokes a jarring awareness in those who hear the call that he is more than merely the member of a community. The awakening into personhood changes everything.

Paradoxically, it results in healthy community. Instead of the covenant community being a static collection of semi-selves, it is a dynamic interaction of authentic persons.

Jewish writers have reflected on biblical personhood from a Hebrew perspective. For example, Martin Buber in *I and Thou*, describes what occurs to individuals when they turn from relating to others as "We" to an "It," and begin to relate as an "I" to a "Thou."

Here's what he means. We are all born (and many of us will die) experiencing ourselves as components of a "We." A child naturally assumes the views of their own tribe and family, in other words. Even as they grow older, they cling to their family, tribe, and nation, not so much because they deliberately choose these communities but because they have never dared to risk the vulnerability of individuated personhood. They mistake their enmeshed codependence for love. They may also choose the path of rebellion as a substitution for the scary process of becoming a person. In that case, they still revolve their life around family and tribe but do so in constant reaction rather than from any real personal independence.

From a biblical standpoint, however, we are meant to embrace both our own individuation and healthy community. That is what being a person means.

Healthy community encourages personhood. They purposefully create the potential for voluntary and joyful participation of persons within community. In *7 Habits of Highly Effective People*, Stephen Covey described this process as beginning with dependence, then moving through independence, and finally into healthy interdependence.

Bishop Zizioulas, in his *Being as Communion: Personhood and the Church*,[1] offers a brilliant and often moving summation of this process from a theological and biblical perspective. In fact, my remarks here owe much to this work.

I found it interesting to contrast Zizioulas's view of personhood with how Charles Taylor describes the contemporary Western view in his *Sources of the Self.*[2] Best known for his book *A Secular Age.* [3] Taylor describes in this earlier book how a postmodern West is altering its definition of "person." For several hundred years after the medieval era, an increasingly secular Western World assumed personhood to be something innate, fixed, and inalienable. As we move away from this traditional view, based upon the theological process I describe here, the more this is changing.

The contemporary Western World tends to view the self as neither fixed nor permanent. Indeed, the self is something one either deliberately constructs or passively accepts from one's culture. In this contemporary view, an individuated self emerges from his own instincts and will. Self begats self by guiding its own evolution through deliberate choices.

A contemporary version of the 100th Psalm might read, "It is not Thou who hast made us but we ourselves."

Christians may experience this viewpoint as hubristic or even as blasphemous. However, if one does not believe in God or an after-life, there is hardly any other way to imagine oneself. Any develop-ment is seen as resulting from an act of existential bootstrapping: self-creating the self through an evolutionary process directed by self.

In this view, if personhood can be evoked by anything outside of us, it can only be the society in which we live. That is the perspective of at least a few neurologists. In my mind, it offers a fruitful place of dialogue with the Christian view of personhood.

In his book *Interpersonal Neurology*, Daniel Siegal describes the human mind as an emergent property of the brain and central nervous system as these interact with one's natural and social envi-ronment. What Christians call personhood, Siegal would describe as a self-aware information-processing system that has learned how to integrate its own inner components into a single (though multifaceted) entity. That will strike most believers as falling far short of "made in the image and likeness of God." However, a deeper look at his perspective reveals considerable compatibility with how Patristic writers described "person."

Is The Human Individual a Unified Whole or A Collection of Persons?

I once saw a cartoon of a man sitting behind an enormous desk. Behind him there were windows looking out over an endless forest of skyscrapers. His secretary has just opened the door of his office. She says meekly, "Your mother is on the phone."

In the next panel, the secretary has closed the door. The man, now hunched over his desk in a near fetal position, says a single word into the phone.

"Mama?"

In an instant, the powerful business tycoon regresses to childhood.

The cartoon is funny because we have all experienced ourselves as changing to meet different kinds of social situations. Our sense of self does seem to depend, at least somewhat, on the social context we are in. I know that I have a distinct sense of personal alteration depending on the language I am speaking at a given time. This is a common experience for most of the bilingual people I've met.

So, we're not always certain whether we will "put on" our self-assured self today or the anxious codependent self. Will we present our professional or personal face? Will we play the romantic or the pragmatist? And so forth.

For most of us, these changes are minor enough that they do not threaten our perception of ourselves as possessing a reasonably stable self. For some people, however, such changes are much more radical and lead one to doubt their own internal unity.

Many years ago, I met with a person who had forgotten his own name. He didn't remember his family members and could not access most of his personal history. This didn't seem to distress him nearly as much as one would expect. In fact, he seemed quite congenial and calm.

Medical examinations had revealed nothing out of the ordinary. There was no tumor, concussion, UTI delirium, or other kinds of issues that could lead to an episode like this.

A few weeks later, his memories suddenly returned as mysteriously as they had gone.

We have several labels for events like this: dissociative amnesia, dissociative fugue (when someone travels to another place because they suddenly disconnect with their identity and their placement in the world), dissociative identity disorder (what we used to call multiple personality), among others. Those whom we assign such labels, are often intelligent and otherwise normal people. They usually carry out the tasks their education and training prepare them to do. They can even gain profound wisdom from their struggle with personal identity.

I believe these dissociative states reveal something that is true of everyone. None of us know ourselves nearly as well as we assume. We have all forgotten things about ourselves, perhaps even banished parts of ourselves. For all sorts of reasons, what we reveal to the world may not include important parts of our own self. In time, we can even seem to lose parts of our self.

Most therapists have witnessed a professional, educated client fade for a few seconds or even longer, suddenly becoming a child or adolescent. The client's voice may change. Their facial features may be altered. Their vocabulary may regress. A sub personality that can be quite different from the person as we know her or him takes over, at least for a portion of the session.

Although that probably sounds bizarre to some of my readers, I can assure you that most of us experience something like this from time to time. The man in the cartoon is only an exaggerated picture of that. Meeting with someone we knew decades before, we will use expressions we haven't used in years. The old acquaintance may call us by a nickname that no one in our present life even knows. As we converse with this old acquaintance, we may recall memories that have not surfaced for a very long time.

All this to say that dissociative disorders are only extreme examples of a phenomena that is common to everyone. However, some individuals seem to fully become themselves. How they present themselves the world seems to be their authentic and whole self. We say that such people have *integrity*. What they present to the world is who they are. What they believe is what they do. Having become aware of their flaws, they neither defend nor hide them. Having become aware of their strengths, they steward them wisely. The person they once were has become fully present to themselves and to others.

These are some of the things we have in mind as we think about personhood.

Every human being is offered personhood through a relationship with God and with others. However, personhood only fully emerges as we become vulnerable enough to expose our various selves—even the sinful and distasteful ones—to the One who heals and transforms these fragments into the whole person we were created to become. That means that we must acknowledge parts of ourselves that we do not like and envision what those parts are meant to play in a whole and undivided self.

The process of integration is complicated. Perhaps it is something we never fully realize in this life.

Sometimes, the reason for one's sense of fragmentation is biological rather than emotional or psychological.

For months after my wife's aneurism in 2004, she suffered through moments in which she felt as though there were two people inside her who were sometimes at odds with one another. The most maddening thing about this was that she did not think of one of the persons as herself and the other person as someone else. Both people were legitimate parts of her.

She would sometimes call me from the shower, distressed because as her right hand had reached for the shampoo her left hand had darted out to restrain it. Neither hand would stop doing what it seemed determined to do. Her hands were like two children in the back of a car fighting over a toy. The same thing would happen as she entered the closet, one hand reaching for a skirt, the other for pants.

What had happened to Trish was that the aneurism had damaged her corpus collosum, the band of brain tissue that connects and coordinates the perception and will of our right and left cerebral hemispheres.

There is considerable research available now on these so-called split-brain patients. Unlike Trish, whose corpus collosum had been damaged but would eventually return to a reasonable level of functionality, split-brain patients undergo a surgical procedure called a corpus callosotomy. This procedure permanently severs the connection between the brain's two hemispheres and is usually performed after all other attempts at controlling the patient's severe seizures have failed.

There are other ways of studying the difference between the cerebral hemispheres. We can anesthetize one of the hemispheres, leaving the other free and unhindered to express itself.

Research with split-brain patients has both clarified our understanding and deepened the mystery of how our two-brains-in-one work separately and together to form our normal sense of an integrated self. Iain McGilchrist, fellow of the Royal College of Psychiatrists, has published his reflections on what split-brain research implies in *The Master and His Emissary: The Divided Brain and the Making of the Western World.*

Although a split-brain patient offers a unique example of a biologically fragmented self, all of us experience some measure of this human reality, usually for psychological or sociological reasons. Full integrated personhood is our ideal, of course. It's just that fatigue, trauma, addiction, anxiety, and other life-events derail or delay it.

Contemporary Western Psychology attempts to point us toward healthy individuation. In many ways though, the work of psychotherapy remains more of an art than a science. Hopefully its practitioners aim for scientific integrity, but that has been challenging to quantify.

Studies do show that long-term counseling can result not only in emotional and behavior changes but even alterations of one's brain structure. Sometimes, medications are helpful or even required. Otherwise, counseling those with acute disorders may find it very difficult to stay engaged. However, both pharmaceutical and therapeutic care—especially when combined—can bring suffering people a new sense of life and vitality, allowing them to imagine and then embrace a fuller identity and deeper experience of life.

Most contemporary people will agree on this view of thera-peutic work. Most of us have either experienced it ourselves or have seen its effects on others. It is important though to state that this is not the only path to healthy psychological life.

Many Christians seem unaware that before the advent of modern psychology, several of the oldest Christian expressions offered what they called spiritual direction. The purpose of this discipline actually was not to direct anyone. It was rather a practice of discernment through which a person could examine their own strengths and weaknesses, discover their vocation, make amends for offenses they had committed, forgive those who had wronged them, and remove the obstacles that might be hindering their spiritual growth. Older Christian traditions, both East and West, still offer spiritual direction, most generally to believer and unbeliever alike. Naturally, any Christian director will assume that one's relationship with God is the core issue of life, so this is not the same as secular therapy.

As we have mentioned elsewhere, for over millennia now, Buddhists have developed effective theories and practices that address the emotional, behavioral, and cognitive disorders of human beings. Although the premise of Buddhism is radically different from that of Christianity—the Buddhist concept of no-self is nearly an opposite belief from the Christian aim of growing into full personhood—Buddhist practice offers insights that are profitable to both secular and Christian caregivers.

As an example, I once heard a psychologist ask the Dali Lama what Buddhist practice might offer to a person suffering from a personality disorder. I recall the questioner specifically mentioned narcissistic personality disorder. Such personality disorders are noto-riously difficult to treat, mostly because those suffering from them tend not to care about the opinions of others. Usually, only the threat of catastrophic loss—perhaps one's children threaten to break off communication—motivates a narcissist to enter treatment.

The Dali Lama replied that only life-long practice can address this sort of intractable disorder. He suggested that the practice could begin with daily compassion-meditation on someone the narcissist truly loves. The patient's mother, perhaps. Over time, the Dali Lama said, this meditation should include another person or two the narcissist would not like to see harmed or removed from his life. Gradually, the circle should grow to include deliberate thoughts of appreciation for all those who have ever demonstrated love or care for the narcissist. In time, this circle can include pets and any other living things that stir at least some bit of empathy and tenderness.

Although I found the Dali Lama's words moving and helpful, a Christian would approach narcissism differently. We would begin with confession to God and to others in something like the words of this old prayer: "I have sinned by my own fault in thought, word, and deed. I have not loved God with my whole heart. I have not loved others as myself. For this, I am truly sorry."

A spiritual director might then ask what this sorrow feels like, seeking to provoke a sense of *compunction,* a felt and acknowledged sense of sorrow and contrition about one's state. The aim would not be to shame or emotionally manipulate a penitent but to help him contact what scripture calls the "godly sorrow that leads to repentance."

Repentance

Repentance, (*metanoia* in Greek) means "beyond thought," or "change of mind." The word implies a desire for cognitive as well as emotive and behavioral change. Christians believe that one's transformation can begin at any of these levels of human life. Wherever it begins, though, change ultimately affects all levels of the self.

The Buddhist example above begins in practice and assumes that an emotive response will either come in time or is not even that important. Contemporary Christians, on the other hand, usually begin at the emotive level, though in past eras Christians would have probably begun with either cognitive change or with an intentional adoption of some spiritual practice.

At least on one occasion Jesus noted that a seeker's emotional response was disconnected from his cognitive and behavioral intent. He had asked the emotionally moved man to make an immediate change in his behavior, "to sell his goods and care for the poor." The young man went away sorrowfully, despite his intense desire to become a disciple. The story shows how an emotional profession is not necessarily a commitment to change. Metanoia, in contrast, is an intense desire for change that affects one's will and daily practice, and therefore, eventually, one's entire self.

Spiritual direction in Reformed Judaism adapts Christian and secular practice. However, Jewish people have always sought the advice of their rabbis and wise people of their community about how to live a covenant life. The Jewish aim is, as in Christianity, not to bring a seeker into dependence upon a practitioner but rather to foster the development of the seeker's own self within community.

I mention Jewish practice because Christian caregivers will usually find considerable insight in the writings of Jewish spiritual directors. I have found the writings of Abraham Joshua Heschel particularly helpful for my own spiritual direction. One of the many memorable things the great rabbi said that has profoundly informed my view of authentic piety was from the telegram he sent his daughter after marching at Selma with Martin Luther King.

The already aged and revered rabbi had bewildered many of his Jewish colleagues by not only acknowledging the justice of King's cause—most Jews agreed with that—but by insisting that King was filling the role of a biblical prophet. At the end of the march, the rabbi sent his concerned daughter a telegram. He told her that he had not had an opportunity to do his devotions that day, but then he concluded with the words: "but my feet prayed."

This idea of "praying feet," is consistent with the advice of New Testament writers like James the Apostle, who tells us that faith in God results in deliberate actions. Being emotionally touched by someone who is hungry demonstrates empathy and concern. That is wholesome and good. However, if we fail to allow our emotion to provoke us to provide food, then our emotional response is incomplete and disordered. Our emotion is, in that case, probably a sign of our own discomfort with the knowledge that others are hungry.

Our move toward integrated personhood nearly always begins with a shock of some sort. Like a man deeply asleep who bolts out of bed after someone pours cold water on his head, our sleepwalking, fragmented self may become distressed when we become aware of our own condition. We may, for perhaps the first time in life, call out for help. What feels like the worst moment in life may then become the greatest moment of life. This is what happened to the slave-trading John Newton, who seeing his own wretchedness, calls for transformation. Later, he writes, "I once was lost, but now I'm found; was blind but now I see."

Francis of Assisi experienced something similar in response to the Gospel when he heard the daily reading in the village church. Hearing the Gospel, he realized his soul was disordered and in need of change.

Transformational stories like these occur outside Christianity as well.

The story of the young Buddha certainly comes to mind. Having been raised in wealth, the young man had been sheltered from contact with death, sickness, and poverty. When on the same day he witnessed an old sickly beggar and a dead body, his previously happy life became darkened by an awareness of human suffering. This shock led him to make a drastic change of life.

The healing of a human psyche requires one to become aware of his or her dignity as a creature made in God's own image and likeness. It also involves learning that all human beings are born bent and without God's intervention remain bent. The journey toward wholeness then includes addressing the obstacles that hinder or obstruct one's embrace of God's undeserved gift. The transformative work continues as one assumes the joys, responsibilities, and disappointments of full personhood as he goes ever deeper into relationship with God and with other human beings.

One becomes fully "person" by embracing first his or her independence and then enters voluntary interdependence with others. This journey is never quite complete, at least in this life.

To exist as one who is both different from but also united with others, is a life-long commitment. So, it is to that subject we now turn.

20

A Community of Persons

The full expression of one's personhood requires both individuation as well as responsible participation within community.

I WAS ONCE STRANDED FOR A WEEK IN THE SOUTHERN ECUADORIAN desert.

I was in my late teens at the time and had been traveling with a friend across terrain that was barely accessible, even in our rugged four-wheel-drive vehicle. The roads were mostly dried up creek beds and cattle paths.

Our original plan had been to stay for a couple of days in a primitive structure used for church services. Those plans abruptly changed while eating lunch one afternoon. Two of our Jeep tires exploded, one after the other with a loud bang. They had probably been pierced by one of the many sharp objects along the way. Either that, or it may have been the heat.

We found a couple of young guys with mules who were willing to take the tires to the nearest town.

Knowing it would be a couple of days before they would return, I thought about how worried my parents would be, far away in Quito. That's why I started walking toward the Peruvian border about three hours away, just after sundown. There was a small settlement there where I figured I could send a telegram.

As I was walking, my Ecuadorian companion abruptly stopped. He grasped my arm and said, "Don't move." Surprised, I looked at him for an explanation. He then pointed to the path ahead of us. That's when I saw the small snake.

"It's just a tiny snake!" I said.

"Yeah," he replied. "One bite from that snake and you'll be dead in half an hour."

After the snake passed, we continued our journey.

Had I been alone, I would not have stopped. I had no awareness that we were in any sort of danger. Even if I had seen the snake, I would have paid it little attention. One sees snakes in the tropics. Most of them, especially the small ones, aren't dangerous.

The difference between me and my Ecuadorian friend was this: I was walking and thinking. He was walking and "reading" the desert. For me, the desert was an empty space through which one travels. To him, the desert was a text that communicated with those who live there.

When human beings talk to one another about what they see, they usually assume that the person with whom they are speaking can see the same thing. That's not always true. Human beings see what they learn to see. They experience their environment through their training and experience.

What we see, what we do not see, and the meaning we assign to our experience of our environment differs widely.

When my Ecuadorian companion was very young, he learned from his family how to survive in the desert. He took for granted information of which I was completely unaware. Had I remained for a while in the desert, I might have learned how to live in that environment too. However, children and adolescents often develop intuitive connections to the natural environment that become more difficult to acquire later in life.

I could share other examples from life in the jungle.

People who live in the jungle develop uncanny skill in reading the natural environment. I usually saw endless green stuff where the jungle dwellers saw sources of food. They knew which animals had been where and how long ago. They heard sounds they could interpret as well as I read highway signs. From their earliest years, they had been learning from their elders and through personal experience how to survive and flourish in the rainforest.

A child's natural environment shapes their brain and central nervous system in specific ways. However, one's social environment is at least as influential in forming what we experience and how we interpret what we experience. Genetics and geography, in other words, are not the only (or even the main) factors in determining what we perceive as real or important. Our social environment has a much more influential role in developing these things.

What I mean by the term "social environment" consists of the multiple layers of meaning one receives (mostly unconsciously) from family, tribe, linguistic community, gender, religion, era of history, social class, and other social entities.

Through most of history, people were born, raised, and lived their entire lives within a stable social environment. One learned from their earliest days how to fit into that environment. They learned who was safe and who was not, how to speak to whom about what, and other social rules that governed their community. They rarely felt a need to question the lens through which they saw and interpreted the elements of their world.

As a child, I was aroused by the sound of an ice cream truck and pled for money from my mother. I avoided bees because I didn't want to get stung.

A child born in the forest follows the bees to a hive and eats some honey. They would find the sound of an ice cream truck terrifying.

Neither my childhood reaction, nor that of the child in the forest are examples of premeditated, cognitive decisions. They are barely conscious decisions, formed by a deep awareness of one's social world and its norms.

In *Saving the Appearances*, Owen Barfield calls the deep connection we make to the natural and social environment *participation*. Barfield means a kind of intuitive bonding through which individuals unconsciously receive and react to information coming from their environment. The experiences I had with individuals who *participated* with their natural environment in the way Barfield describes, saw and heard things I did not. Their awareness of nature came across to me as uncanny, nearly supernatural. However, it was a learned skill that most people of earlier ages took for granted.

Contemporary urban individuals observe nature. They may even study it. However, they rarely participate in nature in the way Barfield has in mind.

Barfield believes that the European Enlightenment led to the final loss of deep participation in nature. The shift from participation began with Plato and Aristotle, he says. They taught the West to detach from nature, thereby making nature an object of study. Indeed, that's what we mean by the word objectivity.

The point here is that the natural and social environments in which we come of age shape who we are and how we move through the world. If our social environment participates in nature, we become one sort of person. If our social environment objectifies nature, we become another sort of person. Furthermore, this social training persists throughout our lives, mostly through unconscious participation or unconscious resistance to participation with nature. Because this training is largely unconscious, we will assume that how we interpret the world is the way any intelligent person would do so if they had all the facts.

It is only when we find ourselves in a radically different social environment that we realize other people are not experiencing the world as we are. In an uprooted situation like this, we are shocked at the beliefs and behaviors of the natives of this (for us) novel environment. At first, we will assume that, unlike our new friends, we are experiencing things "just as they are." If our relationships deepen with these new friends though, we began to realize that we, like them, have been trained in how to experience the world.

Our experience of the world is constructed. There is no such thing as an immaculate perception.

Learning that individuals are trained by their native culture in how to experience the world provokes what we call "culture shock."

It is the awareness that human perception is relative rather than fixed. All immigrants understand this. When one first enters a new social environment, they usually find it fascinating. That's what we may call the tourist response. As the weeks and months pass by, however, the fascination turns to alarm. "These people really think and behave like this!"

We can cure culture shock only by returning to our native place or by altering our own sense of self. As new language, food, and social behaviors become familiar and "second nature," the tourist becomes a third culture child, an individual who belongs at some level to two or more cultures but is no longer fully immersed in any specific culture.

Future Shock

Immigrating to a new place is not the only thing that provokes culture shock. In the late 1960's, Alvin Toffler was already warning that we were entering an era in which rapid social change would result in social upheaval and personal disorientation. Individuals would experience culture shock without ever leaving their homeplace.

Toffler's best-selling *Future Shock* warned that Western peoples would soon begin reeling from cultural changes that had once occurred gradually over many centuries. The same kinds of changes would now begin to occur in very short periods of time. Such changes, he said, will soon force people to make serious, continual adjustments to their values and perception of the world. People, Toffler predicted, will have just adjusted to some major change when another change, just as radical, will demand their attention.

The reason *Future Shock* was a best seller was because people already knew, even in 1969, that the world was rapidly changing. Of course, we now know that Toffler grossly underestimated the pace and scope of the social changes he saw coming.

Those changes caught the Christian world particularly off guard. It would not be a stretch to say the much of the Christian community in the Western World suffers from future shock.

Communication technology—television, internet, social media—has thrust all of us, however rural or socially isolated, into future shock. Most of us now experience some level of unrelenting uprootedness and uncertainty. One can become unsure of where he is—even of who he is.

As a third-culture child, I have experienced culture shock several times in my life. What can prepare anyone for future shock? Culture shock leads to a reorganization of self and a familiarity with what was once a strange environment. Future shock doesn't resolve. At best it leads to an acceptance of never-ending social change.

In today's globalized and technologically wired world, we will have hardly reconstructed ourselves before we are thrust anew into new social norms. Words change meanings. Political and social alliances shuffle and then reassemble. Yesterday's way of communicating with one's friends suddenly causes offense. Political labels we only recently used to define ourselves shift meaning, leaving us without a clear label to identify ourselves.

We grow bewildered and infuriated.

A Community We Have Chosen

Without a stable ground of meaning and purpose, it's difficult to psychologically survive the ceaseless changes thrust upon us by our post-modern, globalized, wired world. Without compassionate ears, kind words, and deliberate patience, we have little hope of relating to our neighbors.

We won't always understand our neighbors of course, but we must try. Jesus told us that following him requires learning to love our neighbors as ourselves. That has never been easy. The contemporary world has made it seem impossible. Many of us are about to give up trying. We long for the comforts of our familiar blood and soil.

Christianity offers another way. It claims that we can choose to participate in a community based on something other than blood and soil. Jesus called it the Kingdom of God, a "nation" that transcends geography, language, and even time. However, unlike other kingdoms, this one celebrates the differences it works to unite. One remains a member of their own race, language, and history as they grow beyond the social confines of these things.

Christianity is not only a belief system and a practice. It is a community. A convert chooses not only to follow Christ, but to enter this community. They then learn to participate in the life of this community in the way Barfield has in mind. The Apostles' Creed calls this participation "the communion of saints." It is a transformational relationship with God, with angels, with "the spirits of just people made perfect," and with our fellow disciples still walking through life with us.

As we saw in the last chapter, Christianity teaches that one does not enter fully into personhood without such community. This aspect of Christianity angers many contemporary people, including, strangely enough, some Christians. Western peoples, particularly Americans, tend to imagine that healthy individuals do not need others to complete us.

Christianity in all its forms, disagrees. Our faith is irrepressibly communal. Without community it unravels.

In our last chapter, we talked about individuation, becoming a person rather than a mere "family fragment." In this chapter, we're looking at the other side of the coin, at the importance—indeed the indispensability—of community.

Few people today would choose the Athanasian Creed to describe how individuation and community interrelate to form and maintain one's personhood. Contemporary peoples, including most Christians, find Athanasius's statement unbearably laborious. They can't imagine why we should ever recite it. Most of us don't recite it —in church or anywhere else. Many Christians have never actually heard of Athanasius.

However, the reason Athanasius's words have endured is because their repetitious nature forces one to look at two things: how community transforms individuals into persons and how persons form and maintain community. In the words of the creed, it is important that we neither "confound the persons" nor divide the communal essence. In other words, healthy communities encourage individuation and healthy individuals form lasting communities.

It is this reciprocity between communal and individual life that makes Christianity's view of social life unique. Christianity does not achieve unity at the cost of individuation. Indeed, even Divine Unity embraces Divine difference. Difference among individual people can thus be viewed as a means of personal growth rather than a provocation for disunity. Individuals can gather around a common core rather than huddle together against the world.

Athanasius wrote his theological statement to define the Christian view of God: as Divine Unity containing Personal Difference. In the saint's own words, "We worship One God in Trinity, neither confounding the Persons nor dividing the essence." He probably didn't have sociology in mind. The implications are clear, nonetheless.

In many ways, we could interpret Athanasius for a Christian political theory, as indeed the founding fathers of the American republic seem to have done. Athanasius as a philosopher rather than a theologian, might have said that a healthy society maintains its unity while respecting the individual differences of the members that comprise it. Indeed, a healthy society develops and matures from both protecting its differences as well as its unity.

Without difference, a society grows stale. Without unity, the society dissolves into anarchy.

Without a balance of power among judges, legislators, and executives, each branch of government tends to become tyrannical.

Without a balance between local and federal authority, there is no accountability.

Without a balance between rights and responsibilities, the state lurches toward either tyranny or anarchy.

Individuality and Community

Of the two following statements, which do you think the more accurate?

1. Individual persons precede and supersede communities.
2. Communities precede and supersede the individuals that comprise them.

Contemporary Western peoples are more likely to choose the first statement. Our common sense leads us to think of community as something abstract, as an intentional or accidental gathering of individuals. We tend to assume that it is the persons *within* a community who are objectively real. In contrast, a community is merely a subjective idea, something that exists only in human imagination.

Ancient thinkers viewed this quite differently. Aristotle, for example, builds his great work, *Politics*, around the statement: "Man is a political animal." He meant that human individuals require community to become fully functioning persons, that individual humans rarely even survive without community.

This is most clearly true at the physical level. To survive, human infants need human adults. An adolescent may physically survive without other people, though this too is rare. Feral children, even after introduced to human society, do not learn to think, or communicate at the level healthy human beings take for granted.

As we halve already noted, community downloads the assumptions upon which the child constructs his or her own sense of personhood. They acquire language, food, opinions, religion, and social station in their early years. These things are not the result of the individual's personal quest. Indeed, changes made by an individual in any of these areas later in life are nearly always experienced as traumatic and disruptive, as what we call a *conversion*.

If you move a fifteen-year-old from rural Alabama to Kyoto, Japan and leave him there for five years with other Japanese, you can be sure that you will experience the man who returns as seriously altered. He will very likely become what we call a third culture individual and remain so for the rest of his life. After these years away, even his own family members will experience him as somewhat odd. He may not even be sure what "home" means anymore.

You could ask me how I know this to be true, but just take my word for it. This social dynamic is not an abstract or academic bit of knowledge for me or for other missionary children.

The writers of the New Testament agreed with Aristotle about how community precedes personhood. That is why the Church is depicted as "a New Jerusalem, coming down out of heaven," or why the Apostle Paul tells non-Jewish believers that they have become "fellow citizens with the saints." It is why Jesus says, "upon this rock I will build my Church," even before there were any converts for that Church.

For Jesus, the Church preceded the members. The Church was not as we tend to think now, simply a way of describing a gathering of believers. Rather, the New Testament writers describe Christian believers as individuals who had been "grafted in," "invited from the highways and byways," placed like "living stones in the temple of God," and so forth. They were immigrants who had left one society to become citizens in another, to use St. Paul's analogy.

The New Testament assumption was that through baptism, a new believer entered a new family. The convert would be re-socialized, gradually expected to replace his old assumptions about reality, his behavior, and the values he had received from his previous community. Through this change in community, a convert would become a very different person.

The Covenant Community envisioned by the New Testament writers purposefully cut across all other human distinctions. A Jew would become the brother of Egyptians or Persians. A Native American would become family-in-God with Russians and Germans. These relationships would become more intimate than the relationships an individual could have with the unbelievers of one's own natural ethnicity or class. This new Community had "come down from heaven," and included "angels, archangels, and all the host of heaven as well as the living and the dead of all times and places."

These are some of the most essential elements of New Testament faith. A "Christian" expression that fails to affirm them doesn't work. For example, a Christianized form of nationalism, that is to say nationalism that borrows Christian terminology to express itself, is heretical, even anti-Christ. The *piety* of Christian nationalism is more about nationalism than about Christianity, at least as Christian faith was defined by the New Testament writers and early Christians.

That said, Christian Community intentionally takes on elements of any human culture it serves. That is what incarnation means after all. Just as Christ became a human being, so does the Church become American, Russian, Chinese, and African. If this intentional process goes too far, however, the national adjective becomes the noun, which forces the noun (Church) to become the adjective. When this occurs, persons may profess Christianity while failing to become converted. They fail to leave old ties behind to become a "fellow citizen with the saints."

In the end, Christianity, unlike either contemporary liberalism or conservatism, is neither communal nor individualistic, but rather both. It is a community that develops and celebrates the process through which individuals become unique persons. It is also a covenantal relationship through which fully formed individual persons develop healthy community.

This Communal/Individual dynamic is what makes Christianity "utterly other than" the secular, sociopolitical narratives around it. This definition of Christian community needs recovery now. Without it, Christianity ping-pongs from one side of a radicalized culture to the other, becoming in the process ever-more frantic and unhinged.

Dependence, Independence, and Interdependence

In the *Seven Habits of Highly Effective People*, Stephen Covey made a valuable contribution to the way we talk about healthy individuation.

He said that human beings first experience themselves as dependent parts of a collective. Babies, for example, cannot survive without the care of others. For many years, they will function within a community that meets their needs without requiring much in return. At some point, though, the child becomes willing to trade the benefits of dependence for risky independence.

Some never outgrow independence. They remain hostile to any sense of obligation toward others or significant communal involvement.

Other people will slip back into a kind of dependence we call codependence, pretending to be an independent adult while becoming enmeshed in relationships that do not require much mature contribution.

The aim of a healthy human adult, Covey said, is to move through independence, to avoid codependence, and finally to grow into healthy interdependence. That is a state in which mature adult persons provide and receive care and assistance in ways that promote the flourishing of all involved.

It is a secular way of expressing what biblical formation seems to be about: becoming a person who both stands face-to-face with God as an individual and at the same time takes his or her place within a community. The idea here is that Church is something much more than merely a collection of individual believers, but a covenant family in which the Holy Spirit resides. In this community, individuals respond to God both as individuals and as a community of individuals. The community in this way forms healthy individuals who then make possible healthy communities.

Because interdependence requires considerable maturity and maintenance, human societies tend to lean either toward communitarianism or individualism. In many human societies, it's challenging to become a real individual, with views of practices that differ from the group. In Western culture, especially in the United States, one is expected to become an individual, but community is difficult to maintain.

Christianity thus becomes a challenge to both communitarian and individualistic cultures because it promotes both individuation and community. In this way, it resists both Ayn Rand's form of libertarianism and Karl Marx's form of communism. Christian society is modeled after its theological view of God, as unity containing difference and of persons committed to unity.

The Spiritual Nature of Community

We will conclude this chapter with this summation of a Christian sociology: that human community, whether family, nation, religion, or any other association existing over time with discernible aims, values, and assumptions, is a spiritual entity. Community is thus something more than an abstract term describing a collection of individuals. It has life and character of its own that not only develops from the life of its members but that actively sustains itself over time.

Spiritual forces reside within human communities that influence individuals for good and evil. Human cultures are therefore capable of war and peace, good and evil, redemption and decline. Christianity is itself such an entity, existing both among and apart from the nations and all other forms of human community.

Christianity is an eschatological movement, which is to say it exists to proclaim a future state of human flourishing in which the nations will submit to the teachings of Christ, war will cease, and God's intended design for creation will be fully realized. Although no human being knows what that will look like, scripture centers the anticipated future of humankind as one that emerges from the love of God and the love of redeemed human beings for one another.

21

Love is All We Need

Christians are called to offer their unique perspectives of reality to others in winsome rather than in combative ways and to demonstrate willingness to learn from (and cooperate with) others, especially in the work of healing bodies, minds, and societies.

IN AN EARLIER CHAPTER, I PICKED ON JOHN LENNON'S SONG, "Imagine." So, I thought I could redeem myself by reflecting favorably on another Beatle's song. The lyrics are straightforward. Mostly, they repeat just the title: "Love is All You Need." I think the Apostle John would agree. He said that God is love. So, this song is literally a summation of everything: all we need is indeed, love.

The apostle John says that God sent Christ into the world because God loved the world, and so that through Christ, all would be saved. Christians believe that Jesus is God's chosen face to the world. That means that through Christ, God came to love us and to teach us how to love one another.

The truth is, though, that even many Christians find the teachings of Jesus troubling. How is it possible to love as he taught us to love?

We call our faith Christianity, a term built around the word

Christ. We claim to be a community that revolves around Christ. However, for the most part, we prefer talking about what Jesus did or who we believe he was, than about the things Jesus said. Some believers dismiss Mathew's summary of Christ's teachings (in chapters 5, 6, & 7), claiming that Christ's words have little to do with the Christian doctrine and practices that would come after Christ's resurrection.

Even in his own day, Jesus noticed the strange disconnect his followers made between him as a person and the teachings he offered. "Why do you call me Lord, Lord, but do not do what I ask you to do?" (Luke 6:46)

He went on to tell a story about a man who built his house on sand. When the wind and flood came, that house collapsed. Of course, it did. It had no foundation. Clearly, Jesus didn't expect us to thank him for his death and resurrection and then decide that what he had taught was just too impractical for real life.

So, what did Jesus teach?

The message of Jesus revolved around love. He said that love begins in God's radical hospitality. Literally everyone, he said, is invited into a relationship paradoxically requiring nothing and everything. God's radical hospitality accepts us as we are. It then gradually transforms us into something we would never have imagined. All Christ requires us to do is to say yes.

When we do say yes, Christ tells us to extend the same radical hospitality we have received from him to others, including our enemies. We are to constantly forgive ourselves and others. We must endure persecution if it comes our way. We are to do all within our power to avoid our own propensity toward hatred and violence. We keep our word, even when it results in loss. We cannot, even in our imagination, sexually objectify others. We must not disdain others. Jesus acknowledges the difficulty of living by his teaching:

"Enter in by the narrow gate. It is the way that leads to life."

Love, as Jesus defines it, is radical, transformational grace. It is not transactional: "I'll scratch your back if you scratch mine."

Indeed, it is sacrificial. It loves when love is not returned. It serves when that service goes unacknowledged. It is a form of life that involves a cross, a death, and unimaginable trust. This requires a continual stretch toward God. Selfishness, tribalism, and entrenchment into what one already knows and accepts are impediments to the kind of love Christ offers, which makes his teaching a threat to self.

C. S. Lewis's *The Four Loves* may be one of the most helpful studies on the word love. He argues that we use the word in so many ways that we often confuse its meaning. Admittedly, there is something similar in loving ice cream, loving one's dog, loving one's nation, loving one's children, or loving God. Learning to love anything stretches one's attention away from self. However, often the stretch is a means of consenting to something that meets one's own needs.

Lewis explains the meaning of love by categorizing these forms of attraction around four Greek words: storge, eros, phileo, and agape.

Storge is the kind of love we feel when we say something like, "I *love* that old chair," or even "I *love* the kind receptionist that has worked at my doctor's office through the years."

Eros is arousal, as in "Oh! Look at that woman wearing that green sweater and high heels. I think I am *falling in love* with her." Other kinds of strong attraction can also be erotic, as in, "I just can't get enough of that neurology class; I want to know everything I can about the human brain!"

Phileo is love of friends and community, as in "I love my cousin. I will be glad to do whatever she needs me to do." Phileo is also willful obligation, the loyalty one feels for family and clan.

Agape is the kind of love Christ wanted us to have. It is a nontransactional form of personal regard. It seeks the good of the beloved, whether that love is reciprocated, appreciated, or even acknowledged. For example, a mother in labor pleads for the doctor to save her baby's life even if it requires the loss of her own. "There is no greater love than this," Jesus said, "that one would lay down his life for his friend."

When the New Testament writers talk about love, it's usually agape they have in mind. "Hereby we know the love of God," Paul writes, "not that we love God, but that God loved us." In such passages, we are asked to reflect on how God's love (agape) works for our eternal good, whether we are aware of it, appreciate it, or return it.

The Latin vulgate translated agape as *caritas*, which in the King James Version became the word *charity*. Of course, today the word charity points toward something much narrower. It also carries a negative connotation. That is why we rarely use it now even in theological discussions. It is helpful to keep the history of this word in mind, though, because in the much beloved 1 Corinthians 13, St. Paul struggles to define and express the foundational role of agape in the Christian view of life. Even though I realize that the way our language has changed through the centuries can lead us to misinterpret passages in the KJV, I believe this version offers the best overall rendering of the Apostle's teaching about agape.

Paul says charity (agape) is more important than supernatural gifts. "Though I speak with the tongues of men and angels and have not charity, I am a sounding brass and tinkling cymbal. And though I have the gift of prophesy, and understand all mysteries and all knowledge; and though I have all faith so that I could remove mountains and have not charity . . ."

He says that charity (agape) is more important than fund drives or social causes. "Though I bestow all my goods to feed the poor, and though I give my body to be burned and have not charity, it profiteth me nothing." All other forms of motivation fail, but charity never fails. Storge can fail. Eros can fail. Phileo can fail. Agape does not.

Paul concludes the chapter by saying that hope, faith, and love are all eternal qualities. However, the greatest of these is love. Social causes, fund drives, and spiritual gifts are all good things. In fact, we should seek spiritual gifts, if, that is, we are motivated by agape.

Agape, in other words, is the central preoccupation of Christian faith. Without it, other important spiritual things—justice, faithfulness, righteousness, missions—all become twisted. For example, from a Christian perspective, the aim of justice is to restore a community and the individuals who comprise it to a state of shalom —to peaceful flourishing as God defines it. We resist injustice not because we hate those who do unjust things but because we love the people—including the unjust people—harmed by injustice. When our motivation for justice is rage, we never attain justice, at least as scripture defines it.

When we love, we do not do unjust things in the name of justice. When we work for justice because we are enraged at unjust people, we become willing to achieve a state of justice (as we define it) by whatever means available. This results in tyranny, oppression, and violence, not sometimes but always. We replace the unjust people with oppressed people who then repeat the same social conditions as before. As the old saying goes, "During the revolution, when you tear down the statues, be sure to save the pedestals!"

Faithfulness to God is likewise an outgrowth of love, not a fastidious obsession with what we consider keeping God's rules. The Prophet Micah rhetorically asks, "What does God require of you?" Then he answers his own question. "That you love justice, do mercy and walk humbly with your God."

If love is the motivation and aim of justice, one will, as much as humanly possible, seek to love the oppressor as well as the oppressed. That doesn't mean that we do not try or convict people of crimes. It does mean that we keep in mind that sometimes oppressors are unaware that they are oppressing. Perhaps they inherited a social system they never thought to question. Love, therefore, seeks to make unjust people aware of how their injustice is harming others. Reformers motivated by love offer the gift of repentance to those willing to learn the truth. Love seeks to bring oppressor and oppressed into community in a new and healthy way.

Nelson Mandela seemed to have learned this. After the end of apartheid, he knew that the last thing his country needed was a new cycle of violence, resentment, and revenge. He risked his nation's respect to lead them into a process of truth and reconciliation.

Love, in this view, is the cure for the world's afflictions. Love is what motivated God to save humanity from sin (for God so loved the world that He gave his only begotten Son). Having learned the nature of love from God, human beings could learn to forgive one another. They could seek the good of their neighbor, even of their enemy.

Because we live in a fallen world, those who love may find themselves surrounded by people who do not believe that love as "all we need." They may even persecute and oppress. So those who love must be prepared to suffer, "like sheep among wolves."

In the end, however, the meek will inherit the earth. The lovers will win.

Learning to love others equips one to love their community and indeed, all of nature.

Agape leads to practical service. Those gripped by compassion feed the hungry and clothe the naked. They lighten the load of the blind. They create infrastructure that enables otherly enabled people to participate in dignified community. Love motivates a community to keep its water and air as clean as possible for those who will live after us.

Perhaps it seems we are too narrowly defining Christian love as agape. However, the other loves referred to by C. S. Lewis also have redemptive qualities. For example, most of the time, we seek change because we feel personally harmed in some way by the status quo. Longing for relief, we are drawn toward what we think will make a difference. Such a longing is a form of erotic energy. It motivates us to attach ourselves to something or someone we believe can make a positive difference in our lives. Indeed, what draws us toward God is at first erotic, in the sense that we seek God because we want something.

As you will see from these remarks, erotic energy is not always sexual in nature. Sexuality is what usually first comes to mind when we hear the word erotic, though. That can make it challenging to discuss the blessings of eros in a Christian context.

Christianity has often failed to address the goodness of sexual life. After puberty, most people will deal in some way with their own sexual desires. For some, the desire is unwelcome. If they are for some reason unable to find a partner, or believe they are called to celibacy, sexual desire often feels more like a temptation than a jolt of life. Others experience their lack of desire as a burden, particularly if they are married to a partner desiring a sexual relationship. Christianity has rarely faced such situations with enough grace or wisdom.

The Christian moral ethic has insisted that sexual life is not to be idolized. That was an important liberation for many believers in the first century, as the classicist Sarah Ruden so powerfully articulated in her book *Paul Among the People*. However, the Church has often gone to the opposite extreme—demonizing the longing to join one's body to that of another. Traditional Christian morality has insisted that unmarried people should live celibate lives. Most believers have tried to accept this teaching and to live accordingly.

Time has exposed the enormous suffering caused by the often woefully inadequate view of sexual life perpetuated by our faith. If holiness is something more than prepubescence and chastity something more than shame, then humanity is owed something more than what Christianity, especially Christianity in the modern period, has offered.

In times past, the church made room for unmarried people to find at least healthy community through which they might make a meaningful contribution. Monastic life was one of the most important ways Christians of the past did this. In Protestant nations, however, even this avenue for meaningful community was closed to unmarried people. The burden of unfulfilled sexual desire, both within marriage and outside it, has been incredibly challenging for many. Increasingly, people have found it to be unreasonably cruel.

Many Christians have resisted all forms of sexual education, leading to a mostly unspoken sense that sexual life is incompatible with holiness. For those who, for whatever reason, were without any form of legitimate sexual expression (as the Church defined it), silence, shame, and a continual sense of moral defeat have been the nearly unbearable fruit.

This is one of the fault lines that separates believers into either traditional or nontraditional points of view. The truth is, most Christians find themselves somewhere in between these extremes.

We know that for most people, love hungers for sexual embodiment. Even the most traditional believer often struggles to find a way forward to adequately address this reality. Nonetheless, most Christians accept that sexuality is a force that must be managed according to some sort of moral code.

Since this is a book that aims to broaden our ability to communicate with contemporary realities, I'm trying to avoid insensitivity about sexual life. That said, many believers throughout history have embraced celibacy not because they were not a sexual person but because they believed God had called them to do so. For such people, and I am not one of them, the loss of erotic life has led not to an embittered compliance with antiquated rules, but to the flourishing of love for the entire human family.

A comparison between two women will illustrate the difference between how traditional Christians and contemporary secular people view erotic life. One of these women is a fictitious character in a film. The other is an unlikely saint.

In *Good Luck to You, Leo Grande*, Emma Thompson plays the role of a newly widowed elderly woman. The film begins with the widow waiting for someone in a hotel room. She has hired a young sex worker who goes by the name Leo Grande. She explains that she has never experienced full sexual life. Her late husband, she says, was reserved and unimaginative. She goes on to reveal that she has never expressed real sexual passion and has never experienced an orgasm. Most of the film then revolves around a dialogue related to these claims. It ends with a few short scenes that tell us that the widow has achieved her goals through the experienced guidance of Leo Grande.

From a secular viewpoint, it's hard to fault the widow. The film leads the viewer to conclude, "Well, good for you." On further reflection though, we find ourselves asking about the ethics of hiring a person to serve one's sexual fantasies. The widow, for whom we develop a degree of sympathy, seems dismissive of her own children, experiencing them more as burdens than as individuals. She never mentions any friends. She describes her career as a religious instructor in ways that reveal no sense of meaningful vocation.

Recalling her middle school students as disinterested in their own education, she exposes her envy of their youth and sexuality.

The widow's only truly significant memory is about a Greek man who once aroused her when she was a teenager. She had been on vacation with her family and had experienced a passionate moment with the man outside the hotel. She was sexually awakened by his intimate touch, but the moment was interrupted by the arrival of a car. This had left her with an unconsummated longing that had overshadowed the rest of her life.

The week after my wife and I watched *Good Luck to You, Leo Grande*, we watched a documentary about Dorothy Day. As a young woman, Day was a Marxist, concerned about urban poverty in America. An important part of her revolutionary persona was being sexually active. When this led to an unplanned pregnancy, she had a dangerous abortion in an apartment building. When the procedure was over, she discovered that her partner had abandoned her. After she became pregnant again, she refused to abort the child and so became a single mother.

When her daughter was ready for school, Day enrolled her in a Catholic school. While attending an obligatory mass with her daughter, Day experienced the presence of God. So, she decided to become a Christian.

After some time, Day decided to ask God for help in living a celibate life. Although not fully convinced of the reasonableness of celibacy, Day nonetheless submits herself to the Christian path she has professed. She then pours her energy into feeding hungry people and advocating for America's poor and uneducated. She makes a family with those who come to help her in her work.

Several years after her death, Pope John Paul II declared Dorothy Day to be a saint.

Both films are moving accounts about what one does with sexual desire. In one, a woman meets her sexual needs by hiring a sex worker. She treats him well. She is grateful to him for the fulfilling experiences he helps her achieve. As the film concludes, we have the sense that she's ready to live a more fulfilling life, at least as she defines it.

In the second film, another woman deals with sexual desire by reluctantly asking for grace to live a celibate life. She then turns her attention toward the care of others.

What we must notice in both accounts is that erotic life affects one's soul. It, therefore, should not be demonized or underappreciated. Nonetheless, all forms of human love are meant to deepen and evolve. Erotic attraction should either lead to commitment or be respectfully managed, not only in romantic and sexual life but in all areas of life. For example, when we meet someone with the sort of contacts and talents that can help our career, we should acknowledge the transactional nature of the relationship. Of course, once we get to know the person, the relationship may well deepen into a full-blown friendship. Erotic life is transactional by nature. It is therefore prone to manipulation and exploitation.

Storge too can seriously enrich our lives. If we are fond of an old church, we may volunteer to clean or repair it, for example. As we work, we see that people are moved to silence as they enter it. We decide to do all we can to preserve it, which will enrich the lives of future generations. A wholesome affection for objects then need not be idolatrous. It can become a conduit for our care and concern for others.

Once we realize that the core of life is love—love in all its forms —we learn to share it appropriately with others. We come to realize that trying to impose our moral beliefs and practices on others not only fails to advance faith in the world, but it also undermines the redemptive power of faith. As Dorothy Day discovered, only an authentic encounter with God's love moves one's soul to hunger for holiness, the spiritual ground of our being.

In the end, this is the sort of love that truly is all we need.

Common Grace

We begin to understand now what some Reformed writers in the nineteenth century (including Abraham Kuyper) called "common grace."

The concept develops from the words of Jesus: "the Heavenly

Father sends rain on both the just and the unjust." Common grace implies that if a non-Christian offers a tomato to a Christian neighbor, the Christian should accept, give God thanks, eat it, and express gratitude for the gift. Few Christians would disagree with that.

However, the principle holds true in science, philosophy, finances, and in every other field of human life. Atheists and Hindus; Buddhists and Muslims; libertarians and communists; Republicans and Democrats; men, women, boys, and girls, receive the same rain from the same Heavenly Father.

All kinds of human beings make discoveries that benefit others. Hindus discovered the concept of zero. Muslims refined and shared the numerical system used now throughout the Western world. We would be still using Roman numerals, making contemporary mathematics challenging if not impossible, without the concept of zero or the Arabic numerical system. It's difficult to imagine how computers could have ever been invented. Because the Heavenly Father's rain falls everywhere on everyone, humanity continues to develop knowledge and to improve its quality of life.

The view of common grace is grounded in love. It leads Christians to become hospitable to non-Christians and to the gifts they offer the world. This enables Christians to view medical science, neurology, sociology, psychology, physics, the arts, government, and all the other aspects of civilization that alleviate human suffering and advance human wholeness, as allies in the common human struggle against chaos and existential anarchy—the great enemies of all that is good, true, and beautiful.

This leads us to ask an important question about what most characterizes Christian piety: is holiness about withdrawing from human society, as Christians have sometimes assumed, or is it about a redemptive interaction with society?

If love is the defining characteristic of a follower of Christ, if it is the central motivation and aim of Christian belief and practice, then the answer is obvious. Love is not an isolated, self-serving way of life. It is a life lived for God and others through which one's own life becomes abundant.

22

Managing Reality

Human beings in covenant with God and with God's Redemptive Community are responsible for stewarding that portion of creation, social order, and redemptive mission that lies within their own sphere of influence, and to do so to the highest level that their gifts, experience, and placement in the world make possible.

THE 126ᵀᴴ PSALM IS ONE OF MY FAVORITE PASSAGES. IT'S A PRAYER of Thanksgiving by Jews returning from a long captivity in Babylon. When I read it, I always hear the voice of Bob Marley!

"It was like a dream," the Psalmist says. "We couldn't stop laughing; we just kept breaking into song. The people around us kept saying that God had done great things for us, and it was true, God had done great things for us!"

Then comes a bit of advice they had gathered from their long years of exile: "Those who go forth weeping, bearing precious seed" (seed saved for sowing) "will doubtless come again rejoicing, bringing his sheaves with him."

These are the lines that inspired the frontier American hymn, "Bringing in the Sheaves." It reuses the Psalm's farming metaphor. I don't know about you, but I rarely deal with sheaves. I have only a vague notion of what they are. So perhaps contemporary readers will understand it better if we use an investment metaphor.

During the last few hundred years, the Western World gradually learned that small investments incrementally made at compound interest (interest earned on interest) eventually become a great sum of money. I am not particularly gifted or trained in financial management. So, I'm not offering financial advice. However, I have learned that when we *owe* money, especially on credit cards, compound interest works *against* us. That wonderful deal I got last year that cost me "only $99 while supplies last," can end up costing $200 if I pay only the minimum monthly payments.

When I buy on credit, I'm contributing to my bank's investment strategy. I am rarely contributing to my own financial well-being. Therefore, our banks have marble floors, but our houses don't!

On the other hand, if instead of using that $100 to buy the impressive gadget for "$99 while supplies last" I invest it and am willing to not see the money again for several years, my $100 may easily become a thousand dollars.

I know this because in my early 40s I began setting aside 10% of my income for retirement. Through many of those years that was a hard thing to do. In fact, there were a couple of years when I couldn't manage to put aside anything. During the financial meltdown a few years back, I adopted the very mature strategy of not even looking at my investment statements. Nonetheless, I kept on investing during the years of international uncertainty. I certainly don't regret doing it today.

I only wish I had started earlier.

The interesting thing about investment is that the investments I made during the years the market was down grew much quicker (and became larger) than the investments I made while the market was booming. That is what this Psalm is referring to by "sowing in tears." It expresses the determination to keep contributing toward a distant future goal, even though we would prefer to put our resources to a more enjoyable use today.

When I was a young man, an insurance agent once told me that there was an old man counting on me who would starve unless I fed him, and that old man was myself. Life insurance is not the best investment one can make, though it is very important, but that is where I began and even though I'm not that great at it, I have something rather than nothing because I now am that older man the insurance agent was talking about.

Warren Buffett, the great investment guru, is known for putting great sums of money into stock when the market is down, when everyone else is pulling all their money out. That's called a contrarian strategy, and he's done well for himself using it. His approach seems to be what this Psalm is talking about.

Like I said, I'm no financial expert. Other people can give you good advice about managing money. Indeed, they may tell you that what I'm saying is not good advice. What I do know is that the investments we make during lean times, what this passage calls "bearing seed for sowing in times of tears," can become a great harvest down the road. Sowing seed is one of the few things human beings can do about growing fruits and vegetables. We are not in charge of the rain, the sun, or the quality of the soil we are given. This is also true of financial markets.

Adam Smith, in his still important book, *The Wealth of Nations*, calls the economic elements that are beyond human control the "invisible hand." He didn't believe the "invisible hand" of the economy was the hand of God but merely the unpredictable nature of accumulated human action. We can't control that. We can only make decisions for ourselves when that invisible hand tosses us around.

The Bible continually warns us about the spiritual danger of wealth. However, it also warns us about the dangers of political power, alcohol, and sexual life. These dangers are why God calls some people into poverty, or total abstinence from alcohol, or into a career far removed from managing others. God even calls some people to celibacy.

Most of us, on the other hand, are called to learn how to steward these great forces, to manage them, to direct our sexual lives, our food and drink, our money and so forth toward the purpose God has called us to live. So, a "Christian economics" is not mostly related to money or financial management—that's simply the illustration I am using to explain this Psalm. What we want to know is how the principle of sowing and reaping works in other areas of our life: our education, our health, our natural talent, and, most importantly, our spiritual lives. We want to remember that raw products are not finished products, that what comes to us in nature nearly always requires human crafting and care.

For example, it takes a lot of discipline to form a habit and to maintain it until it becomes a part of our everyday rhythm of life. However, making small investments consistently over a lifetime, whether the investment is money, physical fitness, talent—whatever it is that we wish to invest—must become such a habit. Furthermore, we may not see much fruit from our investments for a very long time. That's why it's so easy to abandon our habit of making investments, especially when we pass through a season when we would much rather use our time or our money for some immediate pleasure nearby. This passage of scripture recognizes that and teaches us—and it's not the only scripture that says this—that if we persist, we will one day be shocked by the impact our small, incremental investments have made.

On my trip to Italy, I discovered that I understood 75% of everything I heard or read. Had you asked me a couple of years ago if I spoke Italian, I would have said no. As it turns out, I understand the language fairly well. I can, in other words, carry on conversations with Italian speakers. I'm no expert. I make many mistakes. But I can function in the Italian language if I need to—and I do need to, for buying gelato if for nothing else!

The reason I can function in Italian is that I speak Spanish and French. I have also studied Latin. These are all languages related to Italian. I learned Spanish as a child, French as a young adult. More importantly, I have continued to read in those languages, watch movies in them and so forth.

Then, a couple of years ago, when I began to think about going to Italy, I spent 30 minutes a day, five days a week specifically on Italian, using a powerful language-learning program called

Pimsleur. I did this for four months. On this trip, my nerdy habit paid me some rewarding dividends.

Stewardship involves two things:

1. Knowing your vocation, knowing the thing you are supposed to do in life, and,
2. Aiming your resources toward that calling.

Now, it may not make sense for you to spend a lot of your time studying language. I have sometimes wondered if it's made a lot of sense for me to do it. However, one of the things I am called to do is to serve people of different ethnic and linguistic communities. I have a missionary call and have needed language skills to carry out this vocation. I do genuinely love studying language, but it has also served a practical purpose in my line of work.

The Presbyterian writer Eugene Peterson explained this concept best in the book that made him famous, *A Long Obedience in the Same Direction*. The title alone expresses the importance of continual sowing, during good times and bad, over a long, long time. Peterson knew his vocation. He was called to be a pastoral theologian—a pastor who taught believers how to access the teachings of their faith and put those teachings into practice. Peterson was called to be a pastor who taught, as well as a teacher who pastored.

Once he knew his vocation, Peterson could then steward his resources of time, money, relationships, and intellect, to learn what he was supposed to learn and then share with us not only what he had learned but how to apply the knowledge to our everyday lives. This is the Christian stewardship task for every believer. First, we must learn what it is we are supposed to do. We cannot focus our resources until we know our calling. But once we learn what our calling is, we focus our resources on it, day after day, for the rest of our lives. That's what Peterson meant by "a long obedience in the same direction."

The 126th Psalm tells us that we may not see the full harvest from the seeds we plant. In Italy, we visited the catacombs, where early believers gathered to pray and bury their loved ones. 500,000 believers were buried there over four centuries. We also visited museums and palaces of those who reaped the fruit of the sacrifices made by those earlier generations. We are still reaping the seed that the early believers sowed.

This long obedience in the same direction is the ordinary way God works in our lives.

The Gospel of John tells us that Jesus turned water into wine. That is interesting, of course, but then again God had been turning water into wine since the beginning of time. Jesus only sped up the process!

Charismatic spirituality has reminded us that God can do great things suddenly, unexpectedly, without prior preparation. However, that is not the ordinary way God works. A word of prophecy may tell us something we did not know before, which can be very helpful. Usually though, we learn how to discern the providential instructions that God has folded into nature and into the life situations in which we are placed. We pray for the sick and we often see people improve and occasionally, even dramatically healed. Normally, though, we heal people by studying and practicing medicine. Practicing medicine requires a long obedience in the same direction. It requires sowing in tears while others are just having fun. It's harder than the instantaneous success we all hope for.

Flying over the North Atlantic, I usually experience turbulence. I have learned it rarely affects our scheduled time of arrival. The pilot knows his origin. He knows his destination and his general flight plan. He does not know whether there will be mechanical malfunction or unexpected turbulence. He may get sick. A passenger may die. There may be other situations outside his control. The pilot knows only that the plane constantly adjusts its speed and altitude to keep things on course. In nearly every flight, the plane arrives as planned.

As we live out our vocation, we always face the vicissitudes of life. Numerous forces toss us here and there. Like the pilot, we don't know what we'll face as we live out our vocation. That is why the Psalmist tells us to keep sowing the seed corn into the ground even if we must do it through tears. Although we would rather eat the seed corn, we must steward our resources with wisdom and prudence.

The apostle Paul did this. That is why he could say at the end of his life, "I have fought a good fight. I have kept the course."

I once casually walked by the prison where Paul wrote those words. It's about a 15-minute walk from what's left of the Coliseum, one of the world's most valuable buildings. When I took the tour, no one pointed out that Paul was once there. I too was caught up with the grandeur of the Colosseum. I was not thinking about the unspeakable horrors that occurred in that place. The distraction was even more powerful in Paul's time.

There was little Paul could do about slavery, the brutal gladiator games, the oppression of the poor, and all the other nasty sides of ancient Roman life. Paul was in prison. The emperor was on the throne. Nonetheless, Paul didn't use his imprisonment as an excuse to get off course. He didn't say, "Well, I guess the Empire has won." No, Paul wrote a few letters.

He wrote reflections on scripture and thoughts about his aspirations and anxieties for the future. Today, only scholars read the edicts of the emperors. Millions of people in hundreds of languages read Paul's letters. Few people can think of the emperor's name that ruled when Paul was alive. Most people know who Paul was.

I was wondering this week about Peter and what he was thinking as he awaited execution. As the soldier's dragged him into Nero's Circus to be publicly crucified—this was nothing out-of-the-ordinary for Rome; Peter was just the public entertainment for the day —what went through *his* mind? And as the believers laid his body to rest in a pauper's crave just outside of the great circus, what did *they* think

While in Italy, I visited one of the early Christian cemeteries. The graves were forgotten for centuries and then rediscovered after 1500 years. They just weren't all that important. But why did the people buried in them keep on doing what they were doing, generation after generation?

Today, Peter's grave is covered by one of the world's greatest buildings. It is filled with priceless art, visited by millions of people every year. We can justifiably ask whether it was a good thing to build St. Peter's on the sacrifices that the apostle Peter and other early Christians made. What cannot be denied is the harvest of that seed they sowed into the world, not only a harvest of souls that gather each Sunday around the world but even the powerful art and other products of civilization that have been created because of them.

And what of us?

When I became the pastor of the last church I pastored, I had plans I was excited to accomplish. I worked on doing that as best I could, but circumstances and political realities continually interfered. Changes within and around the church continually required my attention. At any rate, most of my dreams for the church remained unrealized. As a result, I sometimes have felt inadequate. On the other hand, as I was trying to live out my vocation, a new generation of believers grew up. Realizing that younger leaders were ready to step up to the plate, I stepped aside.

I'm in a different stage of life now. I can forget about my dreams and just go fishing. However, since I am not dead, I am not done. I am thus responsible for staying the course, both for my own life and for the sake of those yet to come. I must not eat the seed corn by treating the rest of my life as an extended vacation. I must keep sowing precious seed, even if I do not live to see much of the fruit of what I sow. And what is the seed I am given to sow? It is very likely the gifts and experiences that have arisen from my own unique circumstances and experiences of life.

A few years ago, my parents gave me a journal for my birthday. Rather than keep my day-to-day reflections in it, I began writing some short scenes of life as I had experienced it in the Appalachian Mountains. Slowly, I realized that my writing was becoming a novel. I had started it as a joke, but once I got into it, I discovered that it offered me a place to express my thoughts about faith, Appalachian life, and just life in general. In the novel, I could ask what had been healthy about our faith as we experienced it in mountain culture and what had been unhealthy.

My novel was not *War and Peace* nor *Les Miserables*. However, we do not refuse to do what we can simply because our gifts do not compare well with those of others. Even if I begin to paint today, it is unlikely I will ever produce anything like the Sistine Chapel. I am no Michelangelo. However, that doesn't mean I should not paint at all, if that is what I feel compelled to do. And I feel compelled to write!

Several times a week, I write my reflections about life on social media. Some people like what I write, others don't. I often think I am wasting my time. I don't always enjoy the feedback, but I keep doing it anyway. I believe someone needs to offer something different than regurgitated clichés and propaganda. Some attempt at conversation should be made. I also write books, including my first novel. None of my books have been best sellers, but they have allowed me to offer a contribution.

My point is that a *Long Obedience in the Same Direction*—sowing through times of tears, investing during times of scarcity, making a continual contribution to something one believes in, and doing something one is called to do—never ends. It continues until we are dead. And, sometimes, the harvest comes later—much later.

Perhaps in fifty years, my novel, *The Miracle Worker of Mingo County*, will be lauded as the quintessential novel of Appalachia. I'm not holding my breath about that, but what do I know?

In the meantime, I keep on sowing. Like the old gospel song puts it, we are—

Sowing in the morning, sowing seeds of kindness,
Sowing in the noontide and the dewy eve;
Waiting for the harvest, and the time of reaping,
We shall come rejoicing, bringing in the sheaves.

Sowing in the sunshine, sowing in the shadows,
Fearing neither clouds nor winter's chilling breeze;
By and by the harvest, and the labor ended,
We shall come rejoicing, bringing in the sheaves.

Going forth with weeping, sowing for the Master,

Though the loss sustained our spirit often grieves;
When our weeping's over, He will bid us welcome,
We shall come rejoicing, bringing in the sheaves.

Bringing in the sheaves, bringing in the sheaves,
We shall come rejoicing, bringing in the sheaves,
Bringing in the sheaves, bringing in the sheaves,
We shall come rejoicing, bringing in the sheaves.

I think the greatest statement on Christian stewardship may have been Victor Hugo's *Les Miserables*. The novel's main character, Jean Val Jean, is a convict who finds a new way to live. In time, he becomes moderately wealthy. However, he doesn't fit in with either the urban poor, who suspect him because of his wealth, or the aristocracy, who suspect him because of his concern for the poor. Neither side of the aisle view him as a reliable colleague because his view of economics is based on stewardship instead of either entitlement or envy. He views his resources as tools for carrying out his vocation rather than as his personal property to use only for his own pleasure. He creates companies in which people make a just wage.

There are many examples of this in history. In fact, the Guinness brewing company in Dublin is one of the most successful of these. That one company was probably the single most important factor in the transformation of Dublin into a community of educated, cultured people. That process began because the founder heard a single sermon from John Wesley about stewardship!

At the time of this writing, my country is involved in a bitter dispute about the future of the nation's economy. As with most topics, the loudest voices are on the extremes. At one end, there is a defense for outright socialism, in which the state assumes responsibility for most aspects of the citizen's lives. At the other end is a form of libertarian capitalism in which most communal responsibility toward the citizenry is denied. Understandably, each side of the debate attempts to discredit the other. Less understandably, each side also attempts to demonize moderate forms of its own position.

Thus, any form of capitalism that seeks to provide a measure of safety for the disabled, the aged, or the sick is denied the right to call itself "capitalist" and is maligned as a dishonest form of "socialism."

The same thing occurs on the other side. Any communal response to the needs of the citizenry that encourages personal responsibility and reasonable proof of need can be labeled as "heartless capitalism."

The word "economic" comes from *economia*, or household management. (Oikos means family.) The Christian views his or her responsibilities as radiating out from a center: managing my body and personal resources for the good of my own family, for the community of which my family is a part, and, as much as is within my power, for the entire human family.

So far in this chapter, we have talked mostly about money and entrepreneurship. However, for a Christian, the same principles affect every area of life. Our talents, experience, and influence—all that we have—are given to be wisely and compassionately used to the glory of God and the good of humanity. They are not to be either misused or disused.

Since Christians are called to investigate and to participate in all aspects of human life and culture, we are not given the option to avoid the quest for human flourishing. For this reason, Christians should submit themselves for life-long development in the fields in which they serve. They should function at as high a level of competence as their abilities allow. Although Christians view the world differently than their secular colleagues and those who follow other religions, Christian faith is never an excuse for incompetence, sloth, or the use of ignorance as an expression of piety.

Christians are stewards charged with developing their gifts for the glory of God and the good of humanity. That is what Jesus taught in the parable of the talents.

This stewardship includes the way we develop and use our intellectual gifts.

The central theme of this book has been about how Christianity should engage with the contemporary world, both by offering a contrasting view of reality and by a humble willingness to learn and adapt. We have looked at some of the most important scientific discoveries of our time, acknowledging that some of these discoveries call for a reevaluation of what Western Christians have heretofore assumed about reality. Even after honest and sincere evaluation of such new discoveries, however, we have seen that Christians often come to different conclusions than their non-Christian colleagues about what these discoveries imply.

The reason for this difference is because Christians do not relegate the ethical, moral, and metaphysical assumptions of their faith to merely "the religious part of life." Rather, the Christian revelation functions as a "lens" through which believers experience the entirety of life. In other words, Christianity cannot fit within any worldview alien to its assumptions about reality. Christianity is itself a worldview into which one's experience and discoveries are interpreted.

Indeed, this is the foundation of anything unique Christianity offers to the contemporary world: a different way of viewing and understanding reality that we believe holds up to the increasing data gathered by contemporary scientists and mathematicians.

Of all the things we are given to steward for the glory of God and the benefit of humanity, the most important thing is what the Apostle Peter referred to when asked to heal a beggar at the Temple gate: we do not have silver and gold to give you. What we do have, we will give: in the Name of Jesus Christ of Nazareth, rise and walk.

What we have that's unique is the knowledge that we live in a Creation purposefully designed by a Creator who loves us and came to visit us. That means, things are not as they seem. Something wondrous and life-giving peers through the cracks of a broken world and reminds us that things will not always be as they are.

23

More Than a Water Spot
SPIRITUAL LIFE ROOTED IN REALITY

MARK PELLINGTON HAS BOTH PRODUCED AND HAS BEEN A LEADING collaborator of movies and musical projects for several decades. Critics have usually found his work praiseworthy. His 2008 film, *Henry Poole Is Here*, however, provoked considerable hostility. The reason? In this quirky drama, Pellington ventured too far from the unspoken requirement that serious films treat religion as either comedy, repressive, or abusive.

The film gets off to a slow, nearly depressing start. This connects us to the film's essential essence, for we will eventually learn that Henry Pool has been diagnosed with a terminal disease. Deeply despondent, Henry purchases a house near the one in which he had lived as a little boy. We realize that he's searching for some sort of meaning in these few months he has left. He tries to recall the days before his family split up, thinking this may give him some resolution. Instead, he is drawn into a strange neighborhood drama.

Water damage to an exterior wall of Henry's house forms what his neighbor sees as the face of Jesus. Awed by the unusual stain, the neighbor begins burning candles and praying beside the damaged wall.

Others soon join in.

Angry and disgusted, Poole curses and chases the neighbors away. They respond kindly. Henry is, after all, the person God has chosen to bless. When blood appears on the stain, the drama intensifies.

Frustrated, Poole allows a local priest to visit the site for an official investigation.

Watching the priest look over the wall, Poole decides that the man is educated and reasonable and will probably bring an end to the commotion.

"It's a water spot, right?" Poole asks the priest.

"Of course," the priest responds.

"Finally!" Poole exclaims. "Well, so this craziness is over now?"

"There is no question about it being a water spot, Mr. Poole," the priest says. "The question is whether it is ONLY a water spot."

Mr. Poole begins moving from hostile disbelief toward a skeptical openness. He doesn't find faith exactly. Before it's all over, Poole destroys the shrine. Nonetheless, he experiences a skeptical but slightly hopeful "just maybe but probably not" kind of proto-faith. Many contemporary unbelievers experience something like this when they begin their own long journey Godward.

It is not the kind of conversion we were taught to expect. Acknowledging its authenticity requires a Christian to cultivate an attitude of noncontrolling, radical hospitality. We must surrender all forms of Jesus-marketing that many of our denominations have promoted in the last few decades. A spiritual awakening like Poole's is out of human control. Indeed, human meddling can abort it.

We should also be aware that Mr. Poole's stance toward faith is becoming familiar to many Christians. Defining faith as certainty, as a "no questions either asked or permitted" attitude, is simply not available to a growing number of contemporary believers.

Faith rarely explodes in a particular moment or in a predictable way. It is much more common for faith to grow ever so slowly, and by circuitous paths, into real holiness. One author has called that path "a slow-release miracle."

Secular, contemporary, and postmodern culture presents new challenges to Christian faith. Some of them are more subtle than anything we encountered in the modern era. At the same time, the postmodern attitude replaces the modernist sneer toward faith with a sarcastic shrug of the shoulders. "I'll listen," the shrug seems to say. "I'm not buying it, but it's no crazier than anything philosophy or science has to say."

The postmodern attitude opens the door to superstition and magic, to psychedelic experience, and to eroticism as perhaps the only real kinds of meaningful human experiences left to the inhabitants of the digitized, mechanized, dehumanized world we have entered. Christians railing against the ways postmodern people distract themselves from despair will provoke their neighbors' rage. Those who market their faith without concern for the honest questions our culture now asks of faith, will be met with disdain.

In the end, there are only two ways that postmodern, secular people will open themselves for an encounter with Christ. Either they will experience a non-manipulated phenomena of some sort that turns hostility into curiosity and then perhaps to awe, or they will experience holiness through the imperfect life of a believer.

When the opening occurs, it must be met with grace and hospitality. In some cases, this hospitality will involve serious discussions about the nature of reality itself. Serious people often have serious questions. They are unmoved by pious clichés. They want either answers or an honest admission of ignorance.

Such are the things we've been considering in these pages.

This book began with the statement that Christians are uncertain how to respond to the contemporary world. The answer to this uncertainty, or so it seems to me, is for our faith to recover its own roots.

At our roots, we stop treating intellectual sloth as a form of piety. We consult the saints. We recover our practices of prayer and worship. We stop trying to control our neighbors. We cultivate genuine curiosity and respect for honest questions. We serve. We love. We forgive. We demonstrate to the watching world what it means to hunger and thirst after righteousness.

To admit, like the priest in *Henry Poole is Here*, that the water spot is a water spot does not keep us from also believing that the water spot may be something more than a water spot. Indeed, the newborn baby asleep in the hay, normal in every sense, may be nonetheless the door to an utterly different level of reality.

That's exactly what we've been saying for two thousand years. When we truly believe it, everything changes. For if the great Creator has indeed become our Savior and the fullness of God truly dwells in him, this good news transforms our chaos into cosmos—in this age of AI and every age still to come.

THANK YOU FOR READING!

If you enjoyed this book, please leave a review on your eBook retailer's website and tell your friends. Reviews help books find new readers and get advertising.

REVIEW

FREE BOOK OFFER

Are we living in the end times?
Is there anything good about AI?
What are the implications of church scandal?
Dan Scott answers some of the world's most burning questions in his free book, The Great Falling Away.

www.pastordanscott.com

Appendix

A Few Fundamental Christian Assumptions

1. Human Beings are conscious. That is to say that humans are aware of self, of other conscious beings, of the natural world, and of where they are, have been, and may be located in time and space.
2. Human beings live within a created universe, a cosmos
3. The cosmos is the product of a single Intelligence who is a personal being that exists outside as well as inside, time and space.
4. Creation has not only a purposeful origin but a purposeful process and a purposeful end.
5. The ordering of the cosmos—providence—is carried out through systematized patterns that exist at every level of reality, from the cosmic to the subatomic. The cosmos is thus a mystery that arouses the human intellect and demands our thoughtful, thorough observation, and investigation.
6. The patterns and processes that permeate creation make possible, indeed make inevitable, metaphor and allegory,

not merely as communication tools but as meaning-generating structures. These reoccurring patterns make scientific discovery imaginable, compelling, and possible.

7. Metaphor "carries over" information gleaned from these patterns from one realm of creation to another. Metaphor is thus a foundational rather than peripheral component of human intelligence and human communication.

8. Providence can be discerned by human beings seeking to align their thoughts and behaviors with the patterns of creation. That alignment is what is meant by the word *wisdom*. Wisdom, in turn creates a potential for that high state of human flourishing the ancient Hebrews called *shalom*.

9. Complex patterns of information may become integrated in ways that give rise to consciousness (as in the case of animals and perhaps even plants), or even to self-consciousness, as in the case of angels and human beings. Similarly, complex thought-systems (such as human cultures) may present themselves as self-protecting and self-propagating in ways that appear deliberate and personal.

10. Human brokenness makes full alignment with divine providence impossible, even without taking into consideration the existence of malignant non-human forces. As a result, even the most wise and mature human being wrestles with a core radical dysfunction Christians call *sin*.

11. The disruption of the providential structures embedded within creation, whether by neglect and decay or due to the intentional introduction of disorder and misinformation by malignant forces, is the origin of all physical and mental illnesses as well as societal dysfunction. No human being or human society is completely free of these aspects of human brokenness.

12. The cosmos contains forces that hinder, oppose, and distort providence.

13. The Creator's character and will are expressed not only through providential structures, which are accessible and discernible to everyone everywhere, but through a single human person—Jesus Christ. The Creator became human in an act Christians call the *incarnation* and did so to empower the full purposes for which human beings and the entire cosmos had been created.

14. Healing individuals and communities involves restoring providential intent to bodies, minds, societies, and ecological structures.

15. The Creator not only communicates through providence and through the incarnation but through a personal, conscious Divine Presence who is "other than" creation while at the same time permeating creation and all its parts.

16. God inspired individuals in ancient times to write aspects of the Creator's intention for humanity and the rest of creation that had been overlooked or distorted.

17. All human individuals are created in God's own image and likeness. However, full personhood—the development of an individuated sense of agency and responsibility—is a potential that must be purposefully sought and activated. Full adult personhood does not emerge automatically with age.

18. The full expression of one's personhood requires both individuation as well as responsible participation within community.

19. A human community, whether family, nation, religion, or other association existing over time with aims, values, and assumptions, is a spiritual entity. Community is not merely an abstract term describing a collection of individuals.

20. All human efforts to heal and care for creation, even if inadequate, nonetheless contribute to the work of healing.

21. Christians are called to offer their unique perspectives of reality to others in winsome rather than in combative ways and to demonstrate willingness to learn from (and cooperate with) others, especially in the work of healing bodies, minds, and societies.

22. Human beings in covenant with God and with God's Redemptive Community are responsible for stewarding that portion of creation, social order, and redemptive mission that lies within their own sphere of influence, and to do so to the highest level that their gifts, experience and placement in the world make possible.

Notes

What is real?

1. Dumitru Staniloae, *Orthodox Dogmatic Theology: The Experience of God, Vol. 1: Revelation and Knowledge of the Triune God*, 1st edition (Brookline, Mass: Holy Cross Orthodox Press, 1998), xvii.

2. A Mirror That Shapes What It Sees

1. Staniloae, xxi.

3. Participation in Reality

1. Information as defined by Shannon has no relationship to meaning. Ka979mm00, which I have just randomly typed, is, by his definition, information. Logos, in contrast, is what we might call *meaningful information*.

4. The One Beyond Image

1. Jacobs, *The Year of Living Biblically*.
2. Julian Jaynes, *The Origin of Consciousness in the Breakdown of the Bicameral Mind*, 31578th edition (Boston New York: Mariner Books, 2000).
3. Sigmund Freud and Peter Gay, *The Future of an Illusion*, ed. James Strachey, The Standard edition (New York, N.Y.: W. W. Norton & Company, 1989).
4. Pollan Michael, *How to Change Your Mind: The New Science of Psychedelics [Hardcover] [May 17, 2018] Pollan Michael* (London: Allen Lane, 2018).

5. Discovering Personal and Cosmic Meaning

1. John D. Barrow, Frank J. Tipler, and John A. Wheeler, *The Anthropic Cosmological Principle*, Revised ed. edition (Oxford England; New York: Oxford University Press, 1988).

6. A Universe Formed by Word

1. Riley, Henry, Metamorphosis, Cambridge, 1871
2. Abraham Kuyper et al., *Wisdom & Wonder: Common Grace in Science & Art*, ed. Jordan J. Ballor and Stephen J. Grabill, trans. Nelson D. Kloosterman (Grand

Rapids, ID: Christian's Library Press, 2011).

7. Reason, Reality, and Faith

1. *By Dumitru Staniloae The Experience of God: Orthodox Dogmatic Theology, Vol. 2, The World: Creation and Deification* (Holy Cross Orthodox Press, 2005)
2. *By Dumitru Staniloae The Experience of God: Orthodox Dogmatic Theology, Vol. 1, The World: Creation and Deification* (Holy Cross Orthodox Press, 2001), 5.
3. *By Dumitru Staniloae The Experience of God*, 28.

9. Reality's Reflection

1. Mark Johnson, *Embodied Mind, Meaning, and Reason: How Our Bodies Give Rise to Understanding*, 1st edition (Chicago: University of Chicago Press, 2017).
2. Johnson. xi
3. Arthur Herman, *The Cave and the Light: Plato Versus Aristotle, and the Struggle for the Soul of Western Civilization*, 1st edition (Random House Trade Paperbacks, 2014).
4. Owen Barfield, *Saving the Appearances: A Study in Idolatry*, 2nd edition (Middletown, Conn: Wesleyan, 1988). p.xi

10. More on Metaphor

1. Mary Carruthers, *The Book of Memory: A Study of Memory in Medieval Culture*, 2 edition (Cambridge, UK; New York: Cambridge University Press, 2008).
2. Mary Carruthers, *The Craft of Thought: Meditation, Rhetoric, and the Making of Images, 400-1200*, First Paperback Edition edition (New York: Cambridge University Press, 2000).
3. Deirdre Carabine, *John Scottus Eriugena*, 1st edition (New York: Oxford University Press, 2000). p29
4. Carabine. 67
5. Carabine, 69.

17. Above Us More Than Sky

1. Genesis 2:2 Augustine Institute, *The Holy Bible ESV-Catholic Edition* (Augustine Institute, 2020), 1.
2. Eugene F. Rogers Jr, *After the Spirit* (Grand Rapids, Mich: Wm. B. Eerdmans Publishing Co., 2005), 35.
3. Amos Yong, *The Spirit Poured Out on All Flesh: Pentecostalism and the Possibility of Global Theology*, Edition Unstated edition (Grand Rapids, Mich: Baker Academic, 2005).
4. Clark H. Pinnock, *Flame of Love: A Theology of the Holy Spirit* (Downers Grove, Ill: Intervarsity Pr, 1996).
5. Henry T. Blackaby, Richard Blackaby, and Claude V. King, *Experiencing God: Knowing and Doing the Will of God, Revised and Expanded*, Revised, Expanded ed. edition (Nashville, Tenn: B&H Books, 2008).
6. Don Richardson, *Peace Child*, Reprint edition (Bethany House Publishers, 2005).

7. Don Richardson, *Eternity in Their Hearts*, 3rd ed. edition (Minneapolis, Minnesota: Bethany House Publishers, 2006).

18. The Book of Reality

1. Augustine, *Confessions*, trans. Sarah Ruden, Translation edition (New York: Modern Library, 2018), 236–37.

19. Self Beyond the Rabbit Hole

1. Barfield.
2. Charles Taylor, *Sources of the Self: The Making of the Modern Identity* (Cambridge, Mass: Harvard University Press, 1992).
3. Charles Taylor, *A Secular Age*, 1st edition (Cambridge, Mass: The Belknap Press of Harvard University Press, 2007).